The Lost President

un CIVIL WARS

SERIES EDITORS

Stephen Berry
University of Georgia

Amy Murrell Taylor
University of Kentucky

ADVISORY BOARD

Edward L. Ayers
University of Richmond
Catherine Clinton
University of Texas at San Antonio
J. Matthew Gallman
University of Florida
Elizabeth Leonard
Colby College

James Marten
Marquette University
Scott Nelson
College of William & Mary
Daniel E. Sutherland
University of Arkansas
Elizabeth Varon
University of Virginia

The Lost President

*A. D. Smith and the Hidden History
of Radical Democracy in
Civil War America*

RUTH DUNLEY

The University of Georgia Press   *Athens*

Paperback edtion, 2023
© 2019 by the University of Georgia Press
Athens, Georgia 30602
www.ugapress.org
All rights reserved
Set in 10.5/13 Adobe Caslon Pro by Graphic Composition, Inc. Bogart, GA

Most University of Georgia Press titles are
available from popular e-book vendors.

Printed digitally

Library of Congress Cataloging-in-Publication Data
Names: Dunley, Ruth, 1972– author.
Title: The lost president : A.D. Smith and the hidden history of radical democracy in
  Civil War America / Ruth Dunley.
Description: Athens, GA : The University of Georgia Press, [2019] | Series: UnCivil wars |
  Includes bibliographical references and index.
Identifiers: LCCN 2018034315 | ISBN 9780820354545 (hardback : alk. paper)
Subjects: LCSH: Smith, A. D. (Abram Daniel), 1811–1865. | United States—Politics and
  government—19th century. | Republicanism—United States—History—19th century. |
  Presidents—Canada—Biography. | Canada—History—Rebellion, 1837–1838—Biography. |
  Hunters' Lodges (Organization)—Biography. | Cleveland (Ohio)—Politics and government—
  19th century. | Judges—Wisconsin—Biography. | United States. Internal Revenue Service—
  Officials and employees—Biography. | Beaufort (S.C.)—Politics and government—19th
  century.
Classification: LCC E340.853 D86 2019 | DDC 320.973/09034—dc23 LC record available at
  https://lccn.loc.gov/2018034315

Paperback ISBN 978-0-8203-6487-2

Fellow citizens, be not deceived; your rights are now placed in your own hands. Let not your grasp loosen for a moment, that your enemies may snatch them away. Be not inactive. The foe is aroused to his most desperate energies. He is putting forth all his strength and subtlety. The power of self-government is now with you. Let it not depart, lest it depart forever. Come up to the contest with the shout and strength of freemen who know their rights and dare maintain them.

—A. D. SMITH, February 24, 1847

CONTENTS

ACKNOWLEDGMENTS *ix*

INTRODUCTION
  In Search of a Man Named Smith *1*

CHAPTER 1
  New York, Vermont, Ohio:
  The President of Canada *19*

CHAPTER 2
  Wisconsin: When I Think of Him
  I Incline to Spit *51*

CHAPTER 3
  South Carolina: Your Name and Memory
  Will Be Cherished *89*

CONCLUSION
  Act, One and All *121*

EPILOGUE
  Lost and Found *139*

NOTES *145*

BIBLIOGRAPHY *169*

INDEX *185*

ACKNOWLEDGMENTS

It has been a long road to the completion of this book. When editor Stephen Berry first approached me about it, I was nearing a maternity leave. That baby is now well into grade school.

The pace of my progress was so glacial that I suspect it led many to believe the book was a figment of my imagination. For those who trusted that it did indeed exist, who helped me, supported me, and made it possible for me to complete this work—and who made it impossible for me to put it aside—thank you.

I pursued doctoral studies in history at the suggestion of Professor Klaus Pohle, my graduate adviser in journalism. I will always be grateful for his friendship, encouragement, and wisdom.

My application to the University of Ottawa landed in the inbox of Professor Donald F. Davis, who, unlike some, was willing to forgive my background as a journalist and teach me to become a historian. He introduced me to A. D. Smith and urged me to tell his story. Professor Davis was my biggest cheerleader and harshest critic—I thank him for being both. I also thank the other Ottawa professors who encouraged my work on this book and my pursuit of the discipline: Jacques Barbier, Richard Connors, Beatrice Craig, and Chad Gaffield.

This work would not have been possible without the financial support of Fulbright Canada. During my time as a visiting scholar at the College of William and Mary, I benefited from the advice and mentorship of Professors Cindy Hahamovitch, Lu Ann Homza, Scott Nelson, Ron Schechter, Carol Sheriff, Jim Whittenburg, and especially Chandos Michael Brown. They offered ideas and encouragement and welcomed me into their classrooms and homes. I am particularly grateful to Professor Sheriff for supporting my Fulbright application from the beginning.

I am also indebted to those academics and independent historians who were not affiliated with my schools but nonetheless took time to help me or discuss issues examined in this book: Robert Baker, David Blight, Andrew Bonthius, John Carter, Jane Errington, Paul Finkelman, William Freehling,

Donald Graves, Joseph Ranney, Tatiana van Riemsdijk, Michael Wayne, Robert Wheeler, and Stephen R. Wise. The late Michael Fellman played a critical role in helping me revise this biography and introduced A. D. Smith to the University of Georgia Press.

There I owe much to the efforts of editors Stephen Berry, Jon Davies, Ellen Goldlust, Mick Gusinde-Duffy, and Amy Murrell Taylor. When Professor Berry initially approached me about this book, I am certain he did not expect it to become an eight-year conversation. As someone who lacked the backing of an academic institution and had to maintain a day job, I will always be grateful that he held me to historians' deadlines and not journalists' deadlines—and even then, he was more generous than I could have hoped.

I also thank many archivists, curators, and librarians across North America, especially Michael Ruffing, formerly of the Cleveland Public Library; Jane de Broux and John Nondorf, formerly of the Wisconsin Historical Society; Anne Mallek, formerly of the Gamble House; Catherine Butler of Library and Archives Canada; Grace Morris Cordial at the Beaufort County Library; Eva Garcelon-Hart of the Henry Sheldon Museum; Kevin Abing of the Milwaukee County Historical Society; Ann Scheid of the Greene and Greene Archives of the University of Southern California; and Patricia Homer, my Upstate New York specialist.

Numerous friends in Canada and the United States helped me in more ways than I can mention. In particular, I am grateful to Jennifer Cox, Chris Lackner, Joanne Laucius, Augustine Meaher IV, Caroline O'Neill, Tammy Elizabeth Renich, Robert Sibley, Tom Spears, and Laura Stemp. Not only did Reid J. Epstein and Kate Goodloe give me a place to stay in Milwaukee and Washington, but Reid was also my American sounding board and Wisconsin tour guide. Thanks, too, go to the members of the Ottawa Collaborative History Initiative, particularly Anthony Di Mascio, Adam Green, and Samy Khalid, under the direction of Professor Chad Gaffield—their insight helped shape my research and writing in the earliest days.

Although I contacted several of Smith's descendants, only Kathleen Candee of Wisconsin was able to shed any light on their ancestor. I thank her for providing research leads, encouragement, and a willingness to sit down with a stranger to chat about the mysteries of Smith at a Milwaukee pub on St. Patrick's Day. (I'm glad we survived the brawl that broke out in front of us.) I also thank Smith's descendants in the Gamble family for their assistance in locating and sharing the only image of Mary Augusta Smith I have ever seen.

I will always be grateful for the ongoing support of Scott Anderson, the former editor in chief of the *Ottawa Citizen*. It was with some trepidation that I approached him to seek permission to work on a doctorate while simultaneously trying to work full time at the newspaper. Rather than dissuade me, he offered unconditional support. When I subsequently approached him about taking a year's leave of absence to accept the Fulbright, he fulfilled that promise. I was lucky to be working for Scott then and even luckier to work for him again years later.

I can never fully express my gratitude to my family for their ongoing support. My father, who marched me out to read every historical marker along I-75 during our annual family road trips, gave me a love of history that will be with me always and that will always remind me of him. My mother, who spent hours sharing family lore and photographs with me, gave me a better understanding of my own history, a gift I will share with my own daughter. I am also grateful to Paige Dunley for her help with the final proofs.

Finally, Derek Shelly was an advocate for Smith from the beginning and endured his presence in our lives until the end. Forgoing his own scholarship, Derek assisted with research, copyedited draft after draft, searched archives and historical societies, helped me make sense of various documents, and went on many hikes and to many hockey games with our daughter so that I would have the time and solitude required to write.

My daughter has never known a time when her mother was not dealing with "Mumma's book." She put up with A. D. Smith even though she does not yet fully understand who he was or why he often took me away from her.

This book is for her and her father.

The Lost President

INTRODUCTION

In Search of a Man Named Smith

> In the face of Infinity and of Eternity, what is he, but a speck? Is any particular bubble on the ever-flowing stream of Nile or Amazon—an iridescent beam at one moment, and gone the next—singled out for lasting remembrance?
>
> —WILLIAM ROSCOE THAYER, *The Art of Biography*

In a 1998 interview, biographer and historian Stephen Ambrose recalled a life-changing assignment from William B. Hesseltine, his professor. Hesseltine, then working on the *Dictionary of Wisconsin Biography*, asked students to write sketches of people in the state who "were not important enough to have a real biography written about them, but who'd made an impact." Ambrose said he would never forget the lesson he took from the experience: "I'll never forget the feeling I had when I finished that work and wrote the 10-page bio of this guy: 'I know more about Charles A. Billinghurst than anybody else in the world!' I just thought that was marvelous. Now what I soon learned was, the reason for that was that nobody else cared about Charles A. Billinghurst. And then what I learned after that was, 'But I can make 'em care if I tell the story right.'"[1]

Telling a biography "right," especially when it revolves around a character of secondary historical importance, is perhaps not as straightforward as Ambrose's reminiscence might suggest. Theoretical and methodological concerns aside, telling the life story of someone whose historical record is largely unknown creates a thorny set of problems, not the least of which is navigating around the missing information that impedes investigation of lesser-known characters. Antebellum historian Michael Wayne suggests that this deft maneuvering is not a liability but rather forces historians to approach their writing with imagination and originality: "The difficulty of capturing feelings and private thoughts from the kinds of records that survive, the gaps in evidence, so many other obstacles to interpreting the human experience in earlier times necessitate that historians be extraordinarily resourceful and creative."[2]

In searching for the way to tell my story right, I have had endless hours of conversation with friends and colleagues about the nature of life in a century that often seems like a foreign country.[3] But at the heart of this work is a mystery that captured my imagination from the beginning: that of a man named Smith. The mystery sustained me through countless research dead ends, for as seventeenth-century author Sir Thomas Browne said, "We love to lose ourselves in a mystery."[4] Often, as I discovered, the level of enjoyment we receive from a mystery is directly proportionate to the difficulty of solving it.

I first learned of Smith in a conversation with my academic adviser, who quoted aloud to me from a passage in an old American history book by Glyndon Van Deusen, *The Jacksonian Era*. Flipping through the pages of the paperback, my professor stopped and read, "In September, 1838, some 160 Hunters from both sides of the border attended a convention in Cleveland, where they elected one Smith, a resident of that city, President of the Republic of Canada."[5]

One Smith.

The Hunters, my adviser explained, were an obscure, mostly American paramilitary group that had attempted to overthrow Crown rule in the Canadas in the late 1830s. My professor continued, musing aloud about how he often cited the passage to his undergrads and wondered who Smith might have been. Surely someone must have investigated this man's identity, I thought—"one Smith" was at one time a real, specific Smith who very likely had a home and family plus the desire and credentials to lead a country. As I left campus that day, I knew that I must find the identity of the Canadian president who never was. This proved to be a far more difficult venture than I bargained. When I pulled Van Deusen's book off a shelf at the university library, I was greeted with a message from a previous reader. There, in the margin of the weathered book in bright blue block letters next to the reference of Smith, was the exclamation that came to define the reaction I most often received while looking for answers about a man named Smith—"HA!"

It seemed somehow apt, as if Clio were daring me to find this elusive character. I was being asked to scavenge through countless archives for the detritus of a minor life. Very early on in my research, it became clear that finding "one Smith" would have its methodological challenges. For the biographer, "a lot of the time has to be spent seeking trivia—asking for and searching out things that make polite people laugh at you."[6] A trip to the University of Ottawa's library confirmed that the Hunters had existed, that they had held an election, and that they had chosen a Smith as first president of the Republic of Canada. (A book I consulted called Smith a "Canadian refugee," but no subsequent source ever corroborated the assertion that Smith was Canadian.)[7] Over the telephone, librarians and archivists were, more often than not, dismissive of my requests, a sense of futility audible in their voices.

"Smith?" they asked, incredulous.

Yes, Smith. The name alone made the search tremendously complicated. Even in smaller towns of the early nineteenth century, property records usually listed more than one Smith. Eventually, I determined that Smith's initials were A. D., and a day before I left for research in Cleveland, the site of his "election," a volunteer at the Cuyahoga County Archives told me he had stumbled across a reference to an Abram D. Smith who was called to the bar in 1839. In Ohio, I searched as many records as possible in an effort to confirm that A. D. Smith was Abram D. Smith—tax assessments stuffed in boxes under layers of dust at a municipal warehouse, documents in a damp subbasement of city hall and in the archives of the Western Reserve Historical Society. I pestered librarians and archivists and historians, but no one knew anything about A. D. Smith. As the city directories for Cleveland between 1837 and 1845 are no longer extant, the directories I did find were of limited use. Although they indicated that an A. D. Smith had arrived in the city around 1836 or 1837, there was no sign of him in any public records after 1841.[8]

Had he moved to another city? Had he died?

I could not find an obituary. When I entered "A. D. Smith" into the search engine for Cleveland's necrology files, I was greeted by 6,294 possibilities. Probate records yielded the same volume of possibilities for marriage or death certificates.

It was impossible to make progress without a first name, so I consulted a book of baby names and spent hours entering random combinations into online genealogy search engines, guessing at possible names for the mysterious Mr. Smith, an exercise that was both frustrating and futile.

A. D. Smith was listed twenty-eight times in the Annals of Cleveland, an index of newspaper articles from the city, but none of those references produced a name. They did, however, provide one small clue: Smith worked for a time as Cleveland's justice of the peace. Census records revealed that an A. D. Smith living in Cleveland in 1840 was born between 1810 and 1820, but even this document failed to provide a full name.[9]

My adviser surmised that Smith's obvious reluctance to use his full name could indicate that it was unusual in some way, making Smith loath to commit it to paper. I scoured lists of biblical names, looking for something that might have made this man averse to sharing it with the public. Abaddon? Azariah? Abednego? The mystery only deepened.

The Annals of Cleveland contained advertisements for lectures "Dr. A. D. Smith" gave in the late 1830s about the emerging "science" of phrenology. Was he a physician? There was no simple way to know, as the American Medical Association's records do not go back that far. And in that era, many people who called themselves doctors were not trained professionals.

Smith was not listed in the *Encyclopedia of Cleveland History* or the *Dictionary of Cleveland Biography*. He was mentioned in *Cleveland: The Making of a City*, but only as a trustee of the Cleveland Female Seminary.[10] I thought that if I could locate the seminary records, I might find a more complete reference to Smith's name, but no one could tell me where those records might be, and archivists often confused Smith's seminary with a successor built on the same site.

I also tried to search Smith through his involvement in the Hunters' Lodge, but as it was a secret society, few papers survived in Ohio, and some of them were written in code.[11] With the assistance of a hacker (who had asked to remain anonymous), I decoded some of the documents, but again, while Smith was mentioned as president, his full name did not appear. I surmised that colonial officials in Upper Canada must have known Smith's particulars, but documents in Library and Archives Canada simply referred to him as "Smith" or "President Smith."[12] There was nothing to indicate his given name.

I then tried to find Smith by searching his address, which I knew from Cleveland's city directory to have been No. 9, Farmers' Block, but that address no longer exists, and when I ventured downtown in the December snow to locate the site, its current occupant, a parking lot, offered no clues.

I thought perhaps I might find my Smith through other Smith families: Archibald, Ann, and various other Smiths appeared regularly on tax records, but not A. D. I checked property assessments from 1836 to 1841 as well as promissory notes, small claims, and trespass and assault records. The township paid an A. D. Smith $1.50 in 1837, but the receipt did not say why.

Since I now knew that Smith had been a justice of the peace, locating his docket books at the Cuyahoga County Archives in Cleveland made me certain that I had found my man.[13] He had signed nearly every one of the fifteen hundred or so pages of his docket books—some pages twice—but always with just his initials. About halfway through, I realized that he was never going to sign his full name, but I continued to turn the dirt-encrusted pages. Hours later, my hands blackened, I still had no corroboration that this was the Abram D. Smith who had been called to the bar.

No wonder this man has remained a mystery, I thought. I grew envious every time I read books in which fortunate historians reveled in a surplus of documents, untangling their characters' tales with ease and conviction. Not only did the world know nothing about A. D. Smith, but now, as his would-be biographer, neither did I. Sitting in the Detroit airport on a stopover from Cleveland to Ottawa, I realized that I was coming home virtually empty-handed. Mr. Smith had eluded me again and again.

One of the best parts of historical research is that a new document or clue can immediately take the historian on a different path. The break I needed surfaced not long after my research trip to Ohio, but it was hundreds of miles to the west. Even though I had no way of knowing whether Abram was the correct name, I went back to the Internet, trying numerous sites before I hit a match on politicalgraveyard.com, which included a listing for an Abram Smith in Wisconsin. Further investigation led me to the Wisconsin Supreme Court website, which had a biographical sketch of a former justice, Abram D. Smith. He had been born in 1811, which made him a possible match for the A. D. Smith I had found in the Cleveland census. But I needed something more to either confirm that the Ohio Smith and the Wisconsin Smith were the same man or differentiate them.

Hours of frustrating research later, I found an obscure book, long out of print. *The Story of a Great Court*, a 1912 history of the Wisconsin Supreme Court, cited a short biographical sketch of Smith from an even more obscure 1897 publication intended for lawyers, *The Green Bag*. According to that piece, "Before coming to Milwaukee [Smith] was a justice of the peace in Cleveland, Ohio."[14]

Finally. There it was. *Abram D. Smith*.

This breakthrough enabled me to extend the chronology of Smith's life still further. I learned that after serving as a judge in Wisconsin, he had worked as a federal tax commissioner in the occupied Sea Islands of South Carolina during the Civil War. To verify that the Smith I knew in Cleveland was the same one I had found in the South, I asked a handwriting expert to compare an Ohio signature scratched onto paper more than a century ago with one from South Carolina nearly three decades later: nearly everything aligned, though there were subtle changes, which the analyst attributed to "the impetuosity of youth."[15]

At this point, I finally felt confident that I had found the trail of A. D. Smith, even though it remained difficult to follow because Smith was never still for long and ultimately worked in five states before his life's journey came to a sudden end under unusual circumstances aboard a ship. Armed with this basic chronology of Smith's life and spurred on by a portrait of Smith, I pursued the fine details of the mystery, gradually making my way to the places Smith had known—to the tiny towns of his youth in Upstate New York; to the main square in Cleveland, only a short walk from where his home once stood; to the streets of Milwaukee and Madison, where he worked as a lawyer and judge; and to the South Carolina church where, likely drunk, he had staggered to the pulpit to deliver a sermon to the freedmen of the Sea Islands. In each place, the mystery propelled Smith's story forward in my mind—the desire to ask questions and to construct answers based on the emerging evidence.

I endeavored to conquer the mystery at every turn, stepping up my search with whatever tools I could find. I stretched my research skills, becoming a genealogist through trial and error. Genealogy was popular when I started my research, but it wasn't the thriving industry it has become today, with television shows and software and websites that offer far more services than were available even a decade ago. I hit dead end after dead end in my genealogy searches, hampered mostly by the fact that Smith was such a common last name and to a lesser extent by the disputed location of Smith's birth. For the life of me, I could not determine Smith's parentage.

Frustrated, I turned to ancestry.com, which, for a fee, would connect me with a professional genealogist. I submitted a query, and in no time, I received an estimate from a "client services adviser":

> Level: Moderately Challenging
> Hourly rate: $100–$150
> Estimated hours: 20–25
> Minimum retainer: $2,500
> Duration: 16–20 weeks

I wasn't sure if I should be more amused by the minimum retainer fee or the fact that ancestry.com had evaluated the work involved as "moderately challenging." Either way, I declined the services, unwilling to pay $2,500 (or more) with no guarantee that they would find Smith's parents. I placed an advertisement for a genealogist specializing in Milwaukee family history on the online classified site Kijiji, but no one answered.

All else having failed, I turned to the medium with which I was most familiar: the newspaper. The readership of newspapers skews older, and that demographic tends to have more interest in family history and in history in general. I thought about taking out an advertisement in the *Milwaukee Journal Sentinel* but decided it would be too difficult to encapsulate the story in a small ad. Instead, I emailed one of the paper's editors and pitched a column on my mystery as an appeal to the city: Help me find Abram Smith's diary. The column ran, and I held my breath and waited.

Much to my surprise, I received what I considered a very good response from readers. "I just finished reading your story about researching A. D. Smith," wrote one. "I wish I could offer some help, being a Milwaukee native, but I don't believe I have any connection to the man. However, I really enjoyed the story, and wanted to thank you for writing it."

"Thank you for the fine article and scholarship re A. D. Smith," wrote another man from Wauwatosa, Wisconsin. "Unfortunately, I am not able to add anything to your worthy research. . . . I wish you well in your pursuit of the truth."

A woman who at fifty-seven had recently returned to school to pursue a master's in history also contacted me. "I just wanted to tell you how much I enjoyed your article," she said. "What a great idea, to write an opinion piece to help fill in the missing pieces of a research project. . . . I look forward to reading your book."

I received offers to help index my book. Several kind people volunteered to make library runs for me in Wisconsin. A rep of the Wisconsin Grocers' Association suggested that he could try to find any additional info on Smith's brother-in-law, Herbert, a grocer whose store burned down in a suspected arson. But the messages were generally the same: *What a fascinating story . . . too bad I have no information to help you.*

One reader was so inspired by Smith's story that she left the warmth of her Wisconsin home in February to visit Smith's grave. "Going 2 A. D. Smith's grave today. Gr8 art on yr bio in MKE Journal re Smith using states' rights argument on #FugitiveSlaveAct," wrote my newfound Twitter fan (I think it was the first time I'd ever seen "FugitiveSlaveAct" as a hashtag). I asked her to let me know if she found any clues at the cemetery, though I was pretty sure she would not. "I will!" she tweeted back enthusiastically. "& the missing diary—thrilling."

She didn't find any clues, of course, but she did snap a photo of the grave under a blue, Wisconsin winter sky and publish it via Twitter. And she used the word "thrilling" in reference to a dead judge and the possibility of his long-lost diary. That was enough for me. The Civil War. A radical judge. The prospect of a long-lost diary. If nothing else, the article suggested I was not alone in my fascination with the question marks attached to Smith.

Thinking back to Wayne's advice, it dawned on me that, unbidden, a common and natural thread was beginning to weave its way through my work and through the life of the man named Smith. What made his story—and the stories of so many secondary characters—so compelling, so worthwhile in the end, was their ability to captivate us with the powerful pull of a mystery waiting to be solved. That mystery forces us, as historians, to look for clues not only in the raw evidence untouched by time but also through an examination of the characters of the day through the lens of hermeneutics: What would they have seen, felt, and understood about their circumstances? What made them behave the way they did? What motivated Abram Smith? And above all, what inside his character had pushed him from city to city, state to state? Smith's personal library had included a copy of Cervantes's *Don Quixote*, and in many ways he had lived his own quixotic journey. Considering how far he traveled and how often, Smith emerged from the surviving records as a nineteenth-century knight-errant. In the name of all that was good, the medieval knight-errant saw himself as a wandering hero who championed the oppressed—a brave man who sought and fought the dragons and giants of corruption and immorality. Rushing to new frontiers to fight for his (sometimes misguided) perceptions of justice and truth, Smith behaved like a knight-errant for republicanism and justice, battling the most fearsome foes of an American Yankee: monopolistic banks that exploited workers, monarchical government, and race slavery.

As I trudged through a Wisconsin cemetery on my own pilgrimage to Smith's grave, I knew for certain that mystery was very much the province of history—it would be difficult to pinpoint the motivations behind Smith's errant ways, but his quest for personal greatness surely imbued his story with timeless meaning. I searched along winding pathways for some time before I tracked the grave's location to Lot 2, Block 1, Section 26 of Milwaukee's Forest Home Cemetery. The grave, a tall obelisk that overshadowed the headstones of Abram Smith's wife, Mary Augusta, and son, Marius, was under the boughs of a towering old oak. I had seen pictures of the grave, but this was the first time I had visited. As I knelt by the grave and traced the epitaph with my fingers, there was no sign that anyone had recently stopped by. There were no withered flowers, and for a moment I was sorry that I had not gone to a florist's shop.

Someone watching me on that day in March 2004 could be forgiven for thinking I was there to pray for an ancestor: in fact, however, I was mostly hoping that I would one day be able to tell the story of this man who was perpetually on the move and who left behind few traces. Many biographers of nineteenth-century notables often knew or were related to the subjects, but Abram Smith is not my ancestor. Yet like other biographers before me, I felt a connection to Smith that was at once real and deep.[16] This man, I realized, had convinced others of the need to change the course of both Canadian and American history. It seemed impossible to me that a man of such great strength and conviction could have been reduced to a forgotten grave in Milwaukee—no book, no statue, no postage stamp to rescue him from obscurity.

Smith followed a journey to restore republican values and justice: first as the man who wanted to be the president of Canada in the late 1830s, next as the judge who touched off a legal firestorm by declaring the Fugitive Slave Act unconstitutional in the 1850s, and finally as the tax commissioner who demanded that former slaves have an opportunity to preempt land in South Carolina during the Civil War in what historian Willie Lee Rose called a "Rehearsal for Reconstruction."

Smith understood law and classical languages; named his son after Marius, a great Roman general and consul; read poetry and Darwin; and orated for hours.[17] He was clearly a man of intelligence, wit, and passion, yet he had also fallen short, in both his political and personal life, on many occasions. He could be quarrelsome and supercilious, an insufferable blowhard. Though a Democrat, he was alleged to have hated Catholics, was charged with taking a ten-thousand-dollar bribe, and lectured on temperance while battling his own alcoholism.[18]

The dichotomies of Abram Smith's personality, coupled with the fact that he was only a footnote to everyone other than me, added up to a mystery and what I considered a story worth telling. At a time when shelves are populated by dozens of biographies of the Great Men, another group of men and women linger offstage, waiting patiently for someone to resurrect their stories and hold up their life experiences alongside all the retellings of the lives of powerful emperors, politicians, and generals. As prize-winning journalist and biographer Jean Strouse has written, at one end of the spectrum "are exemplary historical figures whose lives take on mythic proportions in the floodlights of public recognition," while at the other end are "census figures made out of obscure lives that now seem exemplary precisely because they were commonplace."[19] The category of lives that falls between the two, however, is sometimes overlooked. Strouse notes, "In between is a twilight zone, a semiprivate realm occupied by minor poets, lesser dignitaries, hands that rocked important cradles, single flashes of success or fame, and the friends, relatives and disciples of great men and women.... Looking at the lives of individuals in this group enables us to examine two dimensions of history at once, both the public arenas of great figures and events, and the hidden dramas of ordinary private life."[20]

A. D. Smith lived in this biographical twilight zone. Though he achieved some prominence, he failed to make a name for the ages. Often, just when it seemed he might be gaining some notoriety, he slipped into obscurity yet again. In Cleveland, his tenure as president of Canada was short lived and went unnoticed by most. In Wisconsin, where his name was once bruited about as a possible vice presidential candidate, his deeds failed to register. And in South Carolina, he held a federal appointment under Lincoln yet played little more than a cameo role in early attempts at Reconstruction.[21] It is clear that he was comfortable in the public sphere: he sought public office at the local, state, and federal levels. He wrote numerous letters to newspaper editors. He lectured publicly. He participated in well-attended public events. He was always, always on the move, witnessing some of the great events of his time in a nimble sort of nineteenth-century Forrest Gumpery.

Smith died a quiet death at the end of the Civil War, and though his life was briefly celebrated in obituaries in Wisconsin, he was quickly forgotten soon after. For all he did, Smith never really stayed on the historical radar long enough for anyone to have contemplated him as a subject of a biography, or, if they did, they soon gave up after discovering the paucity of sources. A. D. Smith was never a Great Man, even though he spent his life trying to become one.

What, then, is the value of telling the story of someone who played a small, unrecognized part in history? The quest for the answers is often as valuable as the answers themselves, as many other historians have illustrated by exploring secondary characters, deeply puzzling aspects of people's lives, what made them tick, and sometimes even what killed them.[22] In *Killed Strangely: The Death of Rebecca Cornell*, historian Elaine Forman Crane examines not just the life of Rebecca Cornell, a New England septuagenarian who turned up horribly burned and dead in her own home in 1673, but also the social aspects of death. A suspect in the case was Cornell's son, Thomas. Crane asks, "Was Thomas Cornell guilty? One reading of the evidence allows us to absolve Thomas Cornell of stabbing his mother and burning her body. Another suggests that Rebecca may have committed suicide or that someone else murdered her. Or her death may even have been accidental. . . . Readers looking for a thesis, an answer, a satisfactory conclusion to the main event will be disappointed, since the Rashomon qualities of this case preclude any easy solution."[23]

Crane propels her narrative through the circumstances surrounding Rebecca's death and its aftermath, ultimately telling a tale about seventeenth-century community and familial relationships through the lens of mystery. Piecing together primary documents with current scholarship about the time and place, Crane offers analysis yet leaves room for readers' interpretations. In the end, the old woman remains very much a secondary historical figure, yet her story merits telling, the author says, in part because it had been neglected and in part because of what interpretation of the mystery can reveal when we look closely enough:

> Thomas Cornell may have killed his mother. On the other hand, it is possible he did not. Either way, the Cornell case is surely one of early New England's darker moments—and doubly so. The nature of Rebecca Cornell's death was ominous to begin with, and the events surrounding the incident have languished in the shadows of historical obscurity. This is unfortunate since it is a compelling tale, one that begs to be told not only because of our fascination with violence at a distance, but because it involves complex historical issues about which there is rarely enough evidence to permit critical analysis.[24]

Wayne also uses the vehicle of detection in his 2001 book, *Death of an Overseer: Reopening a Murder Investigation from the Plantation South*. In this work, which historian James M. McPherson has hailed as a "detective thriller," Wayne investigates the death of Duncan Skinner, a Mississippi overseer. Skinner's death was originally ruled an accident, but local planters believed that he was murdered by slaves egged on by a local carpenter. Echoing Ambrose, Wayne recalls a life-changing episode in his academic past that affected his approach to history and prompted him to construct the book as a mystery. While Wayne was a student at Yale, a professor in one seminar dumped dozens of photocopied documents onto a desk and asked his students to recount what had really happened in the event described in the primary material. It was, Wayne writes, "like being a raw recruit in a police force doing detective work under the supervision of a grizzled veteran."[25] Although *Death of an Overseer* could not solve the puzzle of Skinner's death—the evidence is inconclusive—the case offers an effective instrument for examining slavery and plantation society in the Old South.

And mystery need not be employed exclusively to investigate murder and mysterious deaths. Edward Ball's *New York Times* best seller and National Book Award winner, *Slaves in the Family*, relates his search for his ancestors.

The descendant of powerful South Carolina planters, Ball casts himself as a detective, seeking the answers to a story long hidden. The gift of a family history from his father prompted the author to undertake his own detective work, often with painful results: "I know my father was proud of his heritage but at the same time, I suspect, had questions about it. The story of his slave-owning family, part of the weave of his childhood, was a mystery he could only partly decipher. With the gift of the book, Dad seemed to be saying that the plantations were a piece of unfinished business. In that moment, the story of the Ball clan was locked in the depths of my mind, to be pried loose one day."[26] Ball's search for the descendants of slaves his family once owned, old plantation property records, and artifacts from "a bygone world" met with such acclaim that he followed it up with *The Sweet Hell Inside: A Family History*, which narrated the story of his African American relatives, a side of his family he had not known before beginning his quest several years earlier.[27]

Structurally and in theoretical terms, this biography of A. D. Smith takes the shape of a cultural biography, in much the same vein as David S. Reynolds's study of abolitionist John Brown. Reynolds writes, "Cultural biography is based on the idea that human beings have a dynamic, dialogic relationship to many aspects of their historical surroundings, such as politics, society, literature, and religion. The special province of the cultural biographer is to explore this relationship, focusing on three questions: How does my subject reflect his or her era? How does my subject transcend the era—that is, what makes him or her unique? What impact did my subject have on the era?"[28]

The patterns of A. D. Smith's life trace his era in numerous ways. Born in 1811, he was very much a man of the Jacksonian era, a time that has been declared simultaneously gloomy and triumphal.[29] As Arthur Schlesinger Jr. records in *The Age of Jackson*, it was a time of great political change and anxiety that saw the slow death of the Jeffersonian ideal of an America of independent farmers living peacefully across the countryside. "The young republic faced its critical test," Schlesinger notes. "Could it survive the rule of the people? Or were Webster, Clay, Adams and the friends of Van Buren right in their anticipations of disaster?"[30]

In *The Jacksonian Promise: America, 1815–1840*, Daniel Feller argues that although Americans in this era were grappling with rapid demographic and political change, they were also filled with optimistic anticipation and hope for their country. In describing the celebrations that marked the fiftieth anniversary of the Declaration of Independence, Feller declares that most Americans felt not a sense of foreboding about the future but rather confidence and pride: "The chance still lay, as Paine had said in 1776, to 'begin the world over again.' That sense of possibility inspired optimism and exuberance. It also imparted an earnest and even terrible urgency.... Americans saw themselves at a prophetic moment in history, with the fate of the country and even the world resting in their hands. Americans at the Jubilee felt the power to determine their future."[31]

It was a time of fierce protectionism, migration, and improvements in transportation. A. D. Smith was born into this world and in various ways reflected his challenged and conflicted times. He was raised in a Protestant home in a part of Upstate New York that historian Whitney Cross memorably called the Burned-Over District, an area rapidly transformed by the Erie Canal that was swept up in the religious revivals of the Second Great Awakening, "intensifying popular piety and leading to a multitude of new religious institutions. Projects for social reform germinated in the new environment of religious benevolence."[32]

Smith was an active participant in reform movements, and primary documents show that he was involved in efforts to promote temperance, education for young women, and abolition. Smith undoubtedly reflected the optimism of his times, and the "imminent perfection of human society under God's guidance" was a goal that he clearly believed could be attained.[33]

Smith also reflected an intense dedication to republicanism, a faith cherished by Upstate New Yorkers. His home region had suffered tremendous hardship through the War of 1812, fostering an intense aversion to all things British. Smith's desire to bring republican government to Canadians through his involvement in the Hunters' Lodge was yet another example of his status as a man of his time and place. Smith believed that an individual could effect societal change through sheer force of will and personal conviction.

In an era of upheaval, of mass migration toward the western frontier, A. D. Smith remained constantly mobile, ultimately seeking to bring the ideals of optimism, reform, and republicanism to five different states. He saw taking an active part in politics in the communities in which he lived as part of his duty as an American, yet he also contradicted many assumptions about the times. His addiction to alcohol may well have contributed to his early death, yet he campaigned for temperance. Despite his antebellum outspoken devotion to abolition and postwar advocacy of the rights of South Carolina's freed slaves, his early political career included accusations of nativism and a hatred of Catholics—he fought zealously for the rights of some while actively working to deny others their rights. He was a Free-Soil Democrat who believed in states' rights even when that doctrine hindered efforts to fight slavery.

Despite—or possibly because of—his internal contradictions, A. D. Smith had an impact on his era. His work, along with that of northern missionaries and federal agents, in the occupied Sea Islands of South Carolina marked Americans' earliest attempts to offer equality of opportunity to the freed slaves and their progeny. Smith's most dramatic impact on his era was his controversial decision in *Ableman v. Booth*, the only case in which a state judge had the political temerity to declare repugnant the Fugitive Slave Law of 1850.

Beyond the mystery of his life, Smith's political character also provides fodder for historians of secondary subjects. Everything Smith did was informed by a moral code that was developed as a young man and a product of the Jacksonian era. As historian Sean Wilentz notes, "The key to Jacksonian politics" was "a belief that relatively small groups of self-interested men were out to destroy majority rule and, with it, the Constitution. The nonproducing few were able to oppress the productive many, the Democracy proclaimed, because of deliberate political corruptions that thwarted the great principle undergirding American government, popular sovereignty."[34] Smith formed the central philosophy of his life during this time: an absolute commitment to championing the rights of those oppressed by the "nonproducing few" and upholding the beliefs of the far-left Democracy. All of Smith's actions—and the reactions he provoked—must be seen through this lens of radical Democratic politics. As one Democratic pamphlet from the mid-1850s noted, the "Democratic creed was the creed of Jefferson: Absolute acquiescence in the decisions of the majority, the vital principle of republics, from which there is no appeal but to force, the vital principle and immediate parent of despotism."[35]

A. D. Smith held firm to this vision of his party and of his country from the time he was a young Jacksonian until his death. His earliest known formal political affiliation occurred in the 1830s, when he joined the Locofocos, a group that tended to be populated by "men whose careers were characterized by a 'high incidence of social and occupational mobility.'"[36] Indeed, the young, politically active, and ambitious Smith's career and social standing were ascendant. He readily identified with the Jeffersonian spirit of the Locofocos, who believed they were "the original Democratic party" and based their actions on principles of equal rights.[37] Historian Carl Degler has summarized the party's "declaration of principles":

> 1st. "The true foundation of Republican Government is the equal rights of every citizen, in his person and property, and in their management." 2. "The rightful power of all legislation is to declare and enforce only our natural

rights and duties, and to take none of them from us. No man has a natural right to commit aggression on the equal rights of another; and this is ALL from which the law ought to restrain him. Every man is under the natural duty of contributing to the necessities of society; and this is all the law should enforce on him. When the laws have declared and enforced all this, they have fulfilled their functions."[38]

"It turned out," according to historian Edward Pessen, that the Locofocos "had no permanent friends or enemies, only permanent attachment to their principles."[39] The Locofocos were a relatively short-lived political force, but their guiding principles lived on in Smith decades after he spoke at their Cleveland rallies. In fact, this attachment to far-left Democratic politics can be seen throughout his life in one form or another, often in direct conflict with those around him.

In this light, then, it is hardly surprising that his actions alienated many of his contemporaries, as his principles led him to embrace a radical fringe movement that attempted to overthrow colonial governments in Canada, disagree with the U.S. Supreme Court in *Ableman v. Booth*, and finally to land in federally occupied South Carolina during the Civil War, about as far away from the Washington locus of power as possible.

Smith's path most closely aligned with the Van Buren or Barnburner faction of the Democratic Party in the 1840s and the extreme edges of the Republican Party of the 1850s. The extremist Barnburners allegedly took their name from one farmer's willingness to burn down a barn to rid it of rats.[40] Like the earlier Locofocos, Barnburners "revealed a generally restrictive economic outlook and a suspicion of monopoly, loose banking practices, paper money, and speculation; they became the spokesmen for . . . small farmers and mechanics."[41] These radicals quickly garnered a reputation for their "uncompromising determination, even at risk of total loss; practitioners of the art of the impossible," a reputation that accurately describes the personality of Smith.[42]

Many of Smith's contemporaries simply found his ideas too extreme, his acceptance of African Americans and his willingness to appropriate states' rights ideology in their defense too idiosyncratic, and his politics too corrupt. According to one man, Smith's plan to secure property for freed slaves in the Sea Islands "out radicals all the radicalism I ever heard of."[43]

Smith likely was cognizant that some people found his goals too extreme, but he saw his actions as guided by a higher purpose. In many cases, Smith's unfailing sense of right and wrong—his own distinctive, moral compass of radicalism—dictated that the end justified the means: the deaths of innocent men could be excused if they were necessary to overthrow despots blocking democracy in the Canadas; federal law could be violated to take a stand against slavery; railway bond bribes were acceptable if they meant that the tracks went through Milwaukee instead of Chicago; his political career could be torpedoed to uphold the natural rights of African Americans. Smith apparently believed that his actions would ultimately win him not only public favor in his own time but also the admiration of generations to come. Yet no one today or in any era would admire *all* of his positions: support for racial equality as well as invading a friendly neighboring country; opposition to the Fugitive Slave Act based on the doctrine of states' rights, the intellectual and constitutional bulwark of slavery. It is possible that Smith's dichotomies now strike us as either perverse or preposterous only because we live in a world so radically transformed by the collapse of the antebellum party system, by the Civil War, by emancipation, and by the unification and democratization of Canada that we can scarcely imagine the likes of A. D. Smith—at least not clothed in the respected garb of justice of the peace, supreme court justice, or U.S. tax commissioner.

To study Smith is also to study the mind-set of the American "sense of mission."[44] After all, his interest in "liberating" Canadians led to the mention of "one Smith" that initiated this project. It is vital to understand how the reform impulse that led Smith and other politicians to promote racial and gender equality also led them to international intervention and war.

As much as I sought to address Smith's anonymity in American history and his particular brand of radical politics, I was also conscious of the pitfalls inherent in my interpretation of his life. The subject of evidence is obviously key to all biographers: as biographer and historian Paula Backscheider notes, "Just as poets court, bless, fear, and rail at the Muses, so biographers relate to evidence."[45]

The trail of clues left by Smith is fragmented. His parents, for example, have remained untraceable, and little is known about the character or personality of his wife, Mary Augusta Smith. I also cannot account for his whereabouts at various times. His constant restlessness—between careers, between cities, between states—ultimately compromises my ability to tell his story fully. Yet, as Christopher Morley suggests, the missing pieces of the story and the knowledge that more pieces might be found contribute to the allure of biography: "That single piece of evidence by which a lifetime of research falls into place, seldom exists, for the historian does not make his case, plea for his defendant, or prosecute his master villain on the basis of one discovery. The historian works by accretion, adding a bit here and a piece there, until a reasonable likeness of the subject of his pursuit begins to emerge."[46]

Backscheider, in her *Reflections on Biography*, agrees that the search for evidence provides the biographer with a "fierce struggle."[47] As she points out, judging which evidence can be trusted—how we ultimately understand things to be true—varies from discipline to discipline. The scientist has specific modes of understanding knowledge; only some information is categorized as empirical or inherently trustworthy.[48] The historian, by contrast, is challenged by a much wider expectation of interpretation. Gaps in documentary proof necessitate interpretation as well as silence, as Wayne concludes when he is forced to leave his mystery unsolved:

> Historians are not allowed to introduce fictional places or characters or events into their accounts. Nor may they use invented dialogue.... [T]hese restrictions are the price historians believe they must pay to help ensure that illusion does not overtake reality in their attempts to reconstruct the past. But the rules have an ironic side effect. Because of the constraints under which they operate, historians rarely are able to produce narratives as fully realized or richly textured as those dreamed up by skilled novelists. Call it an occupational hazard.[49]

Among the occupational hazards, then, is the danger that our interpretations lead us astray or solve the mysteries in ways that do not do the subject justice. Pulitzer Prize winner William McFeely pondered this difficulty in his biography of General Ulysses S. Grant. McFeely sought to tell "a story of the quest of an ordinary American man in the mid-nineteenth century to make his mark."[50] That quest was part of McFeely's own "exciting journey," one he shared with readers by revealing his own theories about Grant's inspiration.[51] McFeely concluded that Grant derived his determination to push ever forward to greater and greater roles—from common soldier to general to president—from a desperate fear of failure and from having known failure.[52] Yet McFeely cannot prove this hypothesis, and this inherent personal mystery of the character of every human makes new biographies of Grant compelling despite the existence of many other biographies. McFeely concludes, "What is there that we as writers, as readers, can trust in the re-creation of a life? It seems to me, finally, that at least a hint of an answer lies in the riddle, 'Why biography?' Impeccable research, although absolutely essential, does not alone insure that trust. There is another ingredient, one that I think is hinted at by our question, 'Why biography?' To the subject must come the basic human curiosity about our fellow humans."[53]

The life of A. D. Smith stirs that basic human curiosity. It poses questions about the radical politics of the nineteenth century and how Smith and other men of extreme views were seen by their contemporaries. It asks us to contend with questions of human failure and the almost feverish desire to avoid it through a constant agitation and movement that was so common in the era of the "common" man. This movement creates the mile markers for the story of the errant, questing, and quixotic life of A. D. Smith and his times. What follows is my attempt, in the words of Stephen Ambrose, to tell that story right.

CHAPTER 1

New York, Vermont, Ohio
The President of Canada

> Had the Hunters succeeded, some of their leaders might have been awarded a place in history alongside such heroes as Sam Houston, James Bowie and David Crockett, if not even Washington, Lafayette and other immortals of the American Revolution.
>
> —OSCAR KINCHEN, *The Rise and Fall of the Patriot Hunters*

There was no better day than Canada Day to make my public debut with A. D. Smith. After months of research, I finally felt ready to share what I knew with a wider audience, and the newspaper where I worked, the *Ottawa Citizen*, offered to publish this first foray in its July 1, 2003, edition. They gave me five pages to tell the story, a massive amount of journalistic real estate then and unheard-of now.

To piece together the story, I had traveled to Library and Archives Canada in Ottawa (where I lived); to Beaufort, South Carolina; to Lowville, New York; and to Cleveland, Ohio. My travels to the latter two locations took place in December, a time of year I would not recommend for those who wish to pick up the mantle and pursue A. D. Smith. But as my car plowed through the snow belt of Upstate New York on my way to Lowville, I felt a sense of mission, mixed with a feeling that I really was making some kind of progress in determining who Smith was. Readers would be as captivated by his tale as I was, I was sure. My story, all five pages of it, ran as scheduled under the headline, "On the Trail of the Mysterious Mr. Smith." I braced myself for the inevitable onslaught of readers eager to give their own two cents on "the president of Canada." I anticipated phone calls and emails from other historians, bringing fresh eyes, ideas, and perhaps, if I were lucky, new clues to the search.

But I was greeted with silence.

It's a holiday weekend, I thought. People are away.

More silence.

Finally, one letter to the editor arrived: "Congratulations to writer Ruth Dunley on the quintessential Canada Day story. Despite being much less boisterous than our southern friends, our history can be every bit as fascinating. What better format than when the two countries intertwine? Who would have thought that a Yankee named A. D. Smith would have taken such an interest in our humble land? How different would our lot have been today had he succeeded in turning us into a republic. Traditionally the United States has paid scant attention to her northern neighbour. Perhaps that is just as well. I love America, but I love being a Canadian even more."[1]

Complimentary though the letter was, it wasn't the response I had hoped for. But as I look back, more than a decade later, it is perhaps not surprising. The story I had started researching, "A. D. Smith: President of Canada," was really a Canadian story. But as time went by and I returned again to Beaufort and made journeys to Madison and Milwaukee, I began to realize that Smith's story is not particularly a Canadian story at all. All of his activities north of the border were executed from the United States and were noteworthy not so much for what they say about Canada or Canadians as for what they say about Smith's earliest tendencies toward radicalism and reform. Smith is a lovely piece of Canadian trivia, but his more substantive contributions came as part of who he was as an American.

With benefit of hindsight, I can also say that my early understanding of Smith's accomplishments was limited. I had only just discovered his service to the Lincoln administration in the Sea Islands and had really just scratched the surface of his legal maneuverings in *Ableman v. Booth*. I knew almost nothing of his family, his political scheming, the extent of his problems with alcohol, or his sad death at sea. All of that came after years of painstaking—and, at times, thrilling—digging and deciphering in city archives and the smallest historical societies. I followed his trail via bus, airplane, and my car, finding bits and pieces of him in the towns and cities where he had lived.

But before I could start with a place, I had to start with a time.

The year 1811 is not generally remembered as tremendously significant in American history. Yet it was the year of the Battle of Tippecanoe, of freakish earthquakes in Missouri, and of slave revolts in Louisiana. It was also the year that several people who would make their mark on the century ahead were born: Charles Sumner, Horace Greeley, Harriet Beecher Stowe—and Abram Daniel Smith, the New Yorker who went on to become, at least in his own mind, the president of Canada. It was a time, writes historian Gordon S. Wood, when the United States was still grappling with the aftermath of the revolution and the future uncertainties of the young republic:

> [As] Americans were coming to appreciate their capacity to mold and manipulate the culture of their new Republic, they were less and less sure they had that capacity under control. They knew the world had changed and changed radically since the Revolution, but had it changed in directions they had intended? By the early nineteenth century, America had become a huge bustling, boundless nation fascinated with its own expansion—"an expansion of population, of resources, of territory, of power, of information, of freedom, of everything that tends to magnify man."[2]

Other than that he was born on June 9, 1811, in Lowville, New York, little is known about A. D. Smith's early years. The town—a plain and inauspicious place founded eleven years earlier that sits amid the gently rolling hills of north-central New York, about fifty miles from the Canadian border—seems to have no record of his family, though several posthumous tributes to Smith list Lowville as his birthplace. Several Smith families lived in this area of Lewis County at the time, but none of them can be conclusively linked to A. D. Smith. New York lacks birth records before 1881, and although census data at the Lowville clerk's office go back to 1825, when Smith would have been fourteen, the family does not appear. One of Smith's descendants directed me to a research paper by Nellie Rice Molyneux, "Genealogy: Western New York," which indicated Smith was not born in Lowville but Cambridge, about 168 miles southeast in Washington County, New York.[3] But Cambridge also has no record of his birth that I could locate, and Molyneux's research methods have been questioned by genealogists researching other family names. ("When Molyneux had a reliable genealogical text to work from, she was quite good—not perfect, but quite good—at copying off others' work verbatim. When she lacked this crutch, and had to do some genealogy on her own, things dissolve into confusion and witlessness. This is what I call atrocious genealogy," remarked one online critic.)[4] Further, tributes to Smith after his death consistently list Lowville as his place of birth, thus giving the town the best claim to Smith as its progeny.[5]

Of Smith's childhood and teenage years, very little can be determined. Records for the period are notoriously spotty, and matters are complicated by the fact that even small towns often had more than one Smith family, making it difficult to ascertain which family might have been A. D. Smith's. If, as was common, Smith was named after his father, the historical waters are muddied by the early nineteenth-century tendency of record keepers to use the names Abraham and Abram interchangeably. What can be learned about Smith's early years and his family may be drawn from informed inference about the time and place into which he was born. The social and political landscape of Smith's youth provides a foundation of information for surmising how he and his family might have responded to the prevailing attitudes and opinions of the time. As part of what is referred to as the Burned-Over District, an area of Upstate New York that became legendary for its participation in religious revivals of famed preachers such as Charles Finney, Lewis County and Jefferson County, where Smith lived later, had certain defining characteristics. In the early part of the century, they were populated primarily by migrants from other states—particularly western Vermont, Connecticut, and parts of Massachusetts.[6] According to historian Whitney Cross, this "solid Yankee inheritance" gave the people of these counties and the rest of the Burned-Over District particular traits, most notably a deep moral contemplation:

> It was only to be expected that emigration would carry the old traditions westward, most abundantly in the region wherein the migrants settled most thickly. But this natural legacy was reinforced by the purposeful activity of those who remained in the land of steady habits; and a swelling resurgence of evangelistic religion coincided with the period of migration. Consequently, fervent revivalism concentrated in western New York as in no other portion of the country during its pioneering era. Emotional religion was thus a congenital characteristic, present at birth and developed throughout the youth of the section.[7]

Assuming that Smith was not a first-generation American, his parents likely originated somewhere in New England and settled in Lewis County as part of a wave of westward migration that saw whole communities and villages relocate to western New York.[8] Smith's given names, Abram and Daniel, support the idea that his family had not only religious tendencies but also Puritan preferences for biblical names, an onomastic pattern that remained common throughout the early republic in many regions and especially among settlers of Puritan stock.[9] As historian Daniel Scott Smith has written, "The naming of children is culturally never a trivial act."[10] By naming their son Abram, after the father of Israel, and choosing the middle name Daniel, for the slayer of the lion, Smith's parents bestowed upon him a name that conjured images of strength, leadership, and courage in the face of adversity. Even so, Smith may not have liked his given names, since, as my lengthy hunt showed, he almost always signed with his initials rather than his full name, even when writing to his wife.

Since Lewis County's land records do not show what type of property the Smith family owned, it is unclear whether Smith grew up in the town of Lowville or in the surrounding countryside. Since no birth records have been located for Smith, the question of whether he had any siblings also remains unresolved.

The most obvious place to find details about Smith's birth would be in baptismal records, but so far none have been discovered. The Smith family were likely Congregationalists: when Smith married, the ceremony was performed by a Congregational minister, Rev. Joseph Steele, who was a member of the board of trustees of the First Congregational Bethel Church of Milwaukee as well as a member of the "First Congregational Society in the town of Milwaukie."[11] (Evidence indicates that A. D. and Mary Augusta Smith may have briefly attended a Presbyterian church in Lansingburgh, New York. The clerk of the Town of Castleton discovered a note detailing church minutes that contained "a Letter of Dismission and Recommendation to the Presbyterian Chh in Lansingburg, to Augusta Reed, now Mrs. Smith.")[12]

Congregationalism would certainly be consistent with a Yankee upbringing in the Burned-Over District, where Congregationalism, Baptism, Methodism, and Presbyterianism were common.[13] Congregationalist membership in the United States doubled between 1800 and 1830 as the church followed a "traditional Calvinism modified by revivalism" that was supported overwhelmingly by people of New England ancestry.[14] According to David Hackett Fischer, Congregationalists believed their denomination was the "middleway"—a moderate church that combined independent congregations and weak synods.[15] As Fischer describes, "Their theology took a middle ground between Arminianism (which tended toward rationalism and free will) and Antinomianism (the dominion of the spirit). Their formal beliefs were defined by the Synod of Dort (1618–1619) in the five points of Calvinism (total depravity, limited atonement, unconditional election, irresistible grace and the final perseverance of the saints)—a Christian creed of extreme austerity."[16]

Smith was likely born into this world of asceticism and severity, and even if the denomination of his childhood was not Congregationalism, he was undoubtedly raised in a God-fearing home. In the words of historian Perry Miller, "The Old Testament is truly so omnipresent in the American culture of 1800 or 1820 that historians have as much difficulty taking cognizance of it as of the air the people breathed."[17] It is not likely a coincidence, then, that Smith's first name, Abram, is so closely identified with the Old Testament.

On the assumption that Smith was baptized in a Congregational church, I began to focus on the First Congregational Church of Lowville, which later became the First Presbyterian Church of Lowville. I enlisted the help of church archivist Patricia Homer, who spent hours looking through church records but found no records of baptisms of children named Smith between 1811 and 1814.[18] She suggested that I might find more information about Smith by investigating his educational background: anyone who was anyone in Lewis County at the time sent his children to the Lowville Academy.

Without knowing his father's occupation, it is difficult to assess what kind of schooling Smith may have had. As a young man he studied law and medicine, and his career as a lawyer, state supreme court judge, and federal tax commissioner suggests that he received far more than the rudimentary education generally afforded to the children of farmers and common laborers. His extensive library, the contents of which were itemized in his will, suggests a lifelong interest in reading in a broad range of fields, among them history, poetry, and studies of the great leaders, particularly Napoleon.[19] It is consequently likely that Smith's father was a learned man—perhaps a lawyer, clerk, doctor, or clergyman.

Homer also manages the records of the Lowville Academy and offered to check the school's archives. And despite her warning that few records from the early 1800s still existed, she found something—"a wonderful document (fortuitous as there were no others like it of that time period) that listed the students at Lowville Academy for the year 1826, Smith's 15th year." But the list had "no Abram Daniel Smith, no Smith at all."[20]

So far, Lowville had produced no concrete evidence. Inquiries at the Lewis County Historical Society also found nothing. In frustration, I reached out to a professional genealogist, who wrote me a five-page report and said that I was doing all that I could and that her services would not likely shed any further light on Smith's ancestry.

Perhaps, I thought, if I couldn't find Smith in Lowville, I might find him in the next town where he surfaced—Sackets Harbor, in Jefferson County, a key location in the War of 1812.

Smith would have had no memory of the War of 1812, but the postwar world of his boyhood would have left an impression on him, as he would have heard stories from family members and local legends retold by friends and neighbors. The places he called home in his youth and early adulthood had been particularly hard-hit by the war. According to an old legal publication, Smith resided in Sackets Harbor as a young man, though the article did not indicate when he was there.[21] It did say that Smith was there to read law, a common practice in the days before the advent of widespread formalized legal education. The town had been the headquarters for U.S. military forces in the northern theater of the war, and some estimates have suggested that four-fifths of the area's twelve hundred residents suffered some loss during the conflict. During the war, about a third of the American army and a quarter of its navy were stationed in the town's stone barracks, and Sackets Harbor was the site of two celebrated American victories. One of the residual effects of the war was a deeply rooted sense of anti-British sentiment that can be traced back beyond the War of 1812 to the Revolutionary War. Veterans of the revolution were still alive; indeed, Smith's ancestors may well have fought in its battles. Elderly veterans were commonly paraded about on the Fourth of July and gave patriotic speeches to rowdy tavern crowds.[22]

As a young man studying to become a lawyer, Smith would have taken in all of this information as he began to form his own decidedly republican opinions. One story of his fervent republicanism remained a legend in legal circles long after his death. One hot July, Smith became indignant that none of the young men of his acquaintance had any sort of plans to celebrate Independence Day and took matters into his own hands. Armed with a gun and some liquid provisions, young Smith slipped a rowboat into the waters of a nearby bay and made his way to a small island, where he camped under the stars. When the sun rose the next morning, July 4, gunshots startled birds from their branches as Smith began firing skyward in a jubilant salute. By 10:00 a.m., he had set aside his gun and, as the legend goes, began to read the Declaration of Independence aloud—to the lonely woods—and then held forth on the subject of liberty. Finding the ceremony still inadequate, he marched to his rowboat and raised a bottle of liquor and drank thirteen toasts to the original colonies (plus "any number of volunteer" toasts), all the while singing and cheering. He finished up with a silent toast in tribute to George Washington, curled up on the boat's wooden planks, and promptly fell into an inebriated sleep, lulled, no doubt by the soft splash of the waves. He slept until the next morning, when, thirsty and likely nursing a dreadful hangover, he awoke to discover that the tiny boat had not been securely moored and he was now drifting in the middle of the bay. Ever the optimist, he apparently told friends that he "was never more thankful than to find himself where he could get such a bountiful supply of water to quench his thirst."[23]

In addition to being an amusing anecdote, the tale offers some illumination of young Smith's life. One can see many of the passions that guided him throughout his life, including his love of liberty, his belief in the sovereignty of the states, his belief in republicanism, and his wry sense of humor. It also reveals something of an Achilles heel—a taste for alcohol.

Understanding Smith's next actions requires some knowledge of transAtlantic republicanism and the ways in which it manifested itself in American thought. The historiography on this topic is necessarily deep and broad, but six key themes are important in this context. First, republican ideology traded heavily on the idea that the British system of government, in its original state, was the most perfect of political institutions and that the English constitution was the pinnacle of that perfection.[24] However, the early republicans also believed that this system had suffered at the hands of corrupt officials, who had damaged it beyond repair.[25] Republicans saw themselves as rescuing the historic constitution and implementing it in its purest form in the new republic.

Second, the early republicans adhered to a vision that was apocalyptic bordering on paranoid.[26] They believed that taking action was not negotiable but a mandatory and preemptive strike against the burgeoning corruption that was threatening to take hold across the Atlantic world. A failure to act would result in eternal enslavement. This fatalistic vision justified armed resistance against Britain.

Third, the early republicans sought to strike a balance between power and liberty.[27] They fervently believed that this balance, upset by the corrupt hand of England, had to be not only restored but also enshrined in the U.S. Constitution. For early American republicans, the balance of power was also vulnerable to imbalances created by wealth and luxury.

Fourth, the idea of virtue, in all its forms, held enormous importance for early republican thinkers, who saw it as something to be guarded and something for which every good republican must strive. Historians today argue that virtue is central to our understanding of how early republicans in America shaped their society.[28] Wood defines virtue as the "willingness of the individual to sacrifice his private interests for the good of the community," thereby forcing the republic, by its nature, to depend on the goodwill or inherent virtue of the individual.[29] Further, "every state in which the people participated needed a degree of virtue; but a republic which rested solely on the people absolutely required it."[30]

Fifth, religion fit into early American republican ideology not only as a way of achieving virtue but also as an affirmation that the revolution had been guided by God in the name of liberty.[31] The church could not only promote and restore virtue but also combat the spread of corruption. As Wood writes, "Christianity fostered benevolence, a love of one's fellow man and of the community. Religion was the strongest promoter of virtue, the most important ally of a well-constituted republic."[32]

Republicans believed that from the first stirrings of revolution, God had been on the side of liberty and the colonies. Perhaps the best example of appeals to religion in the name of revolution was Patrick Henry's famous

March 1775 "Give Me Liberty or Give Me Death" speech, in which he thundered, "Sir, we are not weak if we make proper use of those means which the God of nature hath placed in our power. The millions of people, armed in the holy cause of liberty, and in such a country as that which we possess, are invincible by any force which our enemy can send against us. Besides, sir, we shall not fight our battles alone. There is a just God who presides over the destinies of nations, and who will raise up friends to fight our battles for us."[33]

Finally, the sixth theme is the influence of previous groups of writers—the ancient Greeks and Romans, Enlightenment thinkers, and English legal minds and libertarians—on the early republican tradition. According to historian Bernard Bailyn, the republicans "found their ideal selves, and to some extent their voices, in Brutus, in Cassius, and in Cicero."[34] (Indeed, Smith's library included several works by classical authors.)[35]

While much of this historiography refers to late-eighteenth-century republican ideology, those views retained their influence in the early nineteenth century and would have helped shape the young Smith's opinions. And yet, as Wood notes, Americans of Smith's generation differed from their republican forebears:

> A new generation of democratic Americans was no longer interested in the revolutionaries' dream of building a classical republic of elitist virtue out of the inherited materials of the Old World. America, they said, would find its greatness not by emulating the states of classical antiquity, not by copying the fiscal-military powers of modern Europe, and not by producing a few notable geniuses and great-souled men. Instead, it would discover its greatness by creating a prosperous free society belonging to obscure people with their workaday concerns and their pecuniary pursuits of happiness—common people with their common interests in making money and getting ahead.[36]

Still one of the "obscure people," Smith next surfaced as a student at the Vermont Academy of Medicine in Castleton, where he arrived in 1830 at roughly age nineteen. Documents do not reveal how long he lived in Sackets Harbor or whether he sojourned elsewhere before enrolling at the academy, and the reasons for his shift from law to medicine are also unknown. However, it was not uncommon for lawyers at the time to pursue medical training "to secure knowledge of use to them in the practice of criminal law."[37] Other than a brief flirtation with phrenology after his graduation from the academy and his lectures on the subject in Cleveland late in the decade, there is no indication that he practiced medicine.

Chartered in 1818, the Vermont Academy of Medicine later became "the first independent degree-granting medical school in New England with legislative authorization to confer degrees."[38] Nevertheless, gaining admission would not have been difficult for Smith, regardless of his academic background: according to one history of the school, "no educational entrance requirements existed at the medical college at Castleton nor at any other American medical college in the period between 1818 and 1862. A few institutions published in their catalogues advice that the prospective medical student should have 'a good English education,' a phrase that meant much, little, or nothing, depending upon who interpreted its meaning. The institution at Castleton did not publish this meaningless advice."[39] Moreover, formal medical training was not necessary to work as a physician at the time, and most "doctors" simply apprenticed with other doctors and then received certificates.[40]

An 1830 Vermont Academy of Medicine catalog lists Smith as one of thirty-three juniors and records his residence as Cambridge, New York (which may explain why that town is sometimes cited as his birthplace).[41] The catalog for the following year indicates that he was a senior residing in "Buskirks Bridge," New York.[42]

In both years, Smith's instructor was identified as Dr. Simeon A. Cook, a graduate of the school who had an interest in homeopathy. One document labels Cook "an example of consistency, integrity, gentleness and earnestness" who was "universally respected by his fellow citizens."[43]

At some point, Smith moved into the Castleton home occupied by Massachusetts natives Seth Reed and Rhoda Fenny (or Finney) Reed (sometimes Read) and some of their eight children. It is not clear whether he had previously known the family or whether he was simply a boarder, but according to a statement Smith made on June 28, 1864, he had come to know Seth and Rhoda's son, Harrison, by 1830: "When I first knew him he lived in Castleton, Vermont. Was an apprentice in a newspaper office. I was a student at medicine; boarded in his father's house; afterwards married his sister."[44]

The Reeds' fourth child and second daughter, Mary Augusta, had been born in Westford, Massachusetts, on May 25, 1811.[45] The Reed family moved to Tyngsboro, Massachusetts, sometime after 1813 and then settled in Castleton, where they ran a hotel and traded cattle.[46]

Records for Mary Augusta are thin, at best, but some information can be gleaned through research into the life of her younger sister, Martha, who married Wisconsin railway tycoon Alexander Mitchell. Martha attended school in Keene, New Hampshire, in 1831, and by 1835, she was enrolled at Emma Willard's Troy Female Seminary in Troy, New York, known for its progressive attitude toward the education of young women.[47] Records at the Rensselaer County Historical Society provide no evidence that Smith ever lived in that city, but Mary Augusta's younger brother, Harrison, appears in the 1832–1833 city directory as a clerk.[48] Mary Augusta probably received an education similar to that of her younger sister, though perhaps at different institutions.

On September 21, 1832, Mary Augusta Reed married A. D. Smith.[49] Nothing is known about the ceremony other than that it took place in Castleton and was conducted by Joseph Steele, the minister at the Congregational Church.[50] Their first child, daughter Mary Frances, was born in nearby Lansingburgh, New York (now part of Troy), on June 4, 1834.[51] It is not known whether the Smiths had relocated to Lansingburgh or were passing through at the time of the birth.

While much of A. D. Smith's life is a mystery, the story of his wife is an even greater enigma. Her personality and until recently appearance remained largely unknown, and none of her letters or diaries is known to exist. In one letter, A. D. referred to her warmly as "Mrs. S.," and in his will he left everything to his "beloved and affectionate" wife.[52] Their thirty-three-year union was thus apparently a happy one, and they had at least four children.

The Smith family's pursuits between 1834 and 1837 remain undetermined, as do their reasons for moving to Ohio, but at some point they joined the westward migration of New Englanders and New Yorkers. Settled earlier than the other states of the northwest frontier, Ohio was populated by a patchwork of migrants from all over the country, but settlement of the northern part of the state, including Cleveland and the Western Reserve, was dominated by Yankees from New England and New York.[53] During the 1820s and 1830s, thousands of people streamed into Ohio and Michigan, traveling by wagon and boat:

> Cleveland reported the westward movement "beyond any former example." Each season saw the numbers increase. In the spring of 1835 fifty-six boats left Buffalo for the West in one week. Six to eight boats with 1,000 to 1,500 passengers passed Erie daily. At this rate the season's total by the lake route would be 200,000. The next year was the same. In October, when Buffalo reported nine boats with 4,000 people having left for the West, they were welcomed with, "There is yet room, and all things are ready. . . ." The western fever was contagious.[54]

Cleveland's growth further accelerated after the completion of the Ohio and Erie Canal in 1832, and the members of the Smith family were among the many newcomers who chose to settle in the city on the Lake Erie shore.[55] Despite its late-twentieth-century reputation as the Mistake on the Lake, 150 years earlier, Cleveland was considered a beautiful and even utopian city with great promise. By the time the Smiths arrived in 1836 or 1837, it had a population of about nine thousand and was drawing comparisons to the great cities of Europe.[56] Gushed the *Cleveland Herald and Gazette* in 1837, "The favorable location of our city, overlooking as it does a broad expanse of waters on the north and west, often gives to the admiring eye an evening perspective outrivaling the famed rose-colored skies of impassioned Italy."[57]

A. D. Smith moved his wife and daughter into a home not far from the public square, in "Farmers' Block," near the intersection of Ontario and Prospect Streets. This area's dirt streets would have bustled with horse-drawn carriages and people traveling on foot to church or meeting friends and business acquaintances in the square. When I landed in Cleveland on one of my first research trips in 2002, such a scene was difficult to imagine—both Smith's home and Farmers' Block were long gone.

Still just twenty-six years old, Smith began to participate in public affairs. Initially, at least, he seems to have worked very hard to carve out a respectable place for himself in Cleveland society. Newspaper accounts indicate that he quickly became involved in local politics, winning election for justice of the peace by eighteen votes in 1838.[58]

At around this time, "Dr. Smith" also gave several public lectures on the "science" of phrenology, which held that an examination of the bumps and contours of a person's skull could provide insight into that person's psychology.[59] The lectures would have enhanced Smith's growing reputation as someone with credibility and knowledge, and the 1837 Cleveland city directory lists him not as justice of the peace or as an attorney but rather as a physician and professor of phrenology.[60]

In the summer of that year, Smith also became involved with the abolitionist movement as a member of the County Anti-Slavery Society.[61] While no further involvement in abolition surfaces in Smith's public records in Ohio, his later activities suggest that antislavery was a lifelong passion. Ohio had a strong history of opposition to human bondage, and the 1835 organizational meeting of the state's Anti-Slavery Society, held in Zanesville, south of Cleveland, attracted an impressive 110 delegates from 25 counties, including the legendary Reverend John Rankin of Ripley, whose hilltop house on the Kentucky border acted as a beacon for runaway slaves.[62]

Abolitionist activity was part of a wider reform movement that was sweeping the United States during the 1830s. Sparked in part by the Second Great Awakening, efforts on behalf of abolition, education for women, and temperance gained a foothold in Cleveland and other cities. Reformers believed that "only those who mastered base impulses and achieved genuine self-control could count themselves truly free," and Smith followed this line of thinking, perhaps influenced by the Arminianism of the Burned-Over District.[63] As put forth by revivalist Charles Finney and others, Arminianism held that "salvation was a matter of individual choice, not divine fiat."[64] Smith and many other members of his generation replaced the rigid Calvinist theology that emphasized predestination with this philosophy, which promoted the idea that society could be improved through individual actions. In fact, these reformers believed, the actions of a good Christian and a good American were one and the same in that they bolstered republicanism: "The idea of human rebirth, the 'new man' was the central point of St. Paul's moral theology. 'Christianity,' wrote William Ellery Channing, '... should come forth from the darkness and corruption of the past in its own celestial splendour and in its divine simplicity. It should be comprehended as having but one purpose, the perfection of human nature, the elevation of men into nobler beings.' ... The prime instrument in this progressive process was the American Republic itself."[65]

This inclination toward reform was a fundamental tenet of republicanism in the generations that followed the revolution. In the *Radicalism of the American Revolution*, Wood argues that this idea was part and parcel of the desire to create a middle class:

> At the same time as ordinary people were reaching upward and vulgarizing aristocratic and genteel culture, the gentry themselves felt increasingly compelled to reach down and embrace wider and deeper levels of the populace. Central to the republican revolution had been the desire by the revolutionary leaders to refine and improve the moral and aesthetic sensibilities of the American people. Like all educated eighteenth-century gentlemen, they had been eager to roll back Gothic barbarism and vulgar manners and extend enlightened civilization and cultivation among the general populace.[66]

By the 1830s, enlightened, civilized reformers did not drink alcohol to excess, a viewpoint that posed a problem for Smith. Moreover, most members of the Congregationalist Church objected to even moderate consumption of alcohol as well as other activities considered detrimental to the soul: "In both Presbyterian and Congregational churches, members were arraigned for such offenses as scandal, Sunday traveling, theft, sexual immorality, profanity, card-playing, running a Sunday boat, using intoxicants, 'attending cotillions and dancing parties,' and neglecting the 'means of grace,' including family prayers."[67] Historian Francis P. Weisenburger notes that "temperance was a subject for much concern, especially on the part of the evangelical denominations." Furthermore, "Congregationalists were probably the most zealous in the movement. Thus, in 1833, for example, the church at Wellington [Ohio] passed a resolution requiring new members to promise entire abstinence in the use and sale of alcohol."[68]

There is no evidence that Smith's drinking, which may have been something of an issue when he was in Sackets Harbor, had become a problem in Ohio. With temperance's prominence among the reform movements of the day and given the prevailing view that "the elimination of drunkenness would prove crucial to avoiding internal civil disruption—thus literally preserving the republican experiment itself," he presumably at least made a show of leading a temperate lifestyle.[69]

Historian W. J. Rorabaugh explains that temperance may have been a response to heavy drinking that was prevalent in the postrevolutionary turmoil of rapid expansion, migration, and economic uncertainty:

> Societies are vigorous and healthy when their institutions and ideologies reinforce one another. When a culture undergoes rapid, disruptive change, its social structure is altered, some of its institutions are weakened, its ideology loses vitality, and stress develops. How a society responds to these conditions determines its future. If a society eases its stress in nonideological ways such as the consumption of alcohol, institutions will be weakened further, and the structure of society may, as in many primitive tribes, disintegrate. If a society handles its stress by developing ideological responses, such as a temperance movement, old institutions can be reinforced, new ones created, and the social structure maintained.[70]

Although Smith himself bore responsibility for most of the "rapid, disruptive change" in his life, he clearly exemplified both the origins of intemperance and the need for temperance. Now with a young daughter, Smith also showed an interest in educational reforms for women, becoming a trustee for the Cleveland Female Seminary, "a private school for young ladies," in 1837, though nothing else is known regarding his involvement.[71]

Smith was also expanding his experience in politics, another of his passions. While in Ohio, Smith's commitment to the far left of the Democratic Party emerged. These "Locofocos" or later "Barnburners" had originated in Smith's home state of New York, and his dedication to republicanism pulled him into association with the Jacksonian Democrats, who as political scientist John Gerring points out, saw themselves as the guardians of freedom:

> In consonance with their general antistatist bent, Democrats assumed the existence of natural rights, that government was instituted to serve basic principles, like private property and liberty, which were therefore *prior* to government. Any infringement of these rights by government constituted an offense against nature.... Well before the outbreak of the Civil War, Democrats were

emphasizing the rights of minorities and the corresponding danger presented by the overweening power of popular majorities.... Throughout the nineteenth century, the Democratic party was much more likely to emphasize the significance of civil liberties and civil rights (as they pertained to white men) than were the Whig and Republican parties. Freedom of the press and of religion, "personal or home rights," as well as the abstract praise of liberty and the ritual invocation of the Kentucky and Virginia Resolutions and the bill of Rights were predominantly Democratic themes.[72]

Smith and other Jacksonian Democrats closely identified with Jeffersonian ideology. According to historian Merrill D. Peterson, after Jefferson's death, his *Memoirs* were "quoted in Congress almost as readily as ministers quoted scripture," and Smith's choice of party indicates he would most certainly have thought of Jefferson as the "Father of Democracy" and would have viewed politics through a Jeffersonian lens.[73] In Peterson's words, "So tight was the association of these three elements—the Jefferson symbol, democracy, and the Democratic party—that one scarcely existed in the public mind apart from the others and attempts to disengage them met with fleeting success."[74]

Smith represented Ward 1 on the Cleveland City Council from October 11, 1837, until March 19, 1838, though the daily newspapers did not document his politics.[75] He is known to have spoken at meetings of Cleveland's Locofocos. A radical wing of the Democratic Party that emerged in the mid-1830s, the Locofocos allegedly took their name from the brand of matches they used to provide light at a meeting after more conservative members of the party had extinguished the gaslights.[76] This faction and their later New York counterparts, the Barnburners, opposed monopolies, banks, corporations, and slavery.[77] Andrew Jackson and the Locofocos believed that "gold and silver were the proper currency... and that a rapid increase in banks and paper money should be discouraged."[78] They also worked "to purge American democracy of the inequities that had crept into its midst and, as a means to that end, to free Jacksonian Democracy of any taint of privilege."[79] They saw monopolies, banks, and corporations as just as inherently exploitative as slavery was.

Historian Carl Degler notes that many Locofoco policies and beliefs set them at odds with other social and political groups of the Jacksonian period: "While the antimonopoly planks of the Locofocos are quite in keeping with the antimercantilistic or 'liberating' interpretations often applied to the Jacksonians, the party's monetary principles point in precisely the opposite direction. It is the Locofocos' monetary views which most clearly reveal that the group was not a part of the expansionist pattern currently alleged to be characteristic of the Jacksonian movement."[80] According to Degler, most Locofocos were either artisans or mechanics, with professionals such as Smith a much smaller part of the movement.[81] Nevertheless, Degler explains, "regardless of the undoubted constrictive effect upon the larger business community, these ... men sought to control inflation by the drastic deflationary device of a metallic currency. It was for this precise reason that the Locofocos thought they saw champions in Andrew Jackson and his successor, Martin Van Buren."[82]

Sprinkled among ads for cures for baldness and hemorrhoids and recipes for "cheap and wholesome" table beer, local newspapers ran articles indicating that Smith was advancing his political causes during the summer of 1837. In August, Smith participated in a "most rambling" debate at the courthouse and then addressed the crowd, making two speeches of the "ultra Locofoco kind," though no further details were provided.[83] At another meeting, "the largest ever convened in Cleveland," townsfolk crowded the courthouse's seats, floor, and galleries to hear various speeches: the remarks, "especially those of Dr. Smith, drew forth strong symptoms of approbation."[84] Smith spoke for about an hour "in a most able and powerful speech ... against the present corrupt system of banking. He clearly and forcibly illustrated the evil effects of banking upon communities in which those institutions are situated, and their evil tendency upon the country generally."[85]

The gathering was a meeting of "the Workingmen," one of many formal and informal assemblies of mechanics, craftsmen, and journeymen that were springing up across the country, particularly after the Panic of 1837 ushered in a six-year depression. Started in urban areas of eastern Massachusetts and sparked by fears of industrialization, the Workingmen's Party shared many of the philosophies of the Locofocos.[86] As historian Walter Hugins argues, the Workingmen's "initial impetus was economic, a protest against unemployment and a defense of the ten-hour day."[87] Historian Sean Wilentz explains that this movement to secure rights for the average workingman "did not originate in party politics or the old mechanics' interest, but its evolution owed a great deal to the Jacksonian political revolution," and the roots of the Workingmen's parties "lay well outside the changing political establishment."[88] Their radicalism may at least explain their appeal for Smith, who often found himself tied up in fringe movements. At this point, he had already cast his lot with several radical causes—not only the Workingmen but also civil rights for women and African Americans. All of these far-left positions were rooted in Smith's support for the laboring classes. Wilentz writes:

In the aftermath of the 1790s, and for a quarter of a century thereafter, New York's masters and journeymen retained and responded to the ideals of the late eighteenth century, for the protection and expansion of their collective political rights against the static, deferential harmony of unquestioned elite supremacy—or, more loosely, for "equality" against "aristocracy." Even as they came to blows in the workshops and the courts, they were as one in politics—the "sinews and muscles of our country," as one Jeffersonian put it—ever prepared to redeem *their* Revolution against any who would trample on their political liberties, against any who would inject "corruption ... through the veins of the body politic."[89]

As Pulitzer Prize–winning historian Arthur M. Schlesinger Jr. points out in his landmark study of the era, *The Age of Jackson*, although "in every state, the reckless expansion of banking facilities provoked widespread popular disgust," Locofocoism, "the expression of that disgust, ... was strongest in the states where issues of currency and incorporation were most vital. It was thus an *Eastern* movement, designed to meet *Eastern* economic difficulties, preoccupied with fears to which the West was largely indifferent."[90] The movement nevertheless had a presence on the frontier and particularly in Ohio, whose economics closely resembled those of the East.[91]

As a New York native, Smith may have been particularly attracted to a radical faction tied to his home state, but the degree of his commitment to fundamental Locofoco beliefs cannot be determined, since his speeches from this time have not survived. Politics aside, however, Smith and other Locofocos saw themselves, in Glyndon Van Deusen's words, as "principled equalitarians, neo-Jeffersonians, men filled with a high sense of justice and fair dealing."[92] In keeping with that "high sense of justice and fair dealing," Smith's later life featured various struggles for equality, campaigns on behalf of state sovereignty in which he quoted Jefferson, and service as a judge, sworn to uphold the principles of justice. Smith's involvement with the Locofocos was, in short, no political flirtation but rather a lifelong commitment to the left wing of the Democratic Party—and very often to the far left. So extreme were his views that he frequently found himself on the wrong side of the politically powerful.

The early 1830s also witnessed a flurry of economic activity that produced flashpoints across the country: Andrew Jackson's Bank Wars, unprecedented purchases of land on credit, the construction of internal improvements such as canals and roads, and rising prices for land and exports. Some people began to fear that prosperity would not last: "To appearances, the country had never thrived so well. But by 1836 the rise was beginning to spin out of control. Some saw symptoms of a speculative cycle and predicted a bad end. Wage-earners and credit-seeking businessmen felt the pressure of higher prices and interest rates. Doomsayers warned of inflated values caused by 'overtrading.' Fears of an imminent, perhaps catastrophic collapse gathered over Jackson's last days as president."[93]

The Panic of 1837 broke early in the year, bringing the suspension of specie payments, increased unemployment, and a massive drop in land values.[94] While businesses in Ohio cities were affected, the state's residents fared better than most Americans, in part as a consequence of the state's largely agrarian economy: 1837 was a good crop year.[95] As a justice of the peace, Smith probably did not feel much of a pinch—his docket books indicate that he remained quite busy. His personal life was also thriving, as Mary Augusta gave birth to a second daughter, Maria Cecilia, in 1839.[96]

One way in which the Panic of 1837 did affect Smith's actions, however, was by facilitating the jingoist movement of which he was to become a part. As historian Oscar Kinchen notes, many Americans looked outward in a search for a scapegoat, and "not a few bankrupt business and professional men held that Britain was largely to blame for the prevailing hard times."[97]

And although Smith appeared to be a respectable, somewhat prominent professional in a growing city, he was also attending clandestine meetings and learning secret codes and handshakes as a member of the Hunters' Lodge, "the most formidable of all the secret associations formed for the forcible republicanization of Canada."[98] Smith was turning his attention away from the local political scene and toward the international stage. Having grown up only a few miles from the Canadian border, Smith would have already been attuned to at least some degree to the issues that were riling Upper Canadians, and by the late 1830s, Cleveland's newspapers were reporting almost daily on the unrest in the predominantly English-speaking colony of Upper Canada (north of the St. Lawrence River) as well as in the mostly French-speaking colony of Lower Canada. Canadians were becoming increasingly vocal in their opposition to the oligarchic ways of the Family Compact, the Toronto-based group of aristocrats who dominated decision making in Upper Canada. Nepotism, political patronage, land grants, favoritism toward the Anglican Church, and a sliding economy all contributed to a seething anger in the province. When political agitation failed, reformers in Upper Canada, led by the fiery William Lyon Mackenzie, resorted to armed conflict in what subsequently became known as the Rebellion of 1837. Mackenzie, using rhetoric reminiscent of the American Revolution, urged Canadians to join his cause: "'Canadians!'—it was a voice that knifed the expectant hush; 'Do you love Freedom?'—and as the answering murmur swelled—'I know you do! Do you hate oppression?—Who dare deny it! I say to you that the farmer toils, the labourer toils, the merchant toils—and the Family Compact reap the fruit of their exertions! What redresses can we expect, while Canada is ruled by a man in a street in London?'"[99]

In December 1837, Mackenzie led a mob of as many as a thousand men to Montgomery's Tavern north of Toronto. Loyalists fired cannons at the building, killing five rebels and forcing Mackenzie and other "rebel refugees" to flee to the United States.[100] A week later, Mackenzie organized a "patriot army" that occupied Navy Island, part of Upper Canada on the Niagara River, its boundary with New York. Mackenzie's army rapidly increased as Americans answered his call for troops. While some of these young men were undoubtedly looking for adventure, others were spurred by loftier goals. Declared one group of participants, "We the young men residents of the city of Buffalo . . . pledge to each other our mutual support and co-operation for the commendable purpose of aiding and assisting our Canadian brethren in their present struggle for liberty and those principals [sic] which have given the world that asylum which we have the honor of calling our homes and built up that fabrick of human might which pronounces to mankind the sacred dogma of equality."[101]

Disgruntled Canadians also made haste to the island, and by late December, as many as one thousand men had assembled and were preparing to proclaim an Upper Canadian republic. They began firing cannons at the Canadian shore, and matters escalated further on December 29, when Canadian troops captured an American steamer, the *Caroline*, with "the slashing of the cutlass and the sharp bang of the pistol" as it ferried supplies to the militants on Navy Island.[102] In the chaos that ensued, passengers were forced ashore and the steamer was set ablaze, with its fiery remains drifting toward Niagara Falls. Recounted one witness,

> It was a splendid sight which shed a light for many miles around,—the rippling of the water made it appear as if gold dust had been sprinkled on its surface, and the gleam of light was so great that the sentinels upon the island perceived some of the boats, fired, but the balls fell short. . . . Her pipe got red hot and stood upright till the last. At the commencement of the rapids she appeared as if hesitating a moment, when plunge she went, rose once, then a sea struck her, she heeled over, sunk in the falls and disappeared forever. It was a sight that made the boldest hold his breath.[103]

The *Caroline* was in American waters at the time of its seizure, and an American was killed in the melee. As an international crisis loomed in early 1838, President Martin Van Buren sent General Winfield Scott to set up a military command along the border. To defuse the situation, Van Buren officially admitted that American citizens had participated in the *Caroline* catastrophe and called on his countrymen to return to their homes, warning that no American could expect help from his government if captured in Canadian territory.[104] Historian Samuel Watson makes the case that cautious Americans during this time saw the filibusterers as "threats to international law and domestic order—a sort of international mobocracy."[105] But the federal government lacked the constitutional and military authority to suppress the rabble-rousers, presenting Van Buren with a delicate situation. In addition, the president was dealing with the Aroostook War over the Maine–New Brunswick border.[106] In his 1837 inaugural address, Van Buren had clearly indicated his intention to keep the United States on a course of neutrality: "We have no disposition and we disdain all right to meddle in disputes, whether internal or foreign, that may molest other countries, regarding them in their actual state as social communities, and preserving a strict neutrality in all their controversies."[107] Nevertheless, many Americans, particularly those living in border areas, saw the destruction of the *Caroline* as a call to war, and "many a violent resolution was adopted at public meetings along the border."[108] In an area already predisposed to animosity toward the British, the American fatality and violation of the U.S. border constituted reason enough to resume the War of 1812. In Cleveland, citizens braced themselves for possible conflict: warned one newspaper in early November 1837, "a crisis is approaching."[109]

In this climate, Americans along the border began forming secret societies devoted to overthrowing Crown rule in the Canadas. More organized than Mackenzie's ragtag groups, the members of these groups saw themselves as taking part in a postscript to the American Revolution and called themselves the Hunters' Lodge. The name may have been taken from Dr. James Hunter, of Whitby, Ontario, who had taken part in Mackenzie's raid at Montgomery's Tavern or may have been derived as a cover story to explain why armed men were gathering in the backwoods.[110] The groups instituted special handshakes and passwords and devised elaborate initiation rites. Candidates reported to secret locations and were blindfolded; then, as the cloth was ripped from their faces, they were told to "behold the light." With a waving of pistols and torches burning, the new Hunter received a final warning: "As you see light, so you also see death, presented to you in the most awful shape and form, from which no earthly power can save you, the moment you attempt to reveal any of the secrets or signs which have, or may be revealed to you."[111] Such mysterious rituals would have appealed to Smith and other men who were already involved in freemasonry or other fraternal organizations.[112]

Kinchen describes the primary purposes of the local Hunters' Lodges as "initiation of candidates for the various degrees, recruiting volunteers for the Patriot army and navy, collecting money, arms, clothing, and other supplies for the movement, and the making of numerous reports and donations to the central committee, or grand lodge, under whose jurisdiction the local society belonged."[113] What exactly took place at the meetings would have varied from lodge to lodge, though the meetings seem consistently to have taken place at night and often in private homes:

> In these meetings the members were harangued by traveling propagandists, who denounced the alleged evils of monarchical government while extolling the blessings of liberty, equality, and brotherly love. Responsible self-government for the Canadians was bitterly denounced as a delusion and a snare to entice liberty-loving people to turn away from the pursuit of democratic institutions and republican government ... bounteous suppers were sometimes served, very likely for the purpose of promoting the attendance of luke-warm members whose waning interest might otherwise have kept them away.[114]

Speeches, often "long and inflammatory" and extending well into the night, were also common at some lodges.[115] Smith's extant writings and speeches show a fondness for verbosity and flamboyancy, a style that may have been influenced by his early involvement in the Hunters' Lodge.

The Hunters' Lodge was not alone in its efforts. A similarly named francophone group, Les Frères Chasseurs, had lodges in the East and support from New England, primarily Vermont. Les Frères Chasseurs elected their own leaders, who acted independently as well as in concert with the Hunters. In Kinchen's words, "These two organizations were necessarily interdependent, since the success or failure of the one was bound up with that of the other."[116] The extent of Smith's involvement, if any, with the New England group remains unknown.

Although the Hunters' Lodges were primarily an American movement, they had roots in the rebellions led by Mackenzie and his Lower Canadian counterpart, Louis-Joseph Papineau. For his part, Mackenzie, insisting "that Canada identify itself with the struggle for liberty being waged in America in the 1830s," was very much influenced by Jacksonian ideology.[117] As historian J. E. Rea writes, Mackenzie held an idealized vision of Jackson as a "great Democratic hero," "not in words only, but in deed and in truth, the friend of the humbler classes against the united rapacity of their more exalted brethren, who, in America, as elsewhere, would willingly concentrate the wealth and power of the republic in a few hands, that it might minister the more securely to the wants of a luxurious and immoral aristocracy."[118]

Mackenzie's "admiration for American democracy grew as rapidly during the 1830s as his affection for British rule declined."[119] His 1833 *Sketches of the United States and Canada*, which recorded his thoughts on American politics, was influenced by both his travels to and his "omnivorous reading" about the United States. As historians S. F. Wise and Robert Craig Brown remark, "The hero of the Sketches is unquestionably Andrew Jackson, the noblest of 'these modern Romans,' whose austere republican virtues, whose rise to greatness through sheer merit, not birth or wealth, and whose advocacy of the cause of 'the humbler classes against the united rapacity of their more exalted brethren,' testified to the moral strengths of American Democracy."[120] As time went on, Mackenzie "increasingly advocated measures derived from contemporary American political forms," and when he and fellow reformers were ignored, violence ensued.[121] This violence, born of frustration and anger, was first seen in the Rebellions of 1837–1838 but later manifested itself in the form of the Hunters' Lodge.

Very little is known about the Hunters: despite their lack of success in achieving their other goals, they did well at maintaining a secret society. Many of their documents were encoded, and they had a standing order to burn all membership rolls and other lodge records in the event that the movement failed.[122] Consequently, few official Hunter records have been found.

Like the men from Buffalo who helped occupy Navy Island, the Americans who joined the Hunters' Lodge seem to have seen liberating their Canadian brethren from the tyranny of the Crown as a fraternal duty. In Kinchen's view, Hunters had been "bred in revolutionary tradition and nourished on Fourth-of-July oratory to the hatred of all things British"; most were "administration men"—Van Buren Democrats.[123] Like Smith, they were also unafraid of radicalism.

Hunters established lodges in Detroit, Buffalo, Cincinnati, Rochester, and dozens of smaller towns in between, with membership estimates varying between twenty thousand and more than two hundred thousand—the clandestine nature of the organization means that no definitive numbers are available.[124] Cleveland, sharing Lake Erie with Upper Canada and handy to ships, became the western headquarters for the Hunters, and less than a week after the *Caroline* debacle, the city became the site of public meetings to rally support for the "Patriot cause."[125] At one such gathering, attendees formed a committee to "receive donations for the benefit of the Patriots." Smith was one of its twenty-one members.[126] The *Cleveland Daily Advertiser* reported on January 4, 1838, "Monday evening, pursuant to a call posted up about the streets of the city, at an early hour the Court House was filled to overflowing by the friends of the Canadian cause.... General Sutherland, from the Patriot Camp at Navy Island, was then announced to the meeting and the loud, long and enthusiastic cheers which welcomed him attested the sympathy of our citizens with his cause."[127]

While most supporters of the Patriot cause did not openly advocate hostilities with Britain, the Hunters' Lodge began stockpiling arms and plotting invasions of Canada, spurred on not only by the example of their forefathers in the American Revolution but also by more recent revolutionary activity in Greece, Poland, Italy, Belgium, and especially Texas. The Hunters sought to spark similar revolutionary activity in the Canadas: as one man wrote to the *Freeman's Advocate*, a Hunter newspaper based in Lockport, New York, "Ask the immortal Washington, and would he not say—give the patriots the chance that the American Revolutionists had—be to them what France was to you.... The Americans have only to say to the Canadians, be ye free and independant! [sic] and it will be done."[128]

Whether the Hunters desired an independent Republic of Canada or the addition of Canada to the United States is not entirely clear. The idea of annexation certainly was not unthinkable to Americans at the time: though the term "Manifest Destiny" did not enter the American lexicon until the 1840s, the ideas inherent in that philosophy had long been percolating. The idea of acquiring Canada went back as far as the 1690 Siege of Quebec and had resurfaced during the American Revolution and War of 1812. In the decades leading up to the creation of the Hunters' Lodge, the United States had undergone massive expansion through the Louisiana Purchase and the acquisition of Florida. By the 1820s, Americans had staked a claim to a full half of the continent.[129]

Through the early winter and spring of 1838, the Hunters gathered strength, amassing weapons and infiltrating low-ranking government posts as sheriffs, postmasters, and customs officers.[130] They also created a bank, the Republican Bank of Canada, in which investors could buy stock to be paid out when the Canadas achieved liberation. (The bank's currency was to bear the words "liberty, equality, and fraternity.")[131] They also created a logo that could be used as the flag of a new Canadian republic: a giant American eagle swooping to Earth and sinking its sharp talons into the back of the British lion. While the Hunters included malcontents and ne'er-do-wells, the group may also have attracted "men of wealth, influence and intelligence": the governors of some Great Lakes states, including Michigan and New York, were rumored to be members.[132] Even Henry Clay was believed to sympathize with the Hunters.[133] Historian Donald E. Graves notes that the Hunters recruited Orrin Scott, the nephew of the General Winfield Scott, whom Van Buren had sent to oversee the border and prevent Hunter incursions from getting out of hand, as well as

Charles Brown, nephew of General Jacob Brown, former commander of the U.S. Army.[134]

Night after night in Cleveland, men stole into the streets. When they were not gathering for meetings, they trained for battle in the woods outside the city: "Parties were drilled at night in all possible secrecy at distances of thirty to fifty miles from the frontier," wrote one informant to Sir George Arthur, lieutenant governor of Upper Canada. Cleveland also had a newspaper dedicated to the Hunters' cause, the *Bald Eagle*. However, neither the *Bald Eagle* nor the mainstream press reported anything unusual during the week of September 16–22 even though dozens of Hunters were arriving in Cleveland for a convention to elect a provisional government of the Republic of Canada. All lodges were expected to report to the meeting.[135]

Attendees elected "one Smith"—A. D. Smith—to serve as president.

A coded Hunter document dated almost exactly one month before the Cleveland election is signed "by the President, A. D. Smith."[136] It is possible that the date was listed incorrectly, or Smith may have been serving as de facto president prior to his formal election. Cleveland grocer Nathan Williams was elected vice president, and Akron lawyer Lucius V. Bierce became commander in chief of the "Army of the Northwest." The group of 160 delegates approved what labor historian Andrew Bonthius describes as "a quintessentially Locofocoite banking plan designed to fund their cause and serve a new republican economy in Canada."[137]

According to Bonthius, the plan

> left little room for mistaking the Hunters' all-encompassing vision for anything less than the refashioning of Canadian civil society along radical republican lines: "All institutions of the country should be for the benefit of the people. There should be no landed aristocracy, no established church, no bank monopoly, no union of the monied aristocracy with the executive." The exigencies of capitalist development, particularly in the U.S., had made this latter call for the separation of state and bank the calling card of radical, democratic republicans.... Thus, even though they were using the word "bank," theirs was obviously not intended to operate in any traditional capitalist sense, and eastern bankers would certainly have scoffed at the ... plan approved by Patriots in Cleveland.[138]

This aspect of Hunter ideology is particularly relevant for understanding A. D. Smith's character. The Hunters' distaste for monopolies and aristocracies mirrors the Jacksonian aversion to "an America of privilege and monopoly," while their banking scheme was classically Jacksonian.[139] "The bank issue," in the words of historian James Roger Sharp, "was the crucible of the

Democratic party. It tested and tempered the metal of Jackson's followers and became the mold from which the party was shaped."[140] In many respects, then, Hunter ideology rested firmly on Jacksonian precedents and would have had direct appeal for Smith, whose left-Jacksonian leanings—particularly his repeated efforts to vindicate society's disenfranchised—welled up at this stage in his life, priming him for his future personal and public battles.

Cleveland's Hunter headquarters and the place where their new president, Smith, did his scheming was located in Millers Block, on Superior Street. The facility featured a spacious meeting hall on its upper floor that was roomy enough for Hunters to drill. In mid-September 1838, President Smith informed at least one man, Ohio cabinetmaker William Jones, that an attack was planned for the following month.[141] In fact, the Hunters were planning many attacks and invasions, though whether Smith masterminded any of them is not known. In November 1838, the Hunters stormed into eastern Ontario near Prescott, triggering the Battle of the Windmill, an event that historian Donald Graves notes would have made "delightful comic opera" had it not involved the loss of life.[142] The Hunters planned to land at Prescott, seize nearby Fort Wellington, and then "arm the thousands of Canadians expected to rally round once news of the invasion had spread."[143]

With sentries in Prescott sounding the alarm, the Hunters' initial night landing was thwarted, as three attempts to dock their schooners failed and they were forced to retreat to the American side of the St. Lawrence until the morning light. By then, HMSV *Experiment* had arrived to defend the town. On their way to safe American waters, the Hunters' ships ran aground, and their lines became entangled.[144] In desperation, the Hunters, "armed to the teeth," swarmed into the New York river port of Ogdensburg and overwhelmed federal officials, hijacking the steamer *United States*.[145] The Hunter at the helm of the pirated *United States* "decided his best course of action was to ram" the smaller *Experiment*, much to the appreciation of his boisterous "crew." According to Graves, the new captain reasoned that, "If he could not sink the *Experiment*, he might damage her enough to keep her out of the way, and on his orders the steamer's pilot, Solomon Foster, steered directly for the little British steamer. As the *United States* came up the river, the militia in Prescott fired at her but the Hunters on her decks, perhaps as intoxicated as her captain, jeered when the rounds fell short."[146]

Evading the attack, the *Experiment* steamed back to the docks at Prescott. Gathering at Windmill Point, about a kilometer and a half east of the town, the Hunters waited for reinforcements. As many as three hundred Hunters may have reached Canada that day and prepared for battle the following morning.[147] Recalled one, "We had full confidence in our cause as a just and noble one. We believed we were about to do our neighbours a deed of charity, such as the golden rule inculcates when it teaches us to do to our fellows as we would they should do to us. We believed our Canadian neighbours to be struggling for that freedom which we were enjoying and with a little aid, they would be successful in securing."[148] But with limited ammunition and food and bereft of the support they had anticipated from Canadians, some Hunters began to sense the futility of the venture and deserted even before the battle began.[149] Then, after several days of exchanging fire with the British, the Hunters ended up hunkered down inside the mill:

> The doors and ground floor windows of the buildings near the mill were barricaded with bricks, stones, furniture, lumber and timber, and just about anything else that could be found until they were completely blocked. To enter the buildings, the Hunters used ladders to climb up to the second-storey windows, and once inside, these were pulled up to deny access to unwanted visitors.... The invaders also collected nails, spikes, door handles, hinges and other metal scrap to use as canister rounds in their artillery pieces.[150]

The Hunters, some wounded, found themselves surrounded by British forces and staring down the barrels of two eighteen-pounder artillery pieces. Faced with an untenable situation, the Hunters surrendered on November 16, 1838.[151] Kinchen estimates that 157 men were taken prisoner and brought to Kingston's Fort Henry to await military trial, where they were prosecuted under "An Act to protect the Inhabitants of this Province against Lawless Aggression from Subjects of Foreign Countries at Peace with Her Majesty."[152] Some of the Hunters who participated in the Battle of the Windmill were sent to penal colonies in Australia; eleven were hanged.[153] In an ironic twist, the Hunters were defended by a team that included John A. Macdonald, a young lawyer like A. D. Smith. Smith never realized his dream of leading Canada, but in 1867, Macdonald became the united country's first prime minister.[154]

Smith apparently had little to do with the Prescott attack—most of the men involved seem to have been from New York—but likely had a hand in a plot to invade Windsor, Ontario, that was planned in Cleveland and guided in part by his commander in chief, Bierce.[155] Seizing the steamboat *Champlain* on December 3, 1838, and locking the crew inside, the invaders crossed the Detroit River and landed in Windsor. In response to Bierce's command to "conquer or die," the Hunters, armed with muskets, bayonets, pistols, and knives, marauded through the village and set fire to the militia barracks, burning alive some of the soldiers inside.[156] The invaders torched a Canadian steamer, the *Thames*; set fire to houses; and killed one man who refused to join the rampage. Another man suffered a gruesome fate: he was either shot and then slashed with Bowie knives or mutilated with an axe and then fed to hogs. When the militia arrived, the Hunters were positioned in an apple orchard. According to Kinchen, "Before the invaders could reload, the orchard was filled with militia, firing point blank at the wavering lines of the Hunter force it was only a matter of minutes until Bierce's men were in tumultuous flight, some running southward into the woods while others ... were able to find canoes and skiffs and to make their way across the river while bullets whizzed by on their right and left."[157] Twenty-one Hunters died in the battle, and twenty-four were captured. Four of them were shot without trial.[158] The Hunters who returned to the United States were welcomed as heroes in Detroit despite the official U.S. government policy of neutrality.[159]

The incidents in Prescott and Windsor sparked fears of more attacks in Upper Canada, but subsequent incidents were minor. Canadian homes along the border, particularly those of known supporters of the Crown, occasionally were torched, actions that must have confused many Upper Canadians. While disgusted by what they saw as corruption among colonial officials, most had no quarrel with Crown rule, and they did not abide arson. The raids were a serious miscalculation on the part of the Hunters, who had erroneously believed that they enjoyed the moral and physical support of Canadians. Instead, the raids were met with little to no backing, leaving the Hunters completely alone. As historians S. F. Wise and Robert Craig Brown point out, years of violence—first the Canadian Rebellions and subsequently the guerrilla activities of the Hunters—transformed Canadian opinion of the United States, further reducing the likelihood of support for the Hunters:

> In all regions, the rebellions of 1837 and the ensuing violations of British North American territory by American citizens in support of the rebels, with the apparent sympathy of the United States government, served to telescope colonial opinion toward the right. Favorable views of American institutions were now irretrievably associated with treason, and it required more courage—and more conviction—than most moderate reformers possessed to voice publicly the mildest praise for them. For more than a decade after the rebellions, there would be no major challenge to the dominant conservative position on the nature of the American polity.[160]

Several factors contributed to the Hunters' demise. American forces along the border had been strengthened, making excursions more difficult. As well, General Scott and his men were under orders "to use every measure in their power to prevent any hostile incursions into Canadian territory and officers ... were supplied with funds for the purchase of information about threatened attacks," thus hampering recruitment and any open plotting in taverns.[161] This crackdown was quite effective, given the Hunters' weak leadership.

Furthermore, whatever support the Hunters ever enjoyed faded when the 1839 Durham Report recommended responsible government for British North American colonies and the amalgamation of Upper and Lower Canada to form a united Province of Canada.[162] In 1841, the same year as the Act of Union, U.S. president John Tyler, a Virginian little interested in northern expansion, issued a proclamation denouncing the Hunters and their motives:

> I expect all well-meaning but deluded persons who may have joined these lodges immediately to abandon them and to have nothing more to do with their secret meetings and unlawful oaths, as they will avoid serious consequences to themselves; and I expect the intelligent and well-disposed members of the community to frown upon all these unlawful combinations and illegal proceedings, and to assist the Government in maintaining the peace of the country against the consequences of the acts of their violations of the law.[163]

The Tyler presidency ushered in a new era in American politics and American-British diplomacy. Many historians have commented that the two countries were on the brink of war during much of the time of the Hunters' activities, but in the early 1840s, the relationship took a decided turn for the better as the Whigs took power in the United States.[164] In 1842, the British government sent Alexander Baring, Lord Ashburton, to Washington to broker a settlement of all outstanding disagreements with the United States. His mission was helped along by the fact that Secretary of State Daniel Webster was warm to the idea of peace with England and considered Ashburton a personal friend.[165]

In addition to the Maine border dispute, the Webster-Ashburton Treaty settled one of the unresolved issues stemming from the *Caroline* incident. In 1840, a Canadian deputy sheriff, Alexander McLeod, had bragged over beer at a U.S. tavern that he had been responsible for the sole death aboard the boat, the killing that had sparked most of the cries for retribution on the American side of the border.[166] McLeod was immediately jailed in New York on the charge of murder. Britain protested the arrest, but negotiations stalled when the U.S. federal government refused to intervene in a state court case.[167] At trial, evidence showed McLeod to be a liar, not a murderer: he was acquitted when it was determined that he had been miles away from the *Caroline* at the time of the death.[168] Ashburton expressed some remorse for the whole sad affair, and Webster also made a concession: a new law to give federal courts the right to intervene with habeas corpus when foreigners were arrested by state authorities for acts committed in the accused's home country.[169] With reform in Canada and improved diplomatic relations between the United States and Britain, the Hunters' raison d'être and their tenuous organizational structure crumbled. With no issues to keep their radical fires burning, the Hunters simply faded from the landscape, forgotten as quickly as they had formed. As Shaun J. McLaughlin writes, the Hunters "atrophied into a pathetic club of old men who schemed and dreamed of impossible glories."[170]

The question of what exactly the Hunters meant when they elected a "president of Canada" remains largely unanswered. The extant documentation and contemporary accounts say little about what the title involved, and no private writings from Smith during this time have yet been located. On the surface, Smith's title can be read as a provisional role that would have been activated the moment Hunters took control of Canadian soil. In practical terms, he appears to have been solely an administrator: there is no evidence that Smith himself took part in any military activities. The Hunters may simply have been modeling the idea of a Canadian president after what they had witnessed during the Canadian Rebellions, when Mackenzie declared himself president of a new republic: "Less than a week after he had fled the battlefield, Mackenzie was again on Canadian soil, this time as the chief of state of a new Canadian republic. The first volunteers crossed with him to Navy Island. . . . Here Mackenzie raised the Patriot tricolour, with its twin stars for the two Canadas, and, as 'Chairman, *pro tem.*' of the provisional government, promised rewards of Canadian land and silver for every new recruit."[171]

Part of the difficulty in analyzing Smith's role lies in the murkiness that surrounds the Hunters' goals. Kinchen says simply that their "purpose was none other than to 'give liberty to the people of Canada.'"[172] Edwin C. Guillet states explicitly that "the main aim of this elaborate secret organization was to obtain a republican form of government for Canadians, and they were persuaded that on their arrival the populace would rise to their support."[173] But doing so would have required sparking a full-scale revolution: in the aftermath of such an event, it would seem unlikely that Canadians' first choice for president of the new republic would have been a foreigner such as Smith.[174]

If, on the other hand, Hunters envisioned Canada's annexation by the United States, they might have seen Smith as more like a territorial governor than a president and believed that his precise role could be negotiated once the nasty business of revolution had been set aside. Of course, the answers to these questions hinge on whether the Hunters truly believed they had what it took to overthrow the Crown. The success of such a revolution depended on full support from Canadians, and after their first incursions on Canadian soil, the Hunters realized that they lacked that backing. In addition, their plans would eventually have required support from the U.S. government, which they also knew they lacked. Smith and other men who occupied positions of power within the group must also have been aware that the Hunters' Lodge lacked the organization, military skill, and sheer numbers to succeed, leaving a troublesome question: *Did the Hunters even believe in their own stated purposes?*

Some members—particularly those willing to risk their lives on the front lines—undoubtedly believed strongly that their goal of a Canadian republic was possible. Yet the Hunters also paid (or promised future payment to) many men who fought for the cause.[175]

Why would Smith and others like him have joined the group? This question, like so many others, is also difficult to answer. No diary of Smith's time in Ohio has been located, and even those who must have known Smith well, such as Bierce, apparently did not write about his Ohio exploits. But as one spy reported to Canadian colonial officials, Hunter meetings seemed to be attended mostly by "fellows who delight in hearing themselves speak, but who would never venture to take an active part in an invasion of Canadian territory."[176] Smith seems to fall into this category. While the men drilling in the woods may have been of the working classes, many of those in higher positions of responsibility within the organization were doctors, lawyers, merchants, and politicians, whom Kinchen describes as "seeking personal advancement by associating themselves with the 'crusade for Canadian freedom.' Candidates are said to have announced for office, basing their claim to public favor on the ground of their being identified with the Patriot cause."[177] For Smith, with his obvious political aspirations, participation in the Hunter movement would have served the same purpose as his activities with the Freemasons: providing opportunities to connect with influential men in the community, practice oratory, and sharpen leadership skills. Since Ohio's Hunters were known backers of Van Buren, and since Smith was an avowed Democrat, involvement with the Hunters also presented a chance to socialize with like-minded citizens for the purpose of political organization beyond the lodge's goals: "The discussion of politics and the advocacy of candidates deemed favorably to the Patriot cause occupied no small place in the program at these lodge meetings. During the autumn of 1838, the lodges in New York and Ohio were backing a slate of candidates for the various state offices as well as for representatives in Congress."[178] Nevertheless, even if Smith did not believe that the Hunters could obtain their objectives, he might still have believed in the cause itself. The Hunters' efforts to secure republican virtue in Canada, their absolute dedication to concepts of liberty, and their Jacksonian devotion to the protection of the common man would have held immense appeal for Smith.

Smith's involvement in the Hunters reveals some clues about his personality that are evident in all chapters of his life. Most notably, he apparently was unable to assess realistically the alignment of forces in the border region. Similar misjudgments eventually undid his career in both Wisconsin and South Carolina.

More positively, his embrace of the U.S. "mission" to spread republicanism attested to his lifelong passion to protect those he saw as defenseless and vulnerable to the heavy hand of an oppressor—usually government. The *Washington Globe*, a newspaper that strongly backed the Jackson administration, took as its slogan, "The world is governed too much."[179] According to Hugins, "This became the rallying cry of Jacksonians, North and South, and especially of those party radicals, like the Locofocos, who scolded their more conservative fellow Democrats for departing from the guiding principles of Jefferson and Jackson."[180]

The Hunters' aims would have appealed to Smith. Despite their misreading of Canadian public opinion and lack of military proficiency, the Hunters were motivated primarily by a desire to safeguard and defend the downtrodden—ideals tinged with a decidedly Jacksonian flavor. In December 1838, the *Freeman's Advocate* declared,

> Let us be understood—in principle we are of the ultra-democratic school. Aristocracy and monarchy are equally hideous to us—where the former seeks to make wealth a basis of power independent of intellect—the only true and genuine aristocracy which can be claimed by man. We are disposed to look with an equally cold eye upon the republican aristocrat, as the British tory—time and circumstance alone create the difference—the feelings, the motives are the same—a love of power independent and uncontrolled by their fellow men.[181]

In the aftermath of the Battle of the Windmill, the *Freeman's Advocate* added a quote from Scottish essayist and historian Thomas Carlyle to its banner: "There is an unconquerability in man, when he stands on the rights of man; Let despots and slaves, and all people know this and only them that stand on the wrongs of man tremble to know it."[182] A few months later, when Canadians had still not managed to rise up against "the grossest tyranny," the paper did not suggest that the beleaguered and inactive northerners should take matters into their own hands; rather, the Hunters simply felt that "their helplessness should command our warmest commiseration."[183]

In all of his reform efforts, Smith always offered his "warmest commiseration" for anyone he and others deemed helpless. In Ohio, his involvement in antislavery efforts suggests the stirrings of a desire to help those enslaved in the South. That he became involved in education for women at this time in his life indicates he felt strongly that women deserved expanded opportunities. His secret stand with the Hunters perhaps best exemplifies this will to save a group of people from what he considered unreasonable—and, more important, unjust—treatment.

This stance is consistent with Smith's devotion to the Democratic Party, an organization, Gerring asserts, that saw itself as a champion of the oppressed, "a party of victims."[184] In the end, however, Smith's Canadian "victims" did not see themselves in quite the same terms, and the lawless behavior of the Hunters soon began to disappear from newspaper headlines.

Even as Smith broke the law along the border, he was upholding it in Cleveland, as the hundreds of yellowing pages of Smith's justice of the peace docket books attest. On May 5, 1841, Smith signed his name on his last (extant) official document in Cleveland, handing over the dockets to his successor in office, John Barre. Then, like the Hunters, Smith simply disappeared from the city.

There is nothing to indicate that anything in particular acted as a catalyst for Smith's move. While Hunter activity was frowned upon by the U.S. government, there is no evidence that anyone involved in the Hunter cause feared official retribution on U.S. soil, at least as long as they avoided openly engaging in further activity, and Smith seems to have disowned the movement. He likely found his youthful involvement in the Hunters an embarrassment in later life—a radical, reckless episode that he wished to forget. In hindsight, the Hunters were disorganized losers in the fight for the establishment of a Canadian republic, and Smith was the president of Canada who never was. Even his wife, Mary Augusta, may not have understood the extent of his involvement.

In all likelihood, he took that secret to his grave.

CHAPTER 2

Wisconsin

When I Think of Him I Incline to Spit

> Why was it Wisconsin and not some other northern state, which struck down the 1850 Act and embraced states' rights? The answer does not lie in any unique feature of Wisconsin politics or society. Wisconsin happened to have one man on its supreme court, Abram Smith, who was willing to shoulder the responsibility of going against all legal precedent—and got the opportunity to do so. If someone other than Smith had been on the bench... the Wisconsin states rights movement might well never have been born.
>
> —JOSEPH A. RANNEY, "Suffering the Agonies of Their Righteousness"

When I first wrote about A. D. Smith's life in Wisconsin, I started with an anecdote about a striking oil painting of the famous judge that was hanging in the south stairwell of the Wisconsin Historical Society in Madison. It was a massive painting, and it might sound melodramatic to say it took my breath away when I first saw it, but it was such an unexpected sight when I arrived to conduct research that I believe I really did gasp aloud when I realized it was him.

It was huge—impossible to miss, really—yet people shuffled past it without much of a glance. With a gold frame and swirls of dark paint, the portrait looks like so many of the nineteenth century—an austere-looking man with wavy gray hair, dressed in a black suit, with a vest just a little too snug, a second chin spilling over a too-tight cravat. His blue-gray eyes, in which "an expression of mirth was always lurking," according to one description, instead stare down at viewers with a look of mild disdain that borders on superciliousness, as evidenced by the downturned corners of his mouth and the firm set of his shoulders.[1] He looks every bit "a man of strong and original mind, of imperious will and tireless industry," to be sure.[2] It would be of little surprise to anyone, then, that the man was a lawyer and later a judge, though few would recognize the portrait subject as A. D. Smith and fewer still would bother to investigate further.

In 2009, a year after I defended my dissertation, I got an email from a contact at the Wisconsin Historical Society. "Hi Ruth," the note began, "You will be saddened to learn that the A. D. Smith portrait has been moved from its place on the landing of the WHS building."[3] When I returned to researching Smith after a prolonged absence from the stacks (and archives and computer terminals and microfilm readers), I learned that no one had ever asked where Smith's portrait had gone. Evidently, no one really cared—presumably because no one had noticed the portrait of Smith in the first place. I'm sure the Smith portrait's replacement is meaningful to someone, but for me, the painting's absence serves as yet another reminder that the passage of time has pushed my subject still farther into the shadows.

Wherever it now lurks, the painting is a rare image of Smith. Despite his stature in early Wisconsin society, he failed to leave much evidence of his eminent and generally well-respected position in the state. Ironically, when Smith sat for Milwaukee artist Samuel Marsden Brookes sometime in 1856 ("As a painter of fish," the story goes, Brookes was "unsurpassed in the far west"), the judge was at the height of his prominence in U.S. society. An official report on the collections of the State Historical Society of Wisconsin (as it was then known) declared the portrait "a strikingly accurate one, . . . remarkably correct in preserving the expression."[4] Certainly, it is a look of a man who was "fearless and independent," as he is described in one history of Milwaukee.[5] Smith gave the painting to the State Historical Society the same year Brookes finished it. A. D. Smith clearly believed he would be an important face of the state's history, an expectation that makes his disappearance from general textbooks and state histories all the more intriguing. Was he simply a legend in his own mind?

Smith spent the entirety of the 1850s in Wisconsin, becoming one of the state's most powerful men. He moved in influential circles, was connected to people at the highest levels of government, socialized with the legal elite, and was frequently quoted in newspapers. His landmark legal decision in *Ableman v. Booth* became nationally known and was feted by influential abolitionists—until it was smacked down by the U.S. Supreme Court led by Chief Justice Roger B. Taney, whose *Dred Scott* decision only two years earlier had left the North reeling. Today, *Ableman v. Booth* is still seen as one of the most significant cases in Wisconsin's history, fomenting great anger in the nineteenth century and propelling the state and the country toward the Civil War. The case is the first entry in the *Reader's Companion to American History*, a placement that is both alphabetical and appropriate.[6] Yet the entry does not mention Smith, and he did not merit his own entry in the massive 1,188-page book. Few people in Wisconsin have any knowledge of the man, and even those who are aware of *Ableman v. Booth* seem to know very little about the man who first set it in motion. And none of his descendants whom I contacted was aware of his significance.

Telling Smith's story in Wisconsin begins with the question of what brought him to the state. Like so many other questions involving Smith, this one proves difficult to answer. He simply vanished from public records in Ohio after 1840, with no indication of where he might have gone or why he left. By this time, he had a wife, Mary Augusta, and two children, Mary Frances and Maria Cecilia.[7] Whatever thoughts he had of moving north to Upper Canada must have been dismissed, though the specific reasons why will likely never be known. As he had when he moved from New York to Ohio, Smith did what must have seemed prudent—what so many other midcentury Americans did to improve their lives: he moved westward.

One factor that may well have played a part in the Smith family's decision to decamp to Wisconsin was the fact that members of his wife's family, the Reeds, had long since established themselves in the Wisconsin Territory. Mary Augusta Reed Smith's oldest brother, George, had studied law in Vermont and moved to Wisconsin in 1834. He later became a state senator, founder of the State Historical Society of Wisconsin, and president of the Wisconsin Central Railway. About a year after his arrival, his parents, Rhoda and Seth, and at least some of his siblings—brothers Orson, Harrison, Herbert, and Curtis and sisters Juliana and Martha—joined him in Wisconsin.[8] Harrison Reed promptly established himself as an editor at the *Milwaukee Sentinel* and became one of the founders of the Republican Party. During the Civil War, the Lincoln administration tapped him to serve as a tax commissioner in the occupied South, and he later served a rocky stint as a carpetbagging governor of Florida.[9] Herbert Reed ran a Milwaukee grocery that was damaged by an alleged arson attack in 1857, and Curtis Reed started out as a clerk at a trading post and went on to become a state assemblyman who also held positions as alderman, mayor, and postmaster in the town he helped to settle, Menasha.[10] Orson Reed (sometimes listed on documents as "Orrison") served in the state senate.[11] Martha Reed married railway tycoon Alexander Mitchell in 1841, and Juliana married the president of the Milwaukee County Medical Association, Dr. Thomas Noyes, in the mid-1830s.[12] Thus, by the time Smith arrived in Wisconsin, he had an extensive and well-connected network on which he could rely in his efforts to get ahead.

The Reeds were typical of the settlers who headed west for Wisconsin in the wake of the War of 1812 and particularly after the completion of the Erie Canal through New York state in 1825.[13] Like the Reeds, most of Milwaukee's early settlers came from "the stony soil of New England or the rolling New York countryside."[14] By the 1840s, however, immigrants from Europe—especially Germany and to a lesser extent Ireland—began to make their way to Wisconsin, and by the time Smith arrived, their influence would have been evident in German advertisements and German newspapers. In addition, German immigrants such as Edward Weisner, who served as justice of the peace, were beginning to take on positions of authority.[15] During the summers of 1843 and 1844, between one thousand and fourteen hundred Germans arrived in the city every week.[16] Most of these European immigrants arrived via other areas of the United States, initially settling in New England, New York, Michigan, or Ohio before moving farther west.[17]

Smith seems to have moved to Milwaukee in the early 1840s, with most references suggesting he arrived in 1842. He arrived in a city that was undergoing rapid expansion: dams and canals were being constructed, the dozen stores included a "fashionable tailor" and a meat market, and the city had six law offices and five doctors.[18] A history of the city written about two decades later noted that Milwaukee in the summer of 1842 was a "town branching out into enterprise" as the "blossoms of speculation were giving way to the fruits of utility."[19]

According to legal and constitutional historian H. Robert Baker, Milwaukee was the perfect place for a lawyer at this point in time: "Lawyers were the most directly tied to the city's commerce. Lawyers provided crucial services in a cash-poor commercial town where many transactions went naturally through the courts. Lawyers worked to develop a reputation for fairness, predictability, and fidelity in Milwaukee. In a highly litigious community, they earned good livings and were the most financially successful of the professional classes."[20]

Upon his arrival, Smith "immediately took high rank as a pleader at the bar."[21] He first appears in the *Milwaukee Sentinel* in an 1842 notice about his "very interesting" temperance lecture at Presbyterian House; two years later, he was mentioned again in connection with his activities with the Milwaukee Locofoco group, indicating that he had continued his participation in far-left Democratic politics.[22] Two days before Christmas 1843, Mary Augusta gave birth to a son, Marius (named after the famed Roman general and warrior renowned for his dedication to republicanism), but the child died of unknown causes just shy of his second birthday. Smith appears to have responded to the loss of his son by throwing himself into public life.

Slowly emerging as a member of Milwaukee's elite, Smith came to further prominence when he took an active part in the bitter debate over the ratification of the Wisconsin Constitution. In early 1846, he spoke in Madison as "Governor of the People." His words evoked the U.S. annexation of Texas and carried more than a faint echo of Smith's Hunter past: "A magnificent thought at first tremblingly entertained, has rapidly swollen into a universal sentiment, and already is demanding as a settled policy of the country, the union of the whole North American Continent, with all its dependencies under one, free democratic government. This is our destiny. He that rebels against it will be found warring against the inevitable consequences, of the intellectual and moral energies of the American people."[23]

In four referenda between 1840 and 1844, Wisconsin voters had rejected the idea of statehood, largely because they believed the territory lacked the wealth and population to support a state government and advocated continued reliance on the federal government.[24] This sentiment began to shift as the territory's population swelled, and an 1846 act of Congress authorized Wisconsin to write a constitution and apply for statehood.[25] The demographic makeup of the first convention became a factor: 74 percent of the delegates were from either New England or New York, while 103 were Democrats, 18 were Whigs, and only 3 were independents.[26] As legal historian Joseph Ranney explains, these eastern Democrats "espoused a broad variety of reforms designed to further the Jacksonian ideals of popular sovereignty, dispersion of power, and equal economic and political opportunity for all."[27] These reformers were at odds with the more conservative Democrats, the "Hunkers," from the southwestern part of the state, and might have prevailed at the convention had they not been so fractured, with their "spirit of disunity" apparent from the opening day.[28] After the convention, Smith and the other members of the reform-minded group spoke passionately in favor of the proposed constitution, though Smith's oratory skills were not universally praised: noted one detractor, "After walking out of the hall, [Smith] returned in about five minutes with a long series of bombastic resolutions, which he could not have concocted and written out in an hour, and which no doubt had been prepared [in advance]. The preamble and resolutions, characteristic of the framer of them, full of bombast and fulsome with praise and laudations of the late convention and the constitution, were indeed to any unbiased mind a rather sickly affair."[29]

During the contentious period leading up to the vote on the proposed constitution, Smith often offered public commentary. Some of the main issues that divided Democrats included alien suffrage, banks, and married women's property rights, and Smith addressed all of these topics in a lengthy article that was subsequently printed and distributed in response to an anticonstitution tract published by Marshall Strong, a Racine lawyer and newspaper editor. After labeling Strong an "honorable gentleman," Smith proceeded to take issue with and poke fun at every point Strong had advanced.[30]

In particular, Smith argued in favor of married women's property rights, a topic that had come to the fore in the mid-nineteenth century, when coverture—which dictated that women had no legal existence except through their husbands—was the norm. The economic fallout of the Panic of 1837 had led men to use their wives to shelter assets and had forced more women to work outside their homes.[31] Smith and other reformers believed property rights should be extended to women on the basis of equality, but Strong and other opponents argued that doing so would undermine marriage and might even increase rates of illegitimacy, as had occurred in France.[32] Smith responded, "The objection is that if a woman's rights of property are trespassed upon, the law will give her redress. This is seriously imputed by the learned gentleman as a vital objection. But pray, sir, would you not give her the protection of the law at all? Would you dehumanize her? Would you deny her a legal existence? This monstrous doctrine reduces her to a condition worse than the slave of the South. We had supposed it was the design of popular government to extend security of person and property to all."[33] The topic seemed to stir Smith's anger: "Prevented by law or cowardice from trampling upon the rights of men," opponents of married women's property rights "cling with deathly grasp to the power of tyrannizing over woman.... In their view nothing is so terrible as an uncaged woman. Unchain the lion, let loose the tiger, but there can be no security for breeches while a petticoat flutters in the breeze!"[34]

Also controversial was the proposed Homestead Exemption, which was designed to save homestead property valued at no more than one thousand dollars from the attachment of creditors. Only a decade after Wisconsin's territorial system had done away with imprisoning debtors, reforms sparing debtors were relatively new, and they had Smith's backing: "It is hope, bright, sunny hope, that revives the fallen spirit and raises and sustains the man in misfortune. It is hope and reason that distinguish human nature. It is hope that lights the pathway of time and opens a vista to immortality. Deprive man of hope, and his reason only renders him the more capable and inclined for mischief. God gave hope to man to elevate and inspire him with sentiments of virtue and promise of reward."[35]

Opponents of the proposed constitution also found fault with the proposal for an elected judiciary, believing that judges "would be chosen based on service to their political party rather than legal ability and integrity."[36] Again, Smith countered in support of the constitution, suggesting that the people would "select the man best qualified."[37] In the end, Smith argued, only by accepting the constitution could Wisconsin become "what Nature designed her, the Queen of the West": "Be not deceived; your rights are now placed in your own hands. Let not your grasp loosen for a moment, that your enemies may snatch them away. Be not inactive.... Come up to the contest with the shout and strength of freemen who know their rights and dare maintain them."[38]

By early 1847, Smith had achieved some public popularity, with the *Milwaukee Sentinel* again dubbing him the "People's Governor."[39] His image was suspect in some quarters, though, as someone with "Native American prejudices."[40] Accusations of nativism, which had sprung up in the 1830s and 1840s in response to increased immigration, would have been damaging to Smith in a city with such a substantial foreign-born population. In particular, Irish Catholics were conspicuous against Wisconsin's background of predominantly New England–founded Protestantism. If Smith indeed had nativist views, they would have been at odds with general trends in the Democratic Party at the time. Democratic sympathies for the workingman frequently attracted immigrant voters, who were more likely to be employed as laborers. The Whigs, conversely, embraced Protestantism and tended to be less attuned to the needs of newly arrived Catholics.[41] If Smith were a nativist, he endeavored to cover his feelings, as would be prudent for someone with political aspirations, and instead made obvious overtures to immigrants from Germany, Ireland, and Scandinavia, describing them as "our citizens" and the source of "energy and skill" that was transforming Wisconsin "magic-like from a wilderness to a garden. These are the men whose patriotism is the deep foundation of the state's safety. These are the women who are to bear to Wisconsin her sons and daughters to enjoy and transmit the liberty and equal rights which the friends of the constitution are laboring to secure and establish."[42]

In April 1847, Wisconsin's voters rejected the proposed constitution by a margin of 58.9 percent to 41.1 percent.[43] A December 1847 constitutional convention (to which Smith unsuccessfully sought to serve as a delegate) produced a new document, which voters overwhelmingly approved the following March.[44] Smith's next political foray also ended in failure, as he lost to Whig Francis Randall in an 1849 election for a circuit judgeship.[45] Still dogged by accusations of nativism and facing opposition from Milwaukee's

Irish and Roman Catholics, Smith became the subject of much debate in the *Sentinel*: in the summer of 1848, the paper ran an article that "gravely asserted" "that a report goes the rounds telling us that Catholics, 'as such' are arranging themselves as a body to defeat the election of Mr. A. D. Smith on merely religious grounds."[46] The author recounted an incident in which Smith had supposedly blocked a Catholic nominee for the position of sheriff: "We oppose A. D. Smith because he is A. D. Smith, because we know the man. We have not that confidence in his integrity and purity of character that we wish to have in the man we are to support for Judge. Not because he is, or has been thought to be intolerant.... We do not charge him with that. His solemn apology for refusing to support the Democratic nominee for Sheriff some years since on account of his being a Catholic, we regard as an ebullition of disappointed vanity."[47] The newspaper debate over Smith's anti-Catholicism became so heated that some called for Smith to speak to the issue: "Why does he not like an injured man vindicate his good name? Let him speak to his peers and they will hear him!"[48]

Smith entered the fray by threatening to sue the editors of the *Madison Argus* for libel after they suggested he was "of intemperate habits, immoral character, questionable integrity, and unfit altogether for the office of Judge."[49] The possibility of a lawsuit prompted Solomon Juneau, a Montreal Catholic credited as Milwaukee's founding father, to write a vitriolic letter to the editor of the *Sentinel* denouncing Smith's character: "Mr. Smith by threats of prosecution, cannot force public opinion in his favor. The people will judge and act independently of his threats, and if he does not know his own standing in this community, the approaching canvass will inform him that he is not overrated. As for myself, when I think of him, I incline to spit."[50] Smith seems to have abandoned the lawsuit but campaigned with new vigor, traveling through the counties of the Second District to seek support, "a course," the *Sentinel* sniffed, that was "not only unbecoming the station to which Mr. Smith aspires, but must, we think, be exceedingly revolting to the great mass of the electors in all parties."[51]

Defeated but undeterred, Smith continued his speaking engagements, among them a lecture on "immortality of the body" that attracted a large crowd to the Young Men's Association.[52] In 1851, he garnered the Democratic nomination for the Milwaukee mayor's office but lost to George Walker, a Virginian, by 346 votes.[53]

While engaging in politics, Smith took an active role in various community efforts, including the establishment of a medical college. Plans for the college got under way in 1850, and when officers were elected to run the school, Smith won a spot as professor of medical jurisprudence, though the effort subsequently stalled for more than a decade and he never taught.⁵⁴ In 1851 he threw his hat into the political ring for the position of circuit judge but withdrew a short time later for reasons that were not recorded. In 1849, Smith started a legal practice with Henry L. Palmer, a Pennsylvanian who had moved to Milwaukee via West Troy, New York.⁵⁵ Smith thereafter became known as "one of the ablest men at the bar of the county or state" and found himself in the newspaper on a regular basis for his flamboyant defense work in a high-profile 1851 murder trial.⁵⁶

Now at the zenith of his power as an attorney, Smith aimed for an even more powerful position.⁵⁷ In 1852, when the state held an election for its fledgling Supreme Court, he secured a Democratic nomination and won a seat as an associate justice.⁵⁸ The Democrats had national success as well, with Franklin Pierce trouncing decorated military man Winfield Scott in the race for U.S. president. By the late 1840s, tensions in the Whig Party had become more pronounced, and the 1852 election produced the worst showing in the party's history.⁵⁹ Smith's association with the ascendant national Democratic Party would not have hurt him.

Along with his professional success, Smith enjoyed domestic happiness during these years. Not long after arriving in Milwaukee, he built a house at the corner of Grand Avenue and Tenth Street.⁶⁰ A third daughter, Marion Augusta, had joined the family in 1846, while eldest daughter Mary Frances (known affectionately as Franky or Frankie) was beginning to entertain suitors. Her mother, Mary Augusta, seems to have kept busy organizing social functions and taking part in various charities, serving on the board of trustees of Milwaukee's first "orphan asylum," organized by the Ladies' Benevolent Society.⁶¹ In April 1852, Smith wrote glowingly that with the end of the court term, he was sitting "with Franky on my right, Mrs. S. on my left knitting, the little chick hanging on my knee with all the warm and good feelings and affections glowing within me."⁶² The real reason for the letter became evident a few paragraphs later, however: Smith was seeking backing for his bid for the Supreme Court. "If my friends shall deem me qualified and will help me to it, they know how thankful I should be. I believe it is not vanity in me to say that I have rendered the Democratic Party some service.... [I]n this I have only done my duty, but as Supreme Judge, I could still do duty, not to party merely, but to those free and germane principles of Freedom's Laws, upon which the Democratic Party is organized, and on which alone it can permanently prosper."⁶³

In elections held later that year, Smith won a seat on the Supreme Court by a small margin, with Edward V. Whiton winning the post of chief justice and Orsamus Cole taking the other associate justice slot. Smith began his six-year term as an associate justice on June 1, 1853, with an annual salary of $2,000.⁶⁴ Smith was a well-respected member of the bench—accounts of his time there are generally complimentary:

> As a man, he had a high order of mind, fine native powers, which were developed, improved and adorned by liberal culture. As a lawyer, he was able, learned, earnest, eloquent and successful; always kind, courteous, and obliging. As a judge, he was urbane, dignified, patient, especially considerate towards the younger members of the profession, always ready with a word of encouragement and cheer, and never failed to appreciate the place he so nobly filled upon the bench. He was always a generous, genial and hospitable gentleman.⁶⁵

At around this time, however, Smith seems to have become weary of what he saw as his party's tolerance of proslavery politics. Writing to his wife in the winter of 1853, he expressed frustration with the Democrats' response to the 1849 Resolutions of the Wisconsin Legislature on the Subject of Slavery, known as the Hastings Resolutions after the man who proposed them, Samuel Hastings, a Free Soiler who served two terms in the Wisconsin State Assembly. The document had urged political action against the spread of slavery within the Union, but by 1853, Wisconsin's Democrats were considering rescinding the resolutions, a move that Smith found abhorrent: the resolutions, he wrote, "answered up to the question of a *good* national heart! How just: how glorious, to see a just, a powerful, and more than all, a successful party proclaiming, in harmony with the voice of our God, the principles of human liberty, and the suggestions of justice. But, alas! What do I see now! That same party, my own, my beloved party, a party for whose success, glory, liberal achievements, humane, liberal and glorious career, I have sacrificed so much; and from whose triumphs I have hoped so much, now propose to rescind these resolutions!"⁶⁶

For Smith, there could be no compromise on the question of slavery. But for others, the idea that the North and South should ever agree on such a question was "both unnatural and absurd," and compromise represented the only way to protect the Union: "Then in the spirit of the Constitution, to 'insure domestic tranquility,' should not both sections yield a little for the sake of a compromise? This is the course which has been recommended by the best men of the Republic."⁶⁷

In 1854, Smith had the opportunity to make his voice heard when a matter involving Stephen Ableman and Sherman M. Booth came before the court. It was the pivotal moment in his career, and his decision catapulted him onto the national stage, if only briefly. The case involved the capture of an escaped Missouri slave, Joshua Glover, who had traveled some 350 miles and settled in Wisconsin.[68] Set against a backdrop of northern animosity toward the Fugitive Slave Act of 1850, which forced residents of free states to comply with federal attempts to return runaway slave "property" to southern slaveholders, the case constituted the confluence of antebellum laws, the antislavery movement, and the emerging personality of a liberal northern state. And as historian H. Robert Baker points out, the law's treatment of fugitive slave issues was far from clear, creating an environment that was ripe for legal challenges: "What if a slaveholder traveled with his slave to a free jurisdiction and the slave then fled? Or what if a slaveholder claimed a fugitive slave and her child, but her child had been born in the free state to which she had fled? Could the slaveholder carry these people back across state lines legally? The devil, it might be said, was in the details."[69] This tangle of details created "one of history's great unintended consequences," as each fugitive slave case provided opportunities to foment sectional discord.[70] The act, Steven Lubet notes, "potentially empowered every absconding slave to provoke a minor confrontation between North and South."[71]

The idea that slavery might creep north, particularly into the territories, had heightened tensions in Wisconsin and elsewhere. With northerners still reeling from the passage of the Fugitive Slave Act as part of the controversial Compromise of 1850, news of the Kansas-Nebraska Act, which effectively destroyed the Missouri Compromise of 1820 and opened the way for the expansion of slavery in an area where it had previously been prohibited, started to appear in Wisconsin newspapers in late January 1854. By February, petitions against the measure began to circulate, and opponents began to organize meetings.[72] As Paul Finkelman notes, the Compromise of 1850 had been designed to quell tensions over slavery but instead sparked "a decade of confrontations between northerners and the federal government."[73] While residents on both sides of the Mason-Dixon Line had initially welcomed the compromise as a means of strengthening the Union, the Fugitive Slave Act was seen as an affront to the pervasive northern objection to the peculiar institution.

Wisconsin's population, which included large numbers of Germans and New Englanders who had left their homes to escape political turmoil and persecution and who did not support slavery, offered no support for any part of the compromise.[74] In fact, Wisconsinites "deeply detested the Act," and the atmosphere of discontent in the state and the rest of the North proved a fruitful ground for protest in the form of public meetings and even popular culture, such as Harriet Beecher Stowe's novel, *Uncle Tom's Cabin* (a favorite book of Smith's eldest daughter, Mary Frances).[75] Some eminent writers and scholars, Henry David Thoreau among them, began to broadly suggest civil disobedience when it came to the Fugitive Slave Act, suggesting that no one should feel any obligation to obey a law that was unjust: "The only obligation which I have a right to assume is to do at any time what I think right. Law never made men a whit more just; and, by means of their respect for it, even the well-disposed are daily made the agents of injustice," Thoreau argued.[76]

Some opponents of slavery went even further, arguing that violence was acceptable if necessary to combat the evil.[77] Radical Joshua Giddings, for one, called abolitionists to arms in the defense of fugitive slaves.[78] In communities across the North, abolitionists and free blacks called meetings to discuss the law's "federal assault on freedom."[79] The idea of a "higher law" must have reassured those who felt uneasy about the use of force: "There was a strong belief among evangelicals North and South that human laws were of no force unless they were in accord with God's law. The great majority of such evangelicals did not take violent action based on this belief. But the concept of a 'higher law' did encourage many of slavery's opponents to disregard laws that protected the interests of slaveholders. It provided a few such opponents with the resolve to resist such laws physically in the North and in the border South."[80]

Abolitionists particularly objected to several provisions of the Fugitive Slave Act. Not only were accused fugitives denied a trial by jury and prohibited from speaking for themselves in front of commissioners, but the act itself was inherently biased against runaways. Federal commissioners were paid ten dollars for returning slaves to their former owners (or anyone who claimed to be a slave's owner) but only five dollars for each runaway freed. Consequently, commissioners had personal incentives to deny fugitives their freedom, while free blacks living in the North still faced discrimination and prejudice and lived in what historian Carol Wilson characterizes as a "legal limbo between slavery and freedom."[81]

Incensed northerners engaged in a string of blatant violations of the Fugitive Slave Law that caused great embarrassment for the federal government, angry scenes of mob violence, and in some places death. Many towns and cities organized vigilance committees to assist runaways, often by intimidating those who tried to reclaim them and return them to the South. In 1851, a group of men came to Massachusetts to reclaim Georgia runaways Ellen and William Craft, who had fled three years earlier. In what historian Sean Wilentz calls "the most famous runaway saga since Frederick Douglass's," light-skinned Ellen Craft cut her hair, donned men's clothing, and posed as an ailing southern gentleman traveling north via train with his slave, William Craft.[82] The couple became the darlings of the abolitionist press, prompting their former owner to send slave catchers to Boston to reclaim his "property." They did not succeed, however, and were quickly run out of town.[83] President Millard Fillmore, who had referred to the Compromise of 1850 as the "final settlement" of sectional strife, promised the Crafts' owner that he would do all he could to facilitate the couple's return, but their abolitionist friends helped them escape first to Canada and then to Britain.[84]

While fugitive slave cases were generally local affairs, the increasing animosity between North and South quickly gave them national significance. In 1851, captured fugitive Frederick "Shadrach" Minkins was being held in a Boston courthouse and faced a return to bondage in Virginia until a mob freed him, an act Fillmore called "a scandalous outrage."[85] Though ten men were indicted for their part in Minkins's rescue, juries refused to convict them, and Minkins made his way to Canada.[86] The same year, Edward Gorsuch of Maryland was beaten to death by a black mob when he attempted to reclaim slaves who had fled to Pennsylvania. Gorsuch, using intelligence from a traveling clockmaker, tracked his slaves to William Parker's home in Christiana.[87] There, he and his posse of family members and federal and local officials met the violent rage of Parker's black militia: "The tension broke like a dam, and Parker's men flooded forward with a shout. The yard in front of the house dissolved into chaos. All the white men in the lane then fired. At least two blacks were hit. Shots flew in every direction. Someone struck Edward Gorsuch with a rifle and clubbed him to the ground ... others caught Joshua Gorsuch and clubbed him until the blood ran out of his ears.... [T]he only members of the posse who escaped unharmed, leaped the fence and ran for their lives."[88]

The incident made national newspaper headlines, and President Fillmore responded by calling in marines and federal marshals to track down the slaves' defenders in the so-called Battle of Christiana.[89] Three participants eventually made their way to Canada via the Underground Railroad and evaded extradition, while grand jury indictments of forty-one others for treason and failure to uphold the Fugitive Slave Law were dropped when, as historian James M. McPherson writes, "the government's case quickly degenerated into farce. A defense attorney's ridicule made the point: 'Sir—did you hear it? That three harmless non-resisting Quakers and eight-and-thirty wretched, miserable, penniless negroes, armed with corn cutters, clubs, and few muskets, and headed by a miller, in a felt hat, without arms and mounted on a sorrel nag, levied war against the United States.'"[90]

Less than a month later, in October 1851, yet another fugitive slave case came to prominence in Syracuse, New York. A group of men, including some whites in blackface, rescued a fugitive Missouri cooper, William "Jerry" McHenry, from the courthouse, throwing rocks, shattering windows, and screaming, "Let him go!"[91] McHenry was subsequently smuggled into Canada, leaving behind a bureaucratic mess. The federal government spent fifty thousand dollars and more than a year prosecuting fourteen whites and twelve blacks for their part in the rescue, though only one man was found guilty.[92]

In the decade leading to the Civil War, an estimated eighty well-publicized rescues or rescue attempts of fugitives occurred, while about three hundred bondspeople were apprehended under the Fugitive Slave Law.[93] The combination of damaging publicity and relatively few successes embarrassed the federal government, which suffered a string of humiliations in its attempts to enforce the legislation. In the South, such flagrant violations of a federal law intended to protect what slave owners believed was their God-given right provided further evidence of what they perceived as hateful northerners trying to impose their sanctimonious ways on Dixie. Shortly after the violence in Christiana, the *Savannah Republican* warned "the press and the people of the North that there is a point, not far distant, when forbearance on our part will cease to be virtuous or honorable, and ... they and they alone will be responsible for all the ills that may betide this government."[94]

Wisconsin "provided unusually fertile ground for a challenge to the 1850 Act," in the words of historian Joseph Ranney.[95] Not only did the state's robust immigrant population oppose the act, but all of the state's congressional representatives, regardless of political party, had voted against it "and against all parts of the Compromise of 1850 which were designed to placate the South."[96]

Smith eagerly awaited the arrival of a fugitive slave case in his court. In early 1853, he wrote to his wife, "I earnestly wish that ... some poor fugitive might be brought before the court, in order that I might have an opportunity to make & put upon the eternal record, an argument in favor of human liberty."[97] In 1854, Smith got his chance.

On March 13, 1854, the *Milwaukee Sentinel* trumpeted, "GREAT EXCITEMENT! Arrest of a Fugitive Slave!"[98] That slave was Joshua Glover.

Glover had run away from Benammi Garland, a Missouri slaveholder, in 1852, and had settled in Racine, Wisconsin, where he found a job at a sawmill.[99] On the night of March 10, 1854, he and some friends were playing cards in his modest cabin when they heard a rapping at the door. Though various sources offer differing accounts of what exactly transpired, they all agree that when the door was opened, outside stood Garland; a federal deputy marshal from Racine, John Kearney; and three other armed men.[100] They overpowered Glover and hauled him away, with Kearney's boot on his neck and his own blood seeping onto the wagon floor.[101] In so doing, they catapulted him to national prominence.

Word of Glover's capture spread, eventually reaching Milwaukee abolitionist Sherman Booth via telegram.[102] Booth was an old Barnburner from the ultraliberal wing of the Democratic Party and was now a member of the abolitionist-founded Liberty Party. As a young man at Yale, Booth had helped teach English to the captives in the famous *Amistad* case.[103] In that 1839 incident, a cargo of African slaves aboard the *Amistad* had wrested control of the ship from their captors but found themselves reenslaved when the vessel was seized in U.S. waters. A legal battle ensued, making its way to the U.S. Supreme Court, with former president John Quincy Adams arguing that the Africans should be freed based on the illegality of the international slave trade. The Court agreed.

More than a decade later, Booth had gone on to become a prominent opponent of slavery and the publisher of the *Milwaukee Daily Free Democrat*. Just as with A. D. Smith, the Glover case and more broadly the Fugitive Slave Act "presented Booth with a heaven-sent opportunity to demonstrate his principled opposition to slavery on a larger stage."[104]

Booth arranged the distribution of handbills urging people to come to Glover's aid and mounted a horse (a suitable white steed, according to many accounts) and careened through the streets of Milwaukee, shouting, "Freemen! To the rescue! Slavecatchers are in our midst!"[105]

At about 6:00 on the evening of March 11, a mob of about five thousand people whose indignation Booth had whipped "into a frenzy" descended on the jail to rescue Glover by force.[106] After breaking down the door, the vigilantes paraded the former slave through the streets before spiriting him out of Milwaukee. He then made his way to Canada via the Underground Railroad, "borne away at a speed that under ordinary circumstances would have provoked arrest for fast driving."[107]

Four days after the jailbreak, Booth made a shocking announcement in the *Daily Free Democrat*: he had been arrested for assisting and abetting the escape of a fugitive slave: "We have the honor of being the first person in Wisconsin who has been arrested by the Federal Courts for alleged disobedience to the Fugitive Law and for obedience to the higher law. Our crime, if . . . as set forth in the warrant is true, is that we have helped a human being to escape from bondage. And if the government can make out its case and this Fugitive Law stands, we are liable to be fined $2,000 and be imprisoned six months. We cheerfully meet the issue."[108]

Booth retained a young abolitionist, Byron Paine, to represent him. It was Paine's first major legal case. He applied first to the local courts for a writ of habeas corpus releasing Booth and then appealed to the state supreme court after the writ was denied.[109] Smith issued the writ and the *Daily Free Democrat* published it for all to see. Smith ordered federal marshal Stephen Ableman to bring Booth to the judge's doorstep—literally: "You are hereby commanded to bring the body of Sherman M. Booth, by you imprisoned and detained, as it is said, together with the time and cause of such imprisonment and detention ... before me, Abram D. Smith, one of the Justices of the Supreme Court of the State of Wisconsin, forthwith, at my dwelling in the city of Milwaukee."[110]

In appealing for Booth's freedom, Paine used many of the abolitionists' standard arguments against the Fugitive Slave Act. First, hearings conducted by commissioners rather than judges violated the Constitution, which places federal judicial power in appointed judges. In addition, prohibiting a jury trial was unconstitutional, and since neither the Constitution nor the State of Wisconsin had legislated a mechanism for returning slaves to their owners, the act could not be enforced. However, Paine also added a novel—and bold—argument: the Fugitive Slave Act violated the rights of the State of Wisconsin.[111] In his view, the case was as much about states' rights as about Booth's freedom.

"May it please the Court," Paine began. "In arising to commence the investigation of this case, I do so with those feelings of strong embarrassment which must naturally result from knowing that I undertake to deal with a question more important than any that could be presented to a judicial tribunal. It is a question in which, according to my judgment, are involved, not the liberties of Mr. Booth alone, but the liberties of the whole people."[112] Paine could not have made his case to "a more sympathetic ear," and he got the results for which he had hoped.[113] At 11:00 on the morning of June 7, 1854, Smith delivered his opinion.

Had the case reached the Wisconsin Supreme Court in March, when Glover was sprung from the jail, all of the justices would have heard it. But two months passed as the matter worked its way through the system, and by June, all of the other justices had gone on vacation, leaving Smith alone to deal with it.[114] Smith noted the situation in the preamble to his decision:

> I can not but feel the immense responsibility thrown upon me alone, and may be pardoned for expressing my regret that I am deprived of the aid and counsel of my associates, so much better able to cope with the grave and intricate

questions involved than I am myself. Whether by design or from necessity, this application has been made to me, I meet the emergency with all the anxiety and concern which it cannot fail to excite, and I hope with some share of the firmness which the occasion and the nature of the questions involved imperatively demand.[115]

Smith's decision went on for pages and pages—brevity was never his strong suit. Ultimately, he agreed with Paine's argument, emphatically declaring the Fugitive Slave Act unconstitutional based on the principles of states' rights: "Without the States there can be no Union. The abrogation of State sovereignty is not a dissolution of the Union, but an absorption of its elements. He is the true man, the faithful officer, who is ready to assert and guard every jot of power rightfully belonging to each, and to resist the slightest encroachment or assumption of power on the part of either."[116] As historian Richard E. Ellis explains the argument over central power had been "the central constitutional issue in America" since the Declaration of Independence because the nation's founding documents were ambiguous on the question:

> By creating a national government with the authority to act directly upon individuals, by denying to the states many of the prerogatives that they formerly had, and by leaving open to the central government the possibility of claiming for itself many powers not explicitly assigned to it, the Constitution and Bill of Rights as finally ratified substantially increased the strength of the central government at the expense of the states. But the Constitution did not make the states clearly subservient to the federal government.... [F]urther, by failing to provide for an ultimate arbiter to interpret the Constitution, the new frame of government became open to the logical, although controversial, interpretation that this power rightly belonged to the states.[117]

The states' rights philosophy Paine presented would have held immense appeal for a libertarian such as Smith, particularly in the context of his dalliances with the Hunters in Ohio, who had tried to smash centralized power in the form of Crown rule in the Canadas. Until the Glover case, however, states' rights policy had been largely appropriated by the South, first in the nullification controversy of 1831–1833 in South Carolina and subsequently in defense of slavery and its expansion into the territories. John C. Calhoun, the giant at the center of the nullification controversy, had caught the eye of many a radical Democrat in the early 1840s. As Sean Wilentz notes, "The most surprising development with the Democracy was a growing enthusiasm, among some of the most radical northeastern hard-money advocates, for, of all people, John C. Calhoun.... Saving democracy, they now believed, required uniting the small disciplined group who understood what democracy really was, and upending the demagogic rule of capital by the most direct means necessary—which in 1842, after his own strange left-wing turn, seemed to be Calhoun."[118]

It is not known whether Smith was among those who had entertained the idea of supporting Calhoun, but he would certainly have known of this trend and been familiar with Calhoun's arguments about states' rights. However, historian Michael J. McManus argues that one primary distinction existed between South Carolina's use of states' rights and Wisconsin's:

> South Carolina had originally embraced states' rights principles to safeguard its economic interests. Thereafter, the South took up states' rights to block national interference with slavery within the slaveholding states, and state sovereignty, with decrees such as the Fugitive Slave Act, to demand federal protection for the rights of slaveowners outside the state jurisdictions in which they had been granted. To counteract Southern aggressiveness, Wisconsin, along with other Northern states, employed states' rights to defend individual liberty from legislation regarded as unconstitutional. Most often, resistance took the form of personal liberty laws designed to thwart enforcement of the Fugitive Slave Act.[119]

Smith had accepted a southern interpretation of the Constitution—the "compact theory of the Union"—developed by Thomas Jefferson, James Madison, and John C. Calhoun and used it on behalf of a northern cause.[120] As legal historian Jeffrey Schmitt explains, this theory held that "the states, as opposed to the people, had created the Constitution and thus could decide which powers were ceded to the federal government. The states, as principal actors, could not be subordinate to the agent they had created, the federal government."[121] Echoes of this theory could be heard in Smith's ruling:

> The judicial department of the Federal Government is the creature, by compact, of the several States as sovereignties—That department can exercise no power not delegated to it. All power not delegated and not prohibited to the States, the States have expressly reserved to themselves and the people. To admit that the Federal Judiciary is the sole and exclusive judge of its own powers, and the extent of the authority delegated, is virtually to admit that the same unlimited power may be exercised by every other department of the general government both legislative and executive, because each is independent and co-ordinate of the other. *Neither* has any power but such as the

States have delegated, and *all* power not delegated, remains with the States and the people thereof.[122]

Smith emphasized that the states could not afford to give any ground in the matter and that to do so would have catastrophic consequences for republicanism. "I solemnly believe that the last hope of representative federative government rests with the States," he wrote in his judgment. "Increase of influence and patronage on the part of the Federal Government naturally leads to consolidation, consolidation to despotism, and ultimate anarchy, dissolution and all its attendant evils."[123] By using such terms as "anarchy," "despotism," and "evils," Smith showed that he saw himself as living in dire times that imposed on him the moral obligation to make his historic judgment regardless of the potential consequences for his party or career. If, as he feared, the states were being asked to surrender their natural rights, he did not want to become the historical scapegoat:

> If the sovereignty of the States is destined to be swallowed up by the Federal Government, if consolidation is to supplant federation, and the General Government to become the sole judge of its own powers, regardless of the solemn compact by which it was brought into existence and the source of its own vitality, as an humble officer of one of the States, bound to regard the just rights and powers, both of the Union and the States, I want my skirts to be clear, and that posterity may not lay the catastrophe to my charge.[124]

Schmitt holds that Smith's version of compact theory was more radical than that of even Calhoun, who was not known for being moderate about anything but nevertheless limited the states' right to be final arbiters of the Constitution to their elected representatives assembled in a special convention.[125] In Smith's version of compact theory, that power resided in a transient majority on any state's supreme court. Schmitt contends that Smith probably preferred the idea that state judges should adjudicate the meaning of the U.S. Constitution because this approach "lent the theory the perception of legal credibility." Moreover, as a career politician, he could see the advantage of having to convince only one of his two colleagues on the bench rather than the majority of Wisconsin's people.[126] And in fact, Smith did convince one of his colleagues, Chief Justice Whiton, to go along with this constitutional interpretation, as the Wisconsin Supreme Court confirmed Smith's decision on July 19.[127] The court's third member, associate justice Samuel Crawford, dissented. Crawford agreed that Booth should be released due to the technically defective nature of the writ but believed the Fugitive Slave Act was not unconstitutional because, according to Ranney, "the powers which the Act gave commissioners were not judicial powers."[128] The commissioners, Crawford said, did not make the final decision as to whether a fugitive was indeed a slave; rather, they bounced the matter—and the runaway—back to the South for judicial assessment.[129] Whiton's backing of Smith sustained his ruling.

Schmitt concludes that Smith's primary motive was "a desire to reject the southern legal processes of the Fugitive Slave Act and return to the traditional northern presumption of freedom."[130] Inasmuch as the legal procedures outlined by the act "created a presumption of slavery for anyone alleged to be a fugitive," Wisconsin—in the person of the Honorable A. D. Smith—"wished to return to the common law presumption of freedom for alleged slaves."[131] The case represents a collision of the era's dueling legal mind-sets: "The two independently developing trajectories of antebellum habeas corpus—one on the state level where key Northern states were using habeas in favor of liberty, and one on the national level where habeas was used to thwart state power and defend slaveholding state interests through the power of the federal government—met head-on in this case with important ramifications."[132]

Smith must have realized that in his challenge to the Fugitive Slave Act, the principal southern gain from the bitter Compromise of 1850, he was throwing down the gauntlet not only to the entire South but also to the southern-dominated U.S. Supreme Court, which he must have known would reverse his radical decision. But he saw no alternative: upholding slaveholders' rights in the free states would see "the slave code of every state in the union engrafted upon the laws of every free state," leaving "the rights, interests, feelings, dignity, sovereignty, of the free states . . . as nothing, while the more pecuniary interests of the slaveholder are everything."[133]

The decision highlighted Smith's very liberal views of African Americans and their presumed freedom, views that resurfaced equally dramatically later in his life. That presumption of liberty was central to Smith's final decision: "Let the federal government return to the exercise of the just powers conferred by the constitution, and few, very few, will be found to disturb the tranquility of the nation or to oppose by word or deed the due execution of the laws!" he declared. "I feel a grateful consciousness of having discharged my duty, and full duty; of having been true to the sovereign rights of my State which has honored me with its confidence, and to the Constitution of my country, which has blessed me with its protection; and though I may stand alone, I hope I may stand approved of my God as I know I do of my conscience."[134]

Smith's decision "caught the entire nation by surprise" and prompted much jubilation across Wisconsin.[135] Newspapers heralded it as solid and just, and citizens gathered to cheer the news. Exulted the *Milwaukee Daily Free Democrat*, Smith's decision "will stand like a rock, mid the waves of conflicting and discordant opinions and loom up in the future, as one of the great beacon lights, which have led the people out of the darkness of despotism and the bondage of subjection to slaveholding and pro-slavery interpretations of the Constitution."[136] The *Milwaukee Sentinel* agreed that the opinion gave "great and general satisfaction, and even those who differ from him in the conclusions which he has drawn, admit the force and relevancy of the arguments he has advanced."[137] The *Kenosha Democrat* hailed Smith as "a gentleman of eminent ability and candor. We do not know a man who can bring to the investigation of such a question a more dispassionate judgment," while the *Kenosha Telegraph* proclaimed the "dawning of a new era."[138] In Racine, where Glover had resided for the two years before his arrest, hundreds poured into the streets, and the *Advocate* joyously announced that "Wisconsin is Free!!" and lavished praise on the justice:

> We have no words to express our gratification at this bold decision of so able a jurist as A. D. Smith. Henceforth his name will go down to posterity coupled with the names of those who stand out eminent on the pages of history as the vindicator of laws, and the faithful exponent and defender of his country's Constitution.... Judge Smith will henceforth be named as the man who dared step into the gap, in the face of tyrants and declare this hellish enactment, which is the scourge of our country, and the disgrace of humanity, as a nullity, and of no force.... By this gloriously righteous decision, Wisconsin stands a head and shoulders above all other States in the Union.[139]

Further afield, antislavery senator Charles Sumner later declared that Smith's decision "showed the true metal."[140] New York's *Albany Evening Journal* declared, "This upright Judge in Wisconsin is the first who has had the courage to face the Slaveholding aggression which takes upon itself the semblance of authority, only that it may deny Justice and disregard the Law."[141] The *New York Tribune* published Smith's decision and urged readers, especially those still wavering on the constitutionality of the Fugitive Slave Act, to examine its content: "His judgment has all the bone and muscle, with the strong spirit, in which his youthful state exults. As a composition it is excellent, especially when compared with the dead level of judicial opinions, while it is often lifted by its animating principles into a region of true eloquence."[142] And in Rochester, New York, *Frederick Douglass' Paper* (formerly the *North Star*) hailed Smith's decision, suggesting that his name would go on "to posterity unpolluted by the foul miasma of slaveholding flattery, and be placed in the imperishable archives of our country's *future* glory."[143]

Booth's troubles were not over, however, as he still faced federal charges of obstruction of justice.[144] He again appealed to the state's supreme court, but this time, the justices refused to get involved, saying the matter was out of their jurisdiction:

> In this case, when the prisoner was first brought up on the writ of Habeas Corpus, he was within the State jurisdiction exclusively. It then became our duty to decide upon the validity of the process and of the law, by virtue of which he was held. He was discharged. Thus ended our jurisdiction in the case. But our judgment in that case could not be pleaded in bar to a future indictment found against the prisoner for the same offense. Subsequently, the prisoner is indicted in the District Court of the United States.[145]

The justices thus distinguished between a case that would have put Booth before a commissioner and a case that would be heard by a full court. As Smith wrote in the decision, "In the former case he was held under the process of an officer who had no power to hear and determine upon the validity of the law, or the allegations of the defendant against its validity. But now he is held under process of a Court, a judicial tribunal, having full power and authority to decide upon all the questions or allegations presented in his behalf. The legal and just presumption is that the Court will declare the law as it is."[146] Such legal nuances mattered little to lay observers, leading newspapers to decry Smith's latest ruling and to call him "a blind man groping his way out of a labyrinth."[147]

When the case went to trial in the U.S. district court in Madison in January 1855, the jury was instructed to determine not whether the Fugitive Slave Act was constitutional but simply whether Booth had violated it, and he was found guilty.[148] Booth appealed his conviction to the Wisconsin Supreme Court, which found unanimously in his favor on the grounds that the decision "rested upon defective indictments."[149]

Through all of this, Smith maintained an air of celebrity, particularly among abolitionists, and became a sought-after speaker.[150] When he visited Chicago in the spring of 1855, the *Tribune* declared that he looked "well and hearty" and advised readers that "as a history-maker, the Judge will be conspicuous in the future of this Republic, not that he will write a book, but that he will do what will make others write."[151] On an 1857 visit to New York, some of the city's most influential figures, including Horace Greeley, sought to hold a public dinner in Smith's honor, though he did not receive the invitation in time to attend.[152] Sending his regrets to the organizers, Smith wrote that Wisconsin "will be faithful to all the covenants and compacts of the Constitution, and she will also be faithful to all her high and solemn obligations of a sovereign State, cheerfully conceding to federal authority all the powers delegated, and ready at all times to strengthen the arms of federal functionaries in their execution; but yielding not one jot or tittle of her inherent or reserved powers, alike essential to her own existence and to the liberty and prosperity of her citizens."[153]

Smith seemed a bit uneasy in the spotlight. For him, the matter had simply involved principle, and there was no question that the powers of the federal government must be kept in check. In February 1856, after a glowing reference had appeared in the *New York Tribune*, Smith wrote to his wife, "It is certainly very flattering. I only wish I was worthy of it. What I have done I have done from a sense of duty, and if it has been my fortune to be the one who was to set up barriers against the encroachment of the national government, I feel happy that I am the chosen instrument."[154] Later that month, Smith wrote again of his desire to follow his own moral compass: "As God lives I will do my duty. I desire to have so clear a conviction of the correctness of my judgment as to preclude all doubt in my own mind. If I cannot I must get as near right as possible, and then your husband *will stand*, come what will. No fear, no threats, nothing of the sort can influence me."[155]

Smith's domestic life also appeared to be going well during these years. In 1854, his oldest daughter, Mary Frances, married William Sydney Huggins, a Yale-educated Presbyterian minister twelve years her senior, and the couple settled in Kalamazoo, Michigan. The following year, Mary Frances gave birth to the Smiths' first grandchild, Mary Augusta Huggins.[156]

As the people of Wisconsin watched "with a fanatical anxiety," the *Ableman* case wound its way through the court system, landing at the U.S. Supreme Court in 1859, five years after Joshua Glover's quiet card game outside Racine. The Court was headed by Chief Justice Roger B. Taney, whose "states-rights principles never seemed much in evidence when the interests of slaveholders were at stake."[157] Born in 1777 into the planter aristocracy of Maryland and educated in Pennsylvania, Taney had risen through the ranks from Maryland state senator to state attorney general to U.S. attorney general and secretary of the treasury before President Andrew Jackson nominated him to serve as chief justice of the United States on December 28, 1835.[158]

Taney's appointment provoked mixed reactions. Supporters felt sure of Taney's "loyalty to the president and his apparent commitment to an egalitarian economic vision for the young republic"; naysayers—among them Henry Clay and Daniel Webster—feared that Taney "would threaten the interests of property holders, undermine the strength of the Union and weaken the authority of the Supreme Court."[159]

As a young man, Taney held views on slavery that were consistent with those of early nineteenth-century residents of the border states, where, as historian Timothy S. Huebner notes, "slaves constituted only a small percentage of the population."[160] Taney also inherited a number of slaves, whom he later freed, and supported colonization efforts to return slaves to Africa.[161] In Huebner's words, Taney was "a Southerner who loved his country, a states' righter dedicated to the Union, a slaveholder who regretted the institution and manumitted his slaves, and an aristocrat with a democratic political philosophy" but nonetheless "remained committed to proslavery principles throughout his judicial career."[162] However, according to historian Don E. Fehrenbacher, by the time of *Ableman v. Booth*, Taney "had become as fanatical in his determination to protect the institution [of slavery] as [famed abolitionist William Lloyd] Garrison was in his determination to destroy it."[163]

In his two decades on the Supreme Court prior to the arrival of the *Ableman* case, Taney had considered several cases relating to slavery and to the increasingly strained relationship between the federal and state governments. In 1842, the Court heard *Prigg v. Pennsylvania*, in which a state's personal liberty laws clashed with the Fugitive Slave Law of 1793. Many free states had enacted laws that sought to impede the efforts of southern slave catchers on northern soil, and these laws caused particular concern in border areas such as Taney's Maryland.[164] *Prigg v. Pennsylvania* concerned a cross-border dispute involving Margaret Morgan, whose enslaved parents had been permitted to live "in virtual freedom" by their Maryland owner. The owner never actively claimed Margaret as his property, and she married a free man and moved to Pennsylvania.[165] When the owner died, his estate passed to his niece, who hired Edward Prigg to track down her "property."[166] Prigg found Morgan and her family and brought them before a justice of the peace to obtain a certificate of removal, but the justice refused to complete the required paperwork. When Prigg nevertheless took the woman and her children back to Maryland without proper authorization, he violated an 1826 Pennsylvania personal liberty law and was charged with kidnapping. Prigg was convicted by a local Pennsylvania court and the Pennsylvania Supreme Court upheld the decision. On appeal, however, the U.S. Supreme Court rejected the Pennsylvania decisions. Writing for the Court, Justice Joseph Story, a New Englander who was Taney's fiercest rival, declared that under the Constitution's Fugitive Slave Clause, owners of slaves had "the complete right and title ownership in their slaves, as property, in every State in the Union into which they might escape from the state where they were held in servitude."[167] Thus, Pennsylvania's anti-kidnapping law was unconstitutional.[168] *Prigg* amounted to "a major proslavery decision."[169]

Only Justice John McLean, an Ohioan, fully dissented from the decision. Chief Justice Taney and Justices Smith Thompson and Peter V. Daniel disagreed with the part of the decision in which Story asserted that "the states had no role in enforcing" a federal law.[170] According to Fehrenbacher, Taney believed that although states could not block an owner's claim to slave property, they indeed had the "power and even the obligation to assist in *protecting* those rights."[171]

In 1847 the Court again upheld the constitutionality of the 1793 Fugitive Slave Act in a case involving John Van Zandt, an Ohioan caught spiriting Kentucky slaves on a northbound road out of Cincinnati.[172] Van Zandt was represented by Salmon P. Chase (known at the time as "the attorney general for runaway negroes" and a future governor of Ohio, senator, and secretary of the treasury as well as ultimately Taney's successor as chief justice) and William H. Seward (who went on to become governor of New York, a senator, and secretary of state). The lawyers argued that the federal government was powerless to "create, continue, or enforce" slavery, since those functions fell under state jurisdiction—in short, the Constitution "did not give the federal government the power to enslave anyone."[173] Chase also argued that slavery ran counter to the Declaration of Independence's references to personal liberty and that it violated the Bill of Rights.[174] Citing *Prigg v. Pennsylvania*, Justice Levi Woodbury delivered the verdict in *Jones v. Van Zandt*:

> This court has already, after much deliberation, decided that the act of February 12th, 1793, was not repugnant to the constitution.... In coming to that conclusion they were fortified by the idea, that the constitution itself ... flung its shield, for security, over such property as is in controversy in the present case, and the right to pursue and reclaim it within the limits of another State. This was only carrying out, in our confederate form of government, the clear right of every man at common law to make fresh suit and recapture of his own property within that realm.[175]

Woodbury argued that although some states did not recognize slavery, the Fugitive Slave Law was a sort of compromise "for the safety of that portion of the Union which did permit such property, and which otherwise might often be deprived of it entirely by its merely crossing the line of an adjoining State."[176]

Undeterred, Chase took on Taney's Court again in an 1852 case, *Moore v. Illinois*, which involved an Illinois law that prohibited the harboring of escaped slaves. Chase argued that since *Prigg* had given jurisdiction over fugitive slaves exclusively to the federal government, Illinois was powerless to meddle in a matter involving fugitives.[177] However, in this instance, the Supreme Court upheld the state law as a justifiable means of keeping the peace and as in the best interests of the citizens of Illinois: providing assistance to runaway slaves could lead not only to disruptions of the peace but also to "violent assaults, riots, and murder."[178] In addition, Justice Robert C. Grier noted, state and federal law regarding fugitive slaves could coexist, since only a state law that *interfered* with the return of fugitives was an issue.[179] The Illinois law *complemented* the objectives of the Fugitive Slave Act.[180]

Arguably the most important case to set the stage for *Ableman v. Booth* was *Dred Scott v. Sandford* (1857). Scott was a Missouri slave owned by John Emerson, a U.S. military surgeon who frequently traveled out of state and brought Scott along. Some of these journeys involved extended stays in areas that did not allow slavery, including two long-term visits to Illinois and the Wisconsin Territory. When Emerson died in 1843, ownership of Dred Scott and his family transferred to the doctor's widow, Eliza Irene Sanford Emerson. Three years later, Scott, bolstered by support from abolitionists and using the argument that he had lived for a time in free territory, sought his freedom in the Missouri courts.[181] Scott won his case in circuit court but lost on appeal, with the battle landing in the U.S. Supreme Court in 1855. As Fehrenbacher notes, an "odor of conspiracy" had haunted the case, from contemporaries who believed that it had been orchestrated by proslavery forces to questions that still remain over the ownership of Scott and his family.[182] While many facets of the case remain unclear, the basic problem, as set out in Chief Justice Taney's opinion, was straightforward: "The question is simply this: Can a negro, whose ancestors were imported into this country, and sold as slaves, become a member of the political community formed and brought into existence by the constitution of the United States, and as such become entitled to all the rights, and privileges, and immunities, guaranteed by that instrument to the citizen? One of which rights is the privilege of suing in a court of the United States in the cases specified in the constitution."[183]

The answer from the Court, while couched in a decision that took Chief Justice Taney nearly two hours to read, was equally forthright—no: "In the opinion of the court, the legislation and histories of the times, and the language used in the declaration of independence, show, that neither the class of persons who had been imported as slaves, nor their descendants, whether they had become free or not, were then acknowledged as a part of the people, nor intended to be included in the general words used in that memorable instrument."[184]

This part of the opinion, while it left many northerners and particularly abolitionists disgusted, was not as shocking as the rest of the opinion, which went beyond answering the initial question set forth by Scott and his lawyers. Taney declared not only that Scott was not a citizen and thus lacked the right to have his case heard by the Supreme Court but also that because slaves were property and the government had a right to uphold the property rights of its citizens, the federal government had no right to limit slavery in the territories. By that reasoning, the Missouri Compromise was unconstitutional. Taney concluded, "The right of property in a slave is distinctly and expressly affirmed in the Constitution. The right to traffic in it, like an ordinary article of merchandise and property, was guaranteed to the citizens of the United States, in every state that might desire it, for twenty years. And the government in express terms is pledged to protect it in all future time if the slave escapes from his owner."[185]

The decision further polarized a nation that had already been bitterly divided over the Kansas-Nebraska Act of 1854. Public reaction in the North was "vitriolic in the extreme," with many people fearing that the decision had effectively opened the northern territories to slavery.[186] As historian Michael Holt notes, Republicans in particular found the decision galling because it suggested that one of the party's central tenets—that slavery should not be permitted in the territories—violated the Constitution.[187] Exacerbating the situation, the Court's majority had comprised primarily justices from slave states, offering what many Republicans saw as further evidence of the influence of the southern Slave Power, which made itself felt from the annexation of Texas all the way to the loathsome Kansas-Nebraska Act.[188] Republican legislatures in several northern states "passed resolutions stating that color did not disqualify a resident of the state from citizenship," while newspapers throughout the North denounced the decision.[189] Chief Justice Taney could not "have flung a more hate-packed decree at the Republicans if he had been a zealot for perpetual enslavement and disunion."[190]

For Democrats, the reaction was more complex. Most agreed with Taney's opposition to black citizenship, and southern Democrats especially perceived the decision as a long-awaited validation of their way of life.[191] The sticking point was the issue of popular sovereignty, which had long been advocated by Democratic senator Stephen Douglas, architect of the Kansas-Nebraska Act. The subject figured prominently in Douglas's 1858 debates against Abraham

Lincoln as the two men sparred in the Illinois senatorial election, leading Douglas to develop the Freeport Doctrine, in which he tried to find a balance between the popular sovereignty of the Kansas-Nebraska Act and the blanket ruling of the *Dred Scott* decision. When Lincoln asked whether a territory could exclude slavery before statehood, Douglas replied,

> Whatever the Supreme Court may hereafter decide as to the abstract question of whether slavery may go in under the Constitution or not, the people of a Territory have the lawful means to admit it or exclude it as they please, for the reason that slavery cannot exist a day or an hour anywhere unless supported by local police regulations, furnishing remedies and means of enforcing the right to hold slaves. Those local and police regulations can only be furnished by the local legislature. If the people of the Territory are opposed to slavery they will elect members to the legislature who will adopt unfriendly legislation to it. If they are for it they will adopt legislative measures friendly to slavery.[192]

This was not music to southern Democratic ears, but as David M. Potter documents, Douglas was in a difficult spot. To reject the *Dred Scott* decision would be to alienate southerners, while to support it would cost him the endorsements of northerners who had previously backed him simply because of his advocacy of popular sovereignty.[193]

By the mid-1850s, this political turmoil was joined by escalating violence in Kansas (the horror of the Pottawatomie Massacre and the Sack of Lawrence in 1856) and by the brutal and scandalous caning of Senator Charles Sumner the same year. In March 1857, the *Dred Scott* decision added to the instability of political parties that were already fraying over the myriad issues connected to territorial expansion, ever-growing regionalism, and of course slavery.

In the midst of such an atmosphere, which any number of historians have described with variations on the term "powder keg," abolitionists continued to call for action. In a May 1857 speech to the New York Anti-Slavery Society, Wendell Phillips thundered,

> I want a collision. The little State of Wisconsin, how nobly she is fighting the battle! The United States officers put Booth in jail; she took him out. They took his presses; she took them back again. Seward, Wilson, Giddings, Sumner rolled into one, don't make one Chief Justice Smith, who defied the United States Court to the utmost. (Applause.) Mohammedans say that one hour of justice is worth seventy years of prayer. One act is worth a century of eloquence. When Judge Smith flung himself in the face of the United States

writ, and declared that it should not run in Wisconsin, he commenced the beginning of the end.[194]

Smith was not entirely comfortable in the limelight, though he seemed sure his work would become part of history, as he wrote to his wife:

> I am afraid that Mr. Phillips and others go too far, and are too exultant. It is, indeed true that the effect, the *ultimate* effect, of my decisions can not *now* be estimated—long years hence when you and I are sleeping in our graves their full value, their full weight will be felt and appreciated.... I fear that the exultant, and apparently inconsiderate tone in which they are quoted, will tend to lessen their present weight and importance. But, Dearest, you I trust know that they have gone forth with an honest and faithful purpose, and there we must leave them—on their way in the Providence of God to find their just place in the history of nations, long after you and I their authors are gone and forgotten.[195]

By March 1859, when Taney finally delivered the decision in *Ableman v. Booth* after what must have seemed an interminable wait, the case had acquired new importance in the context of the political events and legal precedents that had unfolded in the days since Joshua Glover had been freed by a mob and Sherman Booth had been incarcerated. Unlike other federal cases involving slavery and fugitives, the justices were unanimous in *Ableman v. Booth*. The state, the Court ruled, could not overrule federal authority. In what has been hailed as "the most significant statement for the supremacy of federal over state courts between *Cohens v. Virginia* (1821) and the mid-twentieth century conflicts over desegregation," Taney outlined his case:

> If the judicial power exercised in this instance has been reserved to the States, no offence against the laws of the United States can be punished by their own courts, without the permission and according to the judgment of the courts of the State in which the party happens to be imprisoned; for, if the Supreme Court of Wisconsin possessed the power it has exercised in relation to offences against the act of Congress in question, it necessarily follows that they must have the same judicial authority in relation to any other law of the United States; and, consequently, their supervising and controlling power would embrace the whole criminal code of the United States, and extend to offences against our revenue laws, or any other law intended to guard the different departments of the General government from fraud or violence.[196]

States could not respond to federal legislation as if it were a type of grocery list, acknowledging some laws and rejecting others. Taney argued the federal government's orders superseded the sovereign rights of the state by virtue of the Constitution's supremacy clause: "This Constitution, and the laws of the United States which shall be made in pursuance thereof, shall be the supreme law of the land, and obligatory upon the judges in every State."[197] Taney acknowledged that state and federal governments might not always agree, but when a state took issue with a federal law, the U.S. Supreme Court must serve as the final arbiter on behalf of the people:

> The importance which the framers of the Constitution attached to such a tribunal, for the purpose of preserving internal tranquility, is strikingly manifested by the clause which gives this court jurisdiction over the sovereign States which compose this Union, when a controversy arises between them. Instead of reserving the right to seek redress for injustice from another State by their sovereign powers, they have bound themselves to submit to the decision of this court, and to abide by its judgment.[198]

Dealing a final blow to Smith's decision, Taney closed his opinion with an unambiguous statement regarding the Fugitive Slave Act so that the Court could not "be misunderstood" on the issue: the law was "in all its provisions" constitutional. "The judgment of the Supreme Court of Wisconsin," he concluded, "must therefore be reversed in each of the cases now before the court."[199]

Outraged, the Wisconsin Supreme Court refused to file the federal verdict in its records. In addition, the state legislature adopted joint resolutions that publicly chastised Taney and his legal colleagues: "*Resolved*, That this assumption of jurisdiction by the Federal judiciary, in the said case, and without process, is an act of undelegated power, and therefore without authority, void and of no force."[200] Still, the decision was not entirely unexpected, since the Supreme Court, according to the *Milwaukee Daily Free Democrat*, was "composed of a majority of slave holders and completely under the control of the Slave Power."[201] Chief Justice Taney had anticipated a flurry of renewed interest in the case, even authorizing the publication of a pamphlet containing the judgment, of which he was quite proud. The pamphlet never materialized, however, a situation that historian James F. Simon theorizes had as much to do with the "precipitous drop in the Supreme Court's prestige" as with the lack of interest in the case.[202]

Nonetheless, the timing of the decision was less than propitious for Smith, who was seeking reelection to the Wisconsin Supreme Court in March 1859, the same month the U.S. Court handed down its decision. In the five years between Booth's arrest and Taney's judgment, the once eminent judge and man about Milwaukee had been sailing stormy political and personal seas.

As the Glover story faded from the headlines, another story in which Smith was equally prominent began to take its place. In the spring of 1857, dozens of Wisconsin officials, including Smith, were implicated in a scandal related to the state's first federal railroad land grant. Several companies had been competing for the 1856 grant, which ultimately went to Byron Kilbourn's La Crosse & Milwaukee Railroad. It later emerged that Kilbourn, one of the founders of Milwaukee, had won the grant via thousands of dollars worth of bribes to public officials.[203] The city buzzed with speculation about who had taken bribes, and the dozens of suspected recipients included Governor Coles Bashford; Smith's former law partner, Henry Palmer; the editor of the *Milwaukee Sentinel*, Rufus King; and Smith's brother-in-law, Alexander Mitchell, the first president of the Wisconsin Bankers' Association.[204] Smith himself was accused of accepting ten thousand dollars in railway bonds, and he and Kilbourn probably knew each other, since Kilbourn had worked extensively with Smith's brother-in-law, George Reed, and the pair had founded the Milwaukee and Rock River Canal.[205] Smith denied the charge, but the man who had brought Wisconsin fame and glory as a place of high principles now stood accused of putting a price on his honor.

In May 1858, Smith testified before a special legislative committee investigating the bribery. Smith never denied receiving the bonds but declared emphatically that he had done nothing wrong: "There never was, at any time, any agreement, understanding, or intimation, suggestion or hint, whatsoever to me, or between me and any other person, touching the receipt by me, or payment, or presentation to me of any La Crosse & Milwaukee Railroad Company bonds or stock of any kind or denomination whatever."[206] Asked to explain how he had come to be in possession of the bonds, Smith said that one morning he had found them in a package on his library table:

> I had no reason that I knew, or could think of, to believe or suspect that they were intended for any unworthy purpose. But although I stood in no official relation to the company, I could perceive that such relation might arise. I could foresee other circumstances wherein I thought it would be my duty, in justice as well to myself as to the State, to retain those bonds, safely and securely within my control, to be produced as circumstances might require. I therefore replaced the bonds in the envelope, took them into the bank where I kept my account, and requested the Cashier to put his seal upon it, and deposit the package in the vault of the bank subject to my order, as a special deposit, and there they remain to this day.[207]

Smith admitted to having discussed with Bashford the land grant to Kilbourn's company, but insisted that he had only done what was "proper and lawful" to prevent a "catastrophe" from occurring: "It was rumored, nay confidently asserted, that the Chicago Company, as it was called, were at Madison urging their claims to the grant, with every probability of success. I thought I foresaw that if the grant of land was given to that company for the purpose of constructing a road through the centre of our State to Chicago, it would not only operate disastrously to Milwaukee and all her interests, but would tend to the disparagement of the State, as a confession of her inability to manage her inheritance or bequest."[208]

The 1858 legislature revoked the grant to the La Crosse & Milwaukee, and the scandal ruined several political careers, though Smith's was not among them. Nevertheless, his credibility had taken something of a hit—suspicions of having accepted a bribe did not paint a Supreme Court justice in a favorable light—and his reelection prospects dimmed considerably. Moreover, his ultra-states'-rights position in the Glover case had alienated Smith from the Democrats, effectively leaving him "a man without a party."[209]

The northern Democrats did not approve of party men criticizing the Fugitive Slave Act, a disagreeable but essential part of the Compromise of 1850, which three-quarters of the party's senators from nonslave states had supported.[210] When the omnibus strategy failed, Douglas, the leading northern Democrat, had rescued the compromise, assuring its passage by breaking it into its separate parts.[211]

In *Ableman v. Booth*, Smith had very publicly embarrassed his party with his explicit description of the compromise as "a wicked and a cruel enactment.... Let the federal government return to the exercise of the just powers conferred by the Constitution and few, very few, will be found to disturb the tranquility of the nation.... But until this is done, I solemnly believe that there will be no peace for the state or the nation, but that agitation, acrimony and hostility will mark our progress, even if we escape a more dread calamity which I will not even mention."[212] Thanks to *Ableman v. Booth*, northern Democrats stood accused of subverting the Union, and the blame fell squarely on Smith's shoulders:

> Judge Smith, who granted the first application of Booth, was a Democrat. One would suppose that his party would stand by him in this extreme assertion of state sovereignty, a cardinal doctrine of Democratic faith. Perhaps this might have been so on an abstract question. But in the conflicts of life there are no abstract questions. Men seldom reason logically or clearly where their feelings are involved. The Democratic party was really a pro-slavery party. So in Wisconsin they sacrificed Judge Smith; and when his term expired, nominated another candidate.[213]

Smith had also earned the enmity of William Barstow, a former governor of Wisconsin and "the kingpin of the state's Democratic party."[214] Barstow, the incumbent, had initially been declared the winner of the 1855 gubernatorial election, but a subsequent investigation determined that some of the returns were forgeries or were from areas that did not exist. When the matter came before the Wisconsin Supreme Court, the justices, including Smith, unanimously declared Barstow's opponent, Coles Bashford, the winner.[215]

According to historian Michael J. McManus, Barstow "and his henchmen powwowed in Madison and resolved to place a candidate in the field against Smith."[216] They chose William Pitt Lynde, who was "well known for his views opposing the decision of the state court and favoring the Dred Scott decree and other proslavery enactments of the federal government."[217]

A move to the Republican Party would have been an obvious strategy for anyone seeking public office in Wisconsin: by 1857, both senators, all three congressmen, most state legislators, and the governor were Republicans.[218] And many Republicans were ready to support Smith—he received endorsements from about forty party newspapers.[219] But the railway scandal caused Republican leaders to worry that he "might harm the party's image and fail to rally the rank and file" and that his sullied reputation would make his election an impossibility.[220] Even Sherman Booth, who had benefited from Smith's support, turned against him. "The Angel Gabriel could not be elected judge with ten thousand dollars of Land Grant Bonds in his possession," Booth wrote in the *Daily Free Democrat*. Smith "stands no more chance of being elected than he does of being struck by lightning."[221]

In addition, the Republicans had an appealing alternative in Booth's dynamic defense attorney, Byron Paine, a "youthful, almost romantic figure" who received the party's nomination at its March 1859 caucus in the state capital of Madison, taking forty-six votes to Smith's fifteen.[222] "Better news for Freedom never, in the long line of history, reached this ancient capital," Charles Sumner wrote to Paine from Rome. "God bless the people of Wisconsin who know their rights, and knowing dare maintain! God bless the champion they have chosen! God bless the cause!"[223]

On March 17, 1859, the *Milwaukee Sentinel* reported that Smith had announced a day earlier that he was withdrawing his candidacy for the court, much to the disappointment of those who supported his ultra-states'-rights position. Smith acknowledged his backing but explained that

> during the last few months, I have frequently been asked whether I would be a candidate for re-election—and if so, whether I would desire a party nomination. My uniform reply to all these inquiries has been that I had served the

people of the State six years—and that if they desired my services any longer they would say so—that in no event would I take a party nomination—that if the people, without regard to party ties or demands, desired my services another term, their will would be obeyed.[224]

The *Racine Journal* lamented Smith's withdrawal: "However much this ... will grieve the thousands of his many friends ... we see in it only further evidence of the magnanimity of the man, and still greater proofs of his fitness for the position to which his friends would have again elevated him."[225] Regrets were short lived, however: Republican newspapers "fell into line" and endorsed Paine.[226]

A vague May 1859 reference in the *Sentinel* suggests that someone thought that Smith should seek the vice presidency, and the following January, the paper declared, "There is not hardly a Republican in Wisconsin who does not desire to see A. D. Smith in the Senate of the United States—No more eloquent and earnest champion of freedom can our State produce."[227]

Smith did not pursue either of these offices, choosing instead to seek the post of chief justice of the Wisconsin Supreme Court. The sitting chief, Edward V. Whiton, had died in April 1859, and Vermonter Luther Dixon, a Republican and an "anti–State Rights man," had been appointed to serve until an election could be held twelve months later.[228] Through the winter of 1859–1860, Wisconsin's newspapers touted Smith's candidacy for the post. "There is no man whom the Republican Party could nominate who would begin to come up to his standard, whether you regard the measure of his ability or the character of his back-bone," asserted one letter to the editor of the *Sentinel*. "His re-election at the present crisis, would be an announcement to the world that Wisconsin takes no steps backward towards Despotism, but is firmly pledged to UNION AND LIBERTY."[229] According to the *Daily Free Democrat*, despite the railway scandal, "the people feel that it is time Judge Smith was restored to his place; they have need of his masterly talents and great experience; they feel that old friends are better than new ones."[230]

As the election approached, Smith continued to bang the states' rights drum. He delivered a lengthy and rousing speech in Madison on March 22, 1859, telling the sizable crowd,

> If this government is to be preserved in its purity and strength, if it is to be saved from the fangs of the spoiler to put forth its vast energies, to effect its legitimate results upon the civilization of the world, upon the development of the race, the elevation of man because he is man, to remain true and steadfast to his sacred character as God declared it "a little (only a little) lower than the angels"—then it can only be done by a firm adherence to, and an ever ready

vindication of the right of the States to maintain and exercise all the powers not delegated or relinquished by the Constitution of the United States.[231]

Smith argued that states' rights should form a fundamental part of the Republican platform because they were vital to the founding fathers' visions of the country's governmental structure.[232] As he had written to Horace Greeley several years earlier, Smith believed the founders had expressly desired that states retain a level of autonomy in the face of federal controls, espousing a "glorious vision ... of an expansive and expanding Union of sovereign and independent States, not an empire composed of dependent provinces. Let these principles be preserved, and union and liberty will continue our happy inheritance. Allow them to be trodden under foot, and consolidation and tyranny will be the inevitable result."[233]

This viewpoint was consistent with earlier resolutions set forth by Republicans in Wisconsin. At an 1857 caucus, for example, attendees declared that the party's mission should be to "restore the action of the Federal Government to the purity of principles of its Republican founders" by adopting the Virginia and Kentucky Resolutions as set out by Jefferson and Madison in 1798–1799.[234] In addition, they saw an "imperative duty" to stand by the Wisconsin Supreme Court in its judgment that the Fugitive Slave Act was unconstitutional.[235]

Particularly noteworthy in Smith's Madison speech was his willingness to push the states' rights agenda even when doing so meant taking an unpopular stance alongside proponents of slavery. Smith referred to an exchange that had taken place about a month earlier when *Ableman v. Booth* had become the topic of a U.S. Senate debate between Wisconsin's James Doolittle, a "highly effective orator," and fiery Robert Toombs of Georgia.[236] Toombs had caustically observed that young Wisconsin, a state for just twelve years, "got rotten before she got ripe" and came to the Senate floor with "her hands all smeared with the blood of a violated Constitution, all polluted with perjury."[237] Most Wisconsinites would have bridled at the insult, but Smith dared to be different, backing Toombs on principle when he spoke to the crowds in Madison: Wisconsin must uphold the states' rights position whether or not doing so was convenient, because it was a fundamental part of being a good Republican. He explained, "However I may condemn [Toombs's] political doctrines, I honor that faithful Senator for his noble fidelity to the dignity of the State which he represents, and cordially sympathize in his patriotic aspirations, and only regret that he should have forgotten that there was another state in the confederacy having equal rights, and entitled to equal consideration."[238]

Partisanship may also have played a role in Smith's backing of the Democrat Toombs against the Republican Doolittle. As this exchange demonstrated, the states' rights doctrine was, in historian Paul Finkelman's words, "a two-edged sword" that could easily be used by both sides of the slavery debate: even Byron Paine had admitted to being influenced by the arguments of John C. Calhoun, surely one of the most intensely disliked politicians of his time in a slavery-hating state such as Wisconsin.[239] The political events of the decade demonstrate, as historian David M. Potter writes, "that the attitudes of various groups in a society toward upholding the law is in direct proportion to their approval or disapproval of the law which is to be upheld."[240]

However, the states' rights argument was beginning to lose its luster in Wisconsin. During the campaign for the chief justiceship, Dixon had said that even though he intensely disliked the Fugitive Slave Act and agreed that it was unconstitutional, Wisconsin had an obligation to fall in line with the decision of the U.S. Supreme Court.[241] His victory in the election marked the demise of the states' rights "faction's dominance of the Wisconsin court" and suggests the beginning of a political shift in the state that made it more receptive to federalism the closer the country inched toward Civil War.[242]

Having been rejected in favor of first Paine and then Dixon, Smith took a break from politics and pursued journalism, taking over the *Milwaukee Daily Free Democrat* in December 1860.[243] The newspaper, hitherto edited by Sherman Booth, was a vehicle for the Republican Party, despite its name.[244]

Despite the dramatic flux in Smith's political fortunes, his family life remained stable. His eldest daughter, Mary Frances, and her husband, William Huggins, had added three children to their Michigan family.[245] A. D. and Mary Augusta Smith continued to live in their Spring Street residence with their younger daughters, Maria Cecilia, now in her early twenties, and Marion Augusta, about ten.[246] The household also included two domestic workers from Europe, Anna Whaling from Ireland and a Prussian, Carl Gratz, as well as Mary Augusta's mother, Rhoda Reed, now in her eighties.[247]

In 1861, Maria Cecilia Smith married banker William Sprague Candee in her parents' home, with "flowers, lights, people standing around the room and a big wedding cake," as one of her nieces recalled.[248]

A. D. Smith was apparently very fond of the groom. "My dear son," he began a November 1861 letter to his new son-in-law, "God, in His infinite wisdom, took from me my only son, born to me, but in His infinite mercy, has given me you to love and cherish with all the intensity of parental affection."²⁴⁹ With the Civil War having begun nearly seven months earlier, he continued, "Before you became a member of my family, I was alone and too old to be accepted as a soldier. Now there are two of us. Your life is yet I hope a long one. I have but few years. Your life is worth more than the remnant of mine, and yet I can do as much service in this war as you can. If I fall it is but anticipating Nature a few short years. Therefore let me render the service to our country that she demands of us now . . . a bullet or shell would not frighten me."²⁵⁰

Smith wrote to Candee from Washington, D.C., where he had recently traveled to collaborate with Doolittle in drafting the Direct Tax Act, which would allow the federal government to collect taxes to support the war effort, not only in the states that had not seceded but also in areas of the Confederacy occupied by U.S. troops.²⁵¹ While their collaboration might seem odd, given Smith's comments on the Toombs-Doolittle debate, the two men from Wisconsin had much in common: Doolittle was born in Upstate New York just four years after Smith and was a lifelong Democrat who had remained in the party until 1856, when he departed over the repeal of the Missouri Compromise. Doolittle and Smith also moved in the same legal circles: Doolittle had served as a judge on the Wisconsin's First Judicial Circuit in 1853–1856. A lukewarm Republican who would vote against the impeachment of Andrew Johnson and return to the Democrats in 1871, Doolittle probably found a soulmate and possibly even a mentor in A. D. Smith.²⁵²

In Washington, Smith seems to have had the ear not only of Doolittle but also of Abraham Lincoln: "I have had talks with nearly all the members of the Cabinet, then with the President, and have been politely requested to call again, to hear more from me (I say this most confidentially). Tomorrow by special appointment I am to call upon 'Old Abe'—when I intend to talk still more plainly with him than I have done on former occasions. But, Will, he would halt the grand army while scaling the ramparts of sesessiondom to listen to, or crack a joke upon rail splitting!!!"²⁵³

At the end of January 1862, Smith announced in the *Milwaukee Sentinel* that he had sold his subscription list for the *Daily Free Democrat* to the *Sentinel*. He took the occasion of his departure from the newspaper business to lash out at the war's "foes on this side of the Slave States": "The undying love of the Union is too deeply rooted in the hearts of the northern people, to permit one star to be stricken from our flag, or one stripe to be removed from its folds, except temporarily to lash traitors into submission. Howl on, ye sympathizers with rebellion; ye are welcome to all the satisfaction you can get from your howlings."²⁵⁴

Smith subsequently refocused on his political goals. Though he had alienated Democrats, he still had a chance with Republicans willing to overlook his connection to the railway-bond boondoggle. He had certainly moved sufficiently toward the Republican Party to warrant a patronage appointment, and by the summer of 1862, he was on the move again. Leaving behind his friends and family, he headed for the federally occupied South Carolina Sea Islands as a member of the Direct Tax Commission. He did not return to Wisconsin until a few weeks after the Civil War concluded, and he did so as a corpse.

A. D. Smith, ca. late 1861, when he was in Washington, D.C., to work on the Direct Tax Act. Library of Congress, LC-BH82-5316A.

A. D. Smith sat for this oil painting by Samuel Marsden Brookes in 1856, when Smith was a justice on the Wisconsin Supreme Court.
Wisconsin Historical Society, WHS-2928.

A. D. Smith, daguerreotype by C. A. Johnson, ca. late 1840s–1850s. This is the earliest known image of Smith. Wisconsin Historical Society, WHS-34860.

A. D. Smith's signature. In the early days of my research, when I was having difficulty determining Smith's name and full identity, I searched hundreds of documents to see if Smith ever signed his full name, but he always signed "A. D."

A. D. Smith and Mary Augusta Reed married on September 21, 1832, in Castleton, Vermont, where Smith had been studying at the Vermont Academy of Medicine. Vermont, Vital Records, 1720–1908 [database online], Ancestry.com, Provo, Utah, USA: Ancestry.com Operations, Inc., 2013.

A. D. Smith and Mary Augusta Smith, ca. late 1840s–1850s. This is the only known image of Mary Augusta Smith. Courtesy of the Gamble family.

The steamer *Arago*, where A. D. Smith died on June 4, 1865. "It was the strongest desire of his soul that every human being, however degraded, should enjoy his natural rights," a former colleague said. National Archives (165-c-592).

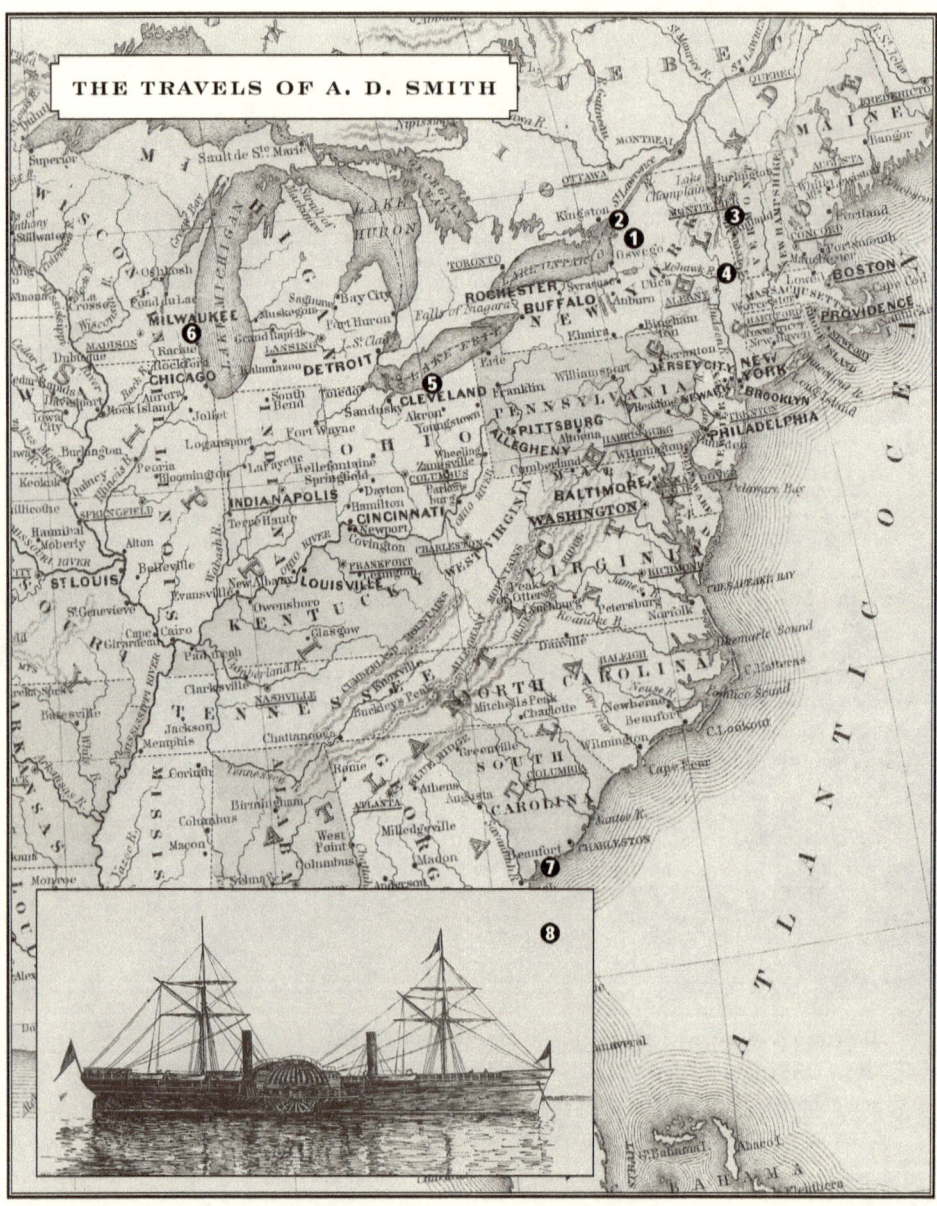

THE TRAVELS OF A. D. SMITH

1. Lowville, N.Y.
Abram Daniel Smith is born, June 9, 1811. Little is known about his childhood or family.

2. Sackets Harbor, N.Y.
Smith reads law.

3. Castleton, Vt.
Smith studies at the Vermont Academy of Medicine and, in September 1832, marries Mary Augusta Reed.

4. Lansingburgh, N.Y.
Smith's daughter Mary Frances is born in 1834.

5. Cleveland, Ohio
The Smith family arrives in approximately 1836, and Smith works as justice of the peace, city councilor, and lecturer in phrenology. Smith leaves Cleveland sometime in 1841.

6. Milwaukee, Wis.
Smith arrives in 1842 and practices law.

7. Beaufort, S.C.
Smith travels to the Sea Islands on a federal appointment as tax commissioner in 1862. He is drinking heavily and clashes with the other commissioners.

8. Aboard the *Arago*
Smith boards this northbound steamer headed for New York. He never makes it, dying on board on June 4, 1865, far from friends and family still in Milwaukee.

A. D. Smith is buried at Forest Home Cemetery in Milwaukee, Wisconsin. His son, Marius, and wife, Mary Augusta, are buried nearby. Darren Hauck, *Ottawa Citizen*.

Mary Frances Smith, Smith's eldest child, and her first husband, the Reverend William Sydney Huggins, who died of typhoid pneumonia in 1862. Schlesinger Library, Radcliffe Institute, Harvard University.

CANADA DAY

OTTAWA CITIZEN

TUESDAY, JULY 1, 2003 · ESTABLISHED IN 1845 · 70 CENTS + GST

The Canadian President

In 1838, a radical group of Americans elected a president of Canada. His name was A.D. Smith.

RUTH DUNLEY
In Cleveland, Ohio, Lowville, New York and Beaufort, South Carolina

F rom his home on Farmers' Block, a young man made his way through the streets of Cleveland under cover of darkness. Past the dry goods shop, the math academy and the school for girls, he moved north along Ontario Street, darted through the public square and then proceeded west on Superior Street until finally he reached his destination.

It was a hot autumn night in the middle of September 1838 and the faint glow of the aurora borealis reflected on the Cuyahoga River. Abram Daniel Smith, 27, was on a mission to change history.

He approached the headquarters of the grand lodge, on Miller's Block, and put a fist to the door, banging precisely three times.

When the door flung open, the man inside didn't take Smith's hand, but asked a simple question.

"Are you a Hunter?"

"Yes," nodded Smith. "On Monday."

With a knowing glance, the man shook Smith's hand, simultaneously pinching his coat sleeve — a secret signal.

With that, Smith entered the lodge, his footsteps pounding up the stairs to a spacious hall on an upper storey.

Inside, a large gathering of men fell silent and watched as one man dropped to his knees and was blindfolded. Slowly, the man began to speak, swearing the oath of the Hunter.

"I solemnly swear in the presence of Almighty God and this Lodge of Hunters that I will not give the secrets of this degree, or any secret that may come to my knowledge, in the body of this lodge, to any person to whom they do not justly and lawfully belong..."

Upon the words "so help me God," the tattered bandages were ripped from his eyes and two pistols were waved in his face. The sharp point of a sword jabbed his breast pocket.

"Behold the light!" another man shouted.

A master of ceremonies took the floor and addressed the trembling man.

"As you see light, so you also see death, presented to you in the most awful shape and form, from which no earthly power can save you, the moment you attempt to reveal any of the secrets or signs which have, or may be revealed to you."

And in that instant, the initiation was over. The man, like Smith, was now a Hunter. He would learn the secret signs, the codes and the plots.

Most important of all, however, he had earned the right to vote in an upcoming election. During this week in September, a select group of Hunters from Upper Canada and various states had gathered in Cleveland to elect a government.

In fact, they were electing the government of the Republic of Canada.

And Smith was elected its first president.

See PRESIDENT on page A3

On the trail of the mysterious Mr. Smith

"Smith died in a time when death was common to this country, when presidents, heroes and statesmen were lost to us by death almost daily, and it was not so much observed as it would have been in times of profound peace; but with him as with the others, history will redeem their memory, and their names will not be forgotten."
— H.S. Orton, July 29, 1865

By RUTH DUNLEY

I t was an obscure reference in an American history book titled *The Jacksonian Era*.

There, on page 158, my professor pointed to a sentence that begged further explanation.

"In September, 1838, some 160 Hunters from both sides of the border attended a convention in Cleveland, where they elected one Smith, a resident of that city, President of the Republic of Canada."

My prof mused aloud about how many times he had cited the passage in his lectures without being able to identify who our would-be president was.

In the weathered copy of the book I snatched from the university library, I looked up the passage again.

In the margin, in bright blue, block letters, a previous reader had added his or her own assessment: HA!

In fact, that was the most common response when I called experts in history, genealogy and at numerous archives and libraries looking for a man named Smith.

No, I didn't know his first name.

More gales of laughter.

How hard could it be? I had a name, a date, a place. That's more than reporters often have when they start to work a story.

I had no idea.

L ooking for a Smith in the 1830s is like looking for a needle in the proverbial haystack. Only worse. Records from that period of the 19th century are incomplete. Files are missing, addresses imprecise, handwriting blurred and often indecipherable. And forget alphabetical order.

But he had to be out there, this Smith. Someone who was alive and well in Cleveland, Ohio, in 1838 couldn't just vanish.

From a preliminary Internet search I was able to determine Smith's initials — A.D. — but not his full name.

See SMITH on page A3

The front page of the *Ottawa Citizen* on Canada Day, July 1, 2003.

CHAPTER 3

South Carolina
Your Name and Memory Will Be Cherished

You can have the assurance that your name and memory will be cherished by these lowly ones, to whom you have spoken cheering words of hope and encouragement, long after the names of those who have slandered you shall have been forgotten, or remembered not for the good they have done here.

—GENERAL RUFUS SAXTON to A. D. Smith, April 18, 1864

On the morning of October 9, 1862, William Lloyd Garrison settled into his seat on a train departing Boston for the town of Randolph, a short journey to the south.[1] Only seventeen days earlier, in the aftermath of the horror of Antietam, the public had learned of President Abraham Lincoln's preliminary Emancipation Proclamation, a plan to make slaves in Confederate states "forever free." The shift from a war about Union to a war about slavery would have been good news to Garrison, publisher of the abolitionist newspaper *The Liberator*, founder of the American Anti-Slavery Society, and a long-standing proponent of equality between the races and of immediate emancipation. Garrison's strong views made him simultaneously beloved and despised in a country torn apart by sectional differences and war. On the previous day alone, another 845 Union troops had died and 2,851 had been wounded at the Battle of Perryville.[2]

As the train whistled and clattered along the tracks through the autumn colors of Massachusetts, Garrison took stock of an unusual scene that made a lasting impression on him.

A man seated behind Garrison began to speak in what he recalled as a clear and emphatic voice. Raising his voice above the clanking of the railcar, the man delivered a short polemic in which he declared the ongoing war was a "just judgment of Heaven" against the United States for its sins of oppression. The man's rhetoric became increasingly heated as he told fellow passengers of his hope that the fire of war "would continue to burn till the dross was removed, and the land thoroughly purified." The man's words "stirred up two others near him," Garrison wrote, recording the episode on a piece of paper on his knee, "Gentlemen in pretence and appearance, one of them the President of the Railroad—who revealed the true democratic [Party] bile, and by their slang about the abolitionists showed they were as secesh in spirit as Jeff. Davis himself."[3]

Garrison wrote that the men obviously recognized him and so "paid Massachusetts a compliment by expressing the wish that she might be set off from the rest of the Union." The man behind Garrison spoke up again, replying "spiritedly" to the two southern sympathizers. What Garrison meant by his choice of the word "spiritedly" is open to interpretation, and according to Garrison, the outspoken passenger who had stirred the exchange with his passionate oratory identified himself only as Dr. Smith, of Wisconsin, formerly of Ryegate, Vermont. "After many years' absence, he was here on a visit to bring up 'the days o'auld lang syne' to his memory," Garrison recorded. "We found him a very hearty abolitionist."[4]

Though Garrison does not provide enough information to confirm the man's identity, this depiction of an outspoken abolitionist, passionate orator, and possibly slightly inebriated and bordering on belligerent rail passenger certainly could apply to A. D. Smith. And Smith indeed could have been on a train in that part of the country, visiting extended family or friends in Massachusetts or Vermont before traveling on to New York City.

The story is just one of many loose-fitting pieces of the Smith puzzle—impossible to prove, impossible to ignore. I have grappled repeatedly with the appropriateness of material in this vein. Is it significant insight or insignificant embellishment? I may never know whether A. D. Smith was aboard a train with William Lloyd Garrison in the fall of 1862, both men unaware of the bloodshed to come. The story is unquestionably much better if the man was Smith, but as has so often been the case, my extensive searches have not yet yielded a document that corroborates his presence.

"Unfortunately didn't find anything of interest to you," came one cheerful reply from an archivist helping me research Smith's Vermont connections. "Keep me posted on how your research develops."[5]

Upon reflection, I have come to see this seemingly inconsequential line in an email as more significant than I initially—and frustratedly—realized. In my storytelling journey with A. D. Smith, the "developing" has perhaps taken on the greatest implications for me. It is not in what I know for certain or what I cannot prove that a picture of Smith emerges, murky at times and crystal-clear at others; rather, it is in the development of his story that I have learned to appreciate the complexities of his character and the multifarious perspectives that are possible in viewing the composite of his life. Like Smith, the story is dynamic, moving, changing. For now, I choose to believe, based on the supporting evidence, that Smith and Garrison traveled on the same train that fall, though evidence may someday prove otherwise.

Eight days after Garrison overheard the mysterious Dr. Smith, A. D. Smith boarded the steamer *Erickson* to make the journey from New York to South Carolina, where he would be stationed for the next year and a half as a federal tax commissioner in the Sea Island town of Beaufort.[6] In one of the lesser-known stories recorded in popular histories of the Civil War, northern abolitionists such as Smith spent much of the war in Union-occupied lands of the South, taking part in what historian Willie Lee Rose labels the Port Royal Experiment—the first attempt at Reconstruction.[7] The area was seized by Union troops early in the Civil War as part of what historian James M. McPherson calls "the salt-water war," as seventeen Union warships, twenty-five colliers, and thirty-three transports snaked their way along the Atlantic seaboard to Port Royal, South Carolina.[8] With "deadly precision," the thousands of Union troops who arrived on those vessels took control of the area on November 7, 1861, forcing plantation owners and Confederate sympathizers to flee, many to nearby Charleston.[9] Those who had been enslaved, now alone on properties they did not own and apprehensive about the Yankees, first sought refuge in nearby swamps and forests, but some later returned to the plantations where they had been enslaved. Finding the properties abandoned and themselves legally free, some of the ex-slaves became destructive. Rose cites a reporter's eyewitness account that appeared in the *New York Tribune*: "We went through spacious houses where only a week ago families were living in luxury, and saw their costly furniture despoiled, books and papers smashed; pianos on the sidewalk, feather beds ripped open, and even the filth of the Negroes left lying in parlors and bedchambers."[10]

To Rose, "Nothing that happened illustrated better the frustrated hostilities of generations than the desecration of the stylish houses in the east end of town."[11] When the white landowners, men and women of what William W. Freehling dubs the "rice aristocracy," abandoned their homes, they left behind more than eight thousand penniless and propertyless slaves who were unable to relocate to areas outside the Union-occupied territory for fear of becoming reenslaved.[12]

Smith later said, "The first necessity was to start a civilization, an education, a domestication of these colored people."[13] In the spring of 1862, northern missionaries descended on the Port Royal area to do just that. Through the coordination of the freedmen's aid societies that had been organized in many major northern cities, missionaries arrived to educate the freedmen and initiate a system of free labor. Many of these emissaries hoped this microcosm of northern reform would prove to skeptics that freed blacks could become self-sufficient and integrated into society. Known as the Gideonites (after the biblical Gideon who led Israel to victory over the Midianites while armed with only pitchers and torches), these men and women from Boston, Philadelphia, and elsewhere in the North left their relatively comfortable homes to embark on an unprecedented social experiment in the South, their work financially supported by well-to-do abolitionists and philanthropists.[14] They arrived, as Allen C. Guelzo writes, with "evangelical fire in their hearts and schoolbooks in their hands."[15]

Smith disembarked at Beaufort several months after the missionaries had arrived and found a world such as he had never before seen. In 1840, just before Smith arrived in Wisconsin, the territory had only 185 blacks; ten years later, that number had increased to 635, which still constituted less than 1 percent of the new state's population.[16] In the Sea Islands, however, blacks outnumbered whites by a ratio of more than one hundred to one.[17] While the instruction of educational and social skills was left to the missionaries, questions relating to the division of property fell to Smith and his colleagues on the Direct Tax Commission.

Both the military officials in Beaufort and the Gideonites likely deemed Smith a logical choice for the position of tax commissioner. First, he had worked with Republican senator James Doolittle of Wisconsin to draft the Direct Tax Act in the spring of 1862.[18] A follow-up to the Confiscation Acts of 1861 and 1862, the measure authorized Washington to seize land belonging to disloyal citizens and free their slaves. The Direct Tax Act also authorized the federal government to collect war taxes from residents of rebellious states—"assessments on individual parcels of land, which would be forfeited to the United States government if the owner failed to pay. Tax Commissioners, appointed by the President for each insurrectionary state, would then assume control, with authority to rent out the property or to subdivide and sell it at auction."[19]

Of greater importance to the Gideonites was the fact that Smith was a well-known and dedicated antislavery ally known for his defiant decision that led to *Ableman v. Booth*. Smith was obviously a sharp legal mind, and he was outspoken—perhaps too outspoken for some.

His outspokenness may have constituted one of the reasons Smith was appointed to the commission. In the early years of the war, the Republican Party had difficulty dealing with its more radical members, many of whom, like Salmon P. Chase and James Doolittle, were former Democrats who had abandoned the party in favor of the fledgling Republicans. As Eric Foner documents, in the decade leading up to the Civil War, at least fifteen ex-Democrats served as Republican governors or senators, a sizable contingent that "had considerable impact on the emergence of a distinctive Republican political program and ideology.[20] In addition, the ex-Democrats "came from a tradition which viewed the states as the locus of most governmental action, and they were extremely fearful of centralized power in Washington."[21]

At a time of war, when federal power was growing inexorably, the Lincoln administration worried about the reaction of this particularly radical wing of the party. The president adopted several strategies to control the former Democrats. For example, he kept Chase at arm's length by adding him to the cabinet as secretary of the treasury.[22] In other cases, Lincoln sent these men as far away as possible. The Department of the South, which maintained bureaus in those areas of South Carolina, Georgia, and Florida that were occupied by federal troops, offered an ideal posting for these loose cannons dedicated to the cause of the Union and with the qualifications needed to perform the difficult tasks required. By installing them far away from the northern stage, Lincoln ensured that their commentary and actions remained largely undetected by the president's critics in Washington. Thus, radicals in the area of states' rights or abolition were often appointed to serve as tax commissioners in the Deep South.[23] And so A. D. Smith went to South Carolina.

Smith had few prospects in Wisconsin when he accepted the position. His ultra-states'-rights views had alienated him from the Democrats but had garnered only limited support among more radical Republicans, who cast him aside in the face of pressure from more moderate members of the party. At the same time, Republicans believed themselves somewhat indebted to Smith for his antislavery stand in 1854 and felt some obligation to toss him a patronage bone: sending him to South Carolina would both appease the radicals and isolate Smith so that he could do no real harm to the Republicans' war effort should he start spouting off about states' rights.

Smith returned from Washington, D.C., in mid-July 1862 and saw the announcement of his appointment "in the newspapers and concluded to accept it."[24] According to the July 19, 1862, edition of the *Milwaukee Sentinel*, "The telegraph reports that Judge A. D. Smith, of Milwaukee, Wm. D.

Wording, of Racine, and Dr. W. H. Brisbane, of Arena, have been appointed the Commissioners under the act for the collection of taxes in the insurrectionary districts, for the District of South Carolina." In addition, the newspaper noted that Smith's brother-in-law, Harrison Reed, had been appointed to the same office in Florida.[25]

It is unclear what Smith's decision meant for his wife and daughters. All indications are that Mary Augusta, Maria Cecilia (who had already married William Sprague Candee), and Marion Augusta remained in the North, where they would have been able to maintain the family's property, stay close to extended family, and avoid the risks of living in an occupied territory vulnerable to Confederate attack. Smith's oldest daughter, Mary Frances, still living in Michigan, had been widowed in March 1862, when her husband, William, succumbed to typhoid pneumonia, leaving her to care for their four children by herself, a situation that apparently did not affect A. D. Smith's decision to move south.[26] In August 1862, Mary Frances's five-year-old son, William Henry Huggins, also died, possibly of the same illness that had killed his father.[27] Recalled Mary Augusta Huggins, his older sister, "There came a day in summer when the house seemed solemn because Brother was very ill and [I] went out under a tree and asked God to make him well, but things happened just as they did when Papa went away and there was no little brother to play with."[28]

On August 6, just four days prior to his grandson's death, Smith wrote to secretary of the treasury Salmon P. Chase to formally accept the appointment to the commission: "Dear Sir," Smith began, "A few days ago I read a note from Sen. Doolittle of Wisconsin, informing me of my appointment as Commissioner of Taxes for South Carolina under the bill for the collection of taxes in insurrectionary districts. Although I had very frequently consulted with Mr. Doolittle in the preparation of the bill, I had had no intimation that I would be called to aid in its execution. Approving as I do of the objects of the bill ... I told Mr. Doolittle that I would not shrink from this duty."[29] Not surprisingly, Smith's letter did not mention the fact that in exchange for the appointment, Doolittle had made Smith promise to abstain "from intoxicating drinks or drugs" while in office.[30]

Apart from occasional letters to the editor of the *Milwaukee Sentinel* remarking on Smith's "intemperate" behavior, references to his drinking habits seem to have subsided during his time as a lawyer in Wisconsin in the 1850s. However, the promises exacted by Doolittle indicate not only that Smith carried a reputation as a heavy drinker but also that he may have been dependent on drugs, though the primary sources contain no other indications that he abused substances other than alcohol. If Smith did have a drug problem, opiates were likely involved. David T. Courtwright's analysis of nineteenth-century opiate addiction shows that one of the most common patterns of abuse involved middle-aged, comfortable or affluent women who nursed their addictions under the guise of treatment for various disorders, among them morning sickness and menstruation. While Smith obviously does not fit into this category, Courtwright suggests that opiates were seen as "a semi-respectable substitute for alcohol," and Smith may well have sought to reduce his alcohol consumption by substituting an opiate such as morphine.[31] His subsequent health problems and activities in South Carolina must thus be considered within the context of possible substance abuse.

On August 20, 1862, as Smith prepared to take up his new post in South Carolina, he wrote to his wife that "Washington is all excitement." He continued, "The two armies have been fighting for the last two days in the neighborhood of Manassas and are at it yet. What the result is, is not known. The City is full of rumors of all sorts and sizes, but nothing definite is known. No one however but the secessionists here have any fears for the safety of the City."[32] Many of those in the capital, including Smith, were speculating that the release of the Emancipation Proclamation was imminent: "Whether or not the President will be equal to the crisis remains to be seen. We are now on the crest of the wave to rush on to safety and glory, or to infamy and perdition. But how can we expect success unless we are willing to proclaim justice to those whom we have all aided to oppress. Three words from the President would scatter rebel forces in 24 hours after they could be heard in Dixie. '*Freedom to Slaves.*'"[33]

Exactly two months later, Smith and his colleagues on the commission, William Henry Brisbane and William Wording, landed in the lush Union outpost of Beaufort, the largest town in the Sea Islands. While completely at home in places such as Cleveland and Milwaukee, Smith must have felt somewhat out of place in South Carolina. Beaufort was a world turned upside down—abandoned plantations, well-meaning missionaries, and a population of former slaves who had never known freedom. Flat, sandy, and dotted with palmetto trees, the islands sit like an unfinished jigsaw puzzle in the waters of the Atlantic, hot and humid in the summer and temperate through the winter. The landscape and climate offered a stark contrast to the brisk winds and harsh winters Smith had known in New York, New England, and the Great Lakes region. Smith might well have wondered at his new surroundings: the crashing surf at Hunting Island, the oak trees dripping with Spanish moss that shaded the opulent homes of the southern aristocracy, the exotic trees and flowers: "Flanked by magnolia and orange trees, furnished with mahogany and rosewood, these mansions attested to the prosperity of a class that had made the great staple crops of South Carolina pay well, if not at all times magnificently, over a number of generations."[34]

The area was what C. Vann Woodward describes as the "seedbed of South Carolina secessionism," but the three new tax commissioners were, Smith reported, received with "the utmost consideration and kindness."[35] In all likelihood, the three men would have crossed paths in Wisconsin. Wording, like Smith, had been a judge, while Brisbane was a doctor and Baptist minister who had grown up in South Carolina. After inheriting property and slaves in the Beaufort area at the age of twenty-five, Brisbane soon sold the land and renounced slavery, marking him as "the most hated man in the Beaufort District."[36] Scott Sandage of Carnegie Mellon University included Brisbane in a book on America's "born losers," noting that a credit agency once said that Brisbane had "been a planter, preacher, publisher, physician, & farmer but has never succeed[e]d at any[thin]g & probably never will."[37] Wandering from Massachusetts to New Jersey to Ohio to Wisconsin, Brisbane also failed financially as a novelist and even as a tavern keeper (as Sandage notes, no one wanted to buy a drink from a Baptist preacher) as well as in numerous business ventures. His "only steady living came from patronage jobs (the last refuge of a man without pluck, people said)."[38]

Brisbane and Smith were related by marriage, which apparently did nothing to prevent rancor from developing on the tax commission. In the spring of 1862, Brisbane's daughter, Phoebe Adeline, married Mary Augusta Smith's younger brother, Herbert Reed. William Henry Brisbane did not initially support the marriage, firing off a frosty letter in which he acknowledged Reed's decent religious, moral, and political principles but nonetheless detailing "two objections to giving you our dear Addie, the one is disparity in your ages; and the other is, not that you are poor, but that you are in debt." In addition, Brisbane reported that his wife was alarmed by the prospective bride's and groom's differing churches, though both were Protestant. However, Brisbane closed the letter by waiving his concerns since his daughter had consented to the marriage.[39] The couple married in March 1862 in Milwaukee.[40] Herbert had previously operated a grocery business but at some point in the early 1860s relocated to New York as an appointee of the New York Customs House.[41]

Despite (or perhaps because of) this tenuous family tie, Smith and Brisbane were at odds from the beginning of their posting to Beaufort. Making matters worse for Smith was the fact that Wording did not have a mind of his own. Instead, as Rose notes, Wording "fell from the beginning under the influence of Brisbane and acted with him in all the business of the Commission."⁴² Originally from Maine, Wording had spent some time in South Carolina in the early 1840s, when he served as the principal of the Cheraw Academy, about two hundred miles north of Beaufort, and later practiced law in Columbia and Charleston.⁴³ Smith's outspoken manner and reputation for drinking would not have endeared him to his abstemious colleagues.

Smith did find an ally and friend in General Rufus Saxton, a fellow Freemason who had been named military governor of the islands. Saxton, a Massachusetts native, was the son of a Unitarian minister with a strong abolitionist pedigree. His brother and aide-de-camp, S. Willard Saxton, also lived in Beaufort, and the two men frequently took Smith's side against Brisbane and Wording. General Saxton had graduated from the U.S. Military Academy at West Point in 1849 and, like Smith, was something of a restless spirit, having taken part in a Rocky Mountain expeditionary force in the mid-1850s.⁴⁴

Despite the fact that the Gideonites had been working on the islands since the spring, the three tax commissioners initially found their surroundings in disarray. Smith told the American Freedmen's Inquiry Commission in 1863 that on his arrival he "found everything at odds and ends;—no system or policy or anything that looked to a permanent plan."⁴⁵ Smith deemed the first priority to be the care and education of the former slaves, who were still adjusting to a life outside of slavery through their participation in activities coordinated by the Gideonites. In keeping with his Jeffersonian principles, Smith believed strongly that land would be required to make the freedmen full-fledged citizens: "They did not want to go away; they were attached to their homes and wanted to stay here provided they could be free and protected," Smith said. "But in order to get that encouragement and hope . . . a homestead must be given them—they *must have land, land.*"⁴⁶

But providing them with land did not prove a simple matter. In their efforts to carve up land through the Direct Tax Act and to ensure that at least some of it went to the freedmen, Smith, Brisbane, and Wording found that they had little data on which to base their assessments. The white residents who had fled the Sea Islands were the only people with information on land deeds and property lines. On November 2, 1862, Smith explained to officials in Washington, "The Commissioners have been able to find scarcely any official data. . . . They have, however found the report of the State Comptroller for the year 1853. This is ancient, even for this ancient commonwealth." He was hopeful that an 1858 report might be found in the Congressional Library.⁴⁷

In addition, the commissioners were working under threat of Confederate attack. Ten days after his arrival in South Carolina, Smith requested that the Treasury Department send the commissioners a rowboat "for the purpose of examining the lands and as a means of transporting the books and documents and other effects of the Commission in any time of sudden attack by the enemy."[48] Although all of St. Helena Parish and a "considerable portion" of St. Luke's Parish were occupied by Union forces, the commissioners were hamstrung as they attempted to function "without a map or plat, a chain or compass, a land mark or a starting point."[49] In sum, as Smith noted in his first official report to Chase, "Out of this chaos and confusion, to bring order, distinctness, definition, valuation, assessment and adequate certainty of description, without the means for survey and measurement, and without the aid of records or maps or sources of reliable information, seemed to be a task of great difficulty as well as of responsibility."[50]

Nevertheless, the commissioners benefited from a stroke of luck: assessment rolls for 1858–1860 were discovered "in a heap of rubbish" in the attic of an abandoned home—left behind as the Rebels hastily departed, the commissioners surmised.[51] With this information in hand, Smith, Brisbane, and Wording scheduled an initial sale of lands for February 1863. The commissioners agreed that in addition to enriching government coffers, the sales needed to provide former slaves with an opportunity to purchase the land they had once worked. As Smith reported to Chase,

> The great impediment in the way of immediate progress appears to be the uncertainty which overhangs the future of the colored population. It is a very great mistake to suppose that they are unmindful of the uncertainty of their present condition, or of their future destiny. Destitute of all means of present livelyhood, powerless to grasp or to use even such means as their rebel masters have abandoned, without a foot of soil or an implement of husbandry to which they could lay claim, they painfully appreciate the fact that though free and capable of earning under present circumstances a daily support, they are nevertheless but tenants at will upon the grace of the Government.[52]

Moreover, according to Smith, the freedmen had a "strong desire" to remain in the region where they were born and raised.[53]

But Smith and his fellow commissioners could not reach a consensus on the best way to help the freedmen obtain land. Smith advocated giving the former slaves preemptive rights, a system of land transfer that had been common in the United States, particularly with westward expansion along the frontier in the decades before the Civil War. As historian Akiko Ochiai explains, preemption "granted first rights of purchase at a fixed price to individuals who had improved and settled on surveyed public lands when those lands were offered at public auction."[54] Advised Smith, "As soon as the government shall have acquired title to the lands, it is suggested that early steps be taken to have them subdivided and offered for sale in small parcels with the privilege of pre-emption, so that the freed man may secure himself and family a home and from his own earnings, that he shall feel its value at an early day."[55] According to Smith, this approach would not only benefit the government but would fulfill a God-given right for the ex-slaves:

> Having the soil—loyal people skilled in its culture, grateful, docile and hopeful—rebels absconded or driven out and refusing allegiance ... their places filled by patriots, their lands yearning for the plow and the spade—arms and hands eager to leap to their joyful because voluntary task—in short, all the elements of reconstruction, reformation, advancement in civilization, happiness, wealth, freedom and assured loyalty, fully devoted and reliable, how can a Government answer to God for its failure to improve opportunities of such a character, means so Providentially furnished ... so humane and magnificent?[56]

Brisbane and Wording, however, raised legal and practical concerns about "squatter sovereignty," creating a rift that hampered the commission's progress.[57]

While the records clearly demonstrate that all the men involved in the debate cared deeply about the issues at hand, particularly the welfare of the former slaves, the repeated clashes among U.S. policymakers and officials speak to a deeper motivation. For Republicans, the issue of land rights for freedmen was a thorny matter that began with the Port Royal Experiment and continued long after the war. Many of those who balked at slavery nevertheless hesitated to grant African Americans the right to own land. However, property rights had long been associated with republican concepts of freedom and liberty. Historian Gordon S. Wood documents that in 1776, for example, Thomas Jefferson lobbied for Virginia to give land to any man who was without property as a means of promoting independence: "Without having property and a will of his own—without having independence—a man could have no public spirit; and there could be no republic. For, as Jefferson put it, 'dependence begets subservience and venality, suffocates the germ of virtue, and prepares fit tools for the designs of ambition.'"[58] Historian Eric Foner notes that eighteenth-century Americans saw ownership of property as the foundation of liberty, and those seeking property rights often justified their position with this argument: "The linkage of property ownership and liberty, previously employed to draw the political nation's boundary so as to exclude those without property, could be transformed into a political entitlement by those seeking land.... Settlers' claims for preferential access to land rested on the idea that possession of property, as a North Carolina congressman put it, was 'a situation incident to freedom and desired by all.'"⁵⁹

In a move that surely would have made Smith's heart glad had he been alive to see it, General William Sherman issued Special Field Order No. 15 in January 1865, offering hundreds of acres of coastal land from the Sea Islands of South Carolina and Georgia all the way south to Jacksonville, Florida, to freedmen looking for a place to settle.⁶⁰ Forty thousand freedmen subsequently came forward to find new homes on that land, most of which had been confiscated from wealthy plantation owners, and Smith's ally, Rufus Saxton, was charged with overseeing the resettlement effort.⁶¹

In the fall of 1865, President Andrew Johnson returned the land to its original owners, and the issue of property rights for freedmen came to divide radical and moderate Republicans even more sharply. For radicals such as Smith and Saxton, the question of whether black citizens of a republic ought to be guaranteed access to property had an unequivocal answer: yes. But after the Civil War, as Foner notes,

> efforts to give the former slaves land failed to receive congressional approval. If emancipation, as [Frederick] Douglass had remarked, represented a convergence of the slaves' interests and those of the nation, eventually those interests, and their respective definitions of freedom, were destined to diverge. Only a minority of Republican policy-makers, most notably Radical congressman Thaddeus Stevens, sought to resurrect the older view—the view put forward by the ex-slaves—that without ownership of productive property, genuine freedom was impossible.⁶²

During Reconstruction, Radical Republicans "hoped to reshape Southern society in the image of the small-scale competitive capitalism of the North," a philosophy that was consistent with Smith's position in Port Royal.⁶³ Stevens, who had called for the confiscation of land owned by Confederates to help offset the costs of the war, advocated property rights for freedmen as a way of integrating them into society, favoring the right to land over the right to vote: "nothing is so likely to make a man a good citizen as to make him a freeholder. Nothing will make them so industrious and loyal as to let them feel that they are above want and the owners of the soil which they till."⁶⁴ Foner writes that Stevens stood virtually alone in this view, with most Republicans believing black suffrage a much more important question than property rights: "It is hardly surprising that many Radicals proved reluctant to support a program that so contravened the sanctity of property as confiscation; what is striking is how few suggested an alternative, other than holding out the prospect of individual advancement in accordance with the free labor ideology."⁶⁵

Smith, Brisbane, and their cohorts could not have anticipated how the Reconstruction debate would play out, but they doubtlessly understood the significance of their own debate and recognized the possibility that they were setting precedents for the treatment of freedmen in a postwar society. The frequency with which both men and their allies lobbied Washington and the urgency they often attached to their entreaties suggests that both the Smith-Saxton alliance and Brisbane and Wording were well aware of the long-term ramifications of the property-rights argument in Beaufort. This understanding added a subtext to the actions and interactions of these strong-willed men: they knew that their actions might set precedents for future policy. That neither side was willing to give an inch consequently is hardly surprising.

The internecine battle of Beaufort began in January 1863 over Lincoln's orders to hold a sale the following month in which tracts of land would be "sold to the highest bidder in lots of up to 320 acres."[66] Both Saxton and Smith as well as the like-minded Reverend Mansfield French, a Methodist minister working in the Sea Islands under the auspices of the American Missionary Association, believed this sale would be disastrous for the freedmen, who could not compete financially with northern investors. French wrote to Salmon P. Chase to express "serious apprehension" about the welfare of the former slaves: "Plans for stock companies are already before the public, and speculators are privately contriving to secure these plantations.... Should legislature be the only way of securing the laws, I beg to suggest that were Genl. Saxton ordered, or permitted, to visit Washington, Congress with the aid of his experience could act in turn to save the law and avert a vast amount of suffering. Much as he is needed here, we could spare him for the few days required."[67] However, before the February sale was advertised, Smith, not Saxton, traveled to Washington in an effort to amend the initial orders to allow the freedmen a better chance of purchasing land. After meeting with Chase and then with a number of high-profile senators, including Sumner and Doolittle, Smith drew up an amendment to the Direct Tax Act allowing the government to "select such lands and purchase them as [Union commander] Gen. [David] Hunter, Gen. Saxton and the Commissioners might deem a necessity for the military, naval, revenue, charitable, educational and police purposes of the Department, and also giving the land Commissioners power, in their discretion, to bid upon any lands up to two-thirds of their assessed value, so that indeed it might not be a change of masters from slaveowners to capitalists, but that Government might have land enough for them all."[68]

In early February 1863, Congress enacted Smith's amendment, thereby reserving some land for the freedmen. Under these provisions, the land sales were rescheduled for March, when twenty-one thousand of the eighty-thousand acres of confiscated land were sold into private hands, with the freedmen procuring about two thousand acres.[69] Smith immediately filed a glowing report, noting that it was "particularly gratifying to be able to state that I do not know of an acre of land having passed into the hands of a speculator, but all have purchased with a view to immediate cultivation."[70]

But this episode represented the beginning of the end for Smith. While his allegiance with Saxton and French had held strong and his efforts in Washington had paid off, his actions seem to have worsened his relations with Brisbane and Wording. The two men staunchly opposed preemption for a number of reasons and questioned "the capacity of the freedmen to become functioning citizens immediately."[71]

Further, Brisbane and Wording believed that the "settlement of freedpeople on small plots all over the islands would devalue property and dissuade white purchasers from residing among them." And by purchasing the land at two-thirds of its value, the government financially disadvantaged itself.[72]

The differences between commission members momentarily disappeared as 1862 turned to 1863. The new year brought some joy as the Sea Islands celebrated Lincoln's Emancipation Proclamation. As Brisbane read aloud the proclamation, freedmen broke into song; General Saxton held a dinner party and dance at his headquarters in Beaufort.[73] But the conflicts between Smith and Brisbane and Wording soon bubbled to the surface again, and their repeated clashes did not go unnoticed. French confided to Chase as early as February 1863 that "a broad and most unfortunate gulf of both opinion and action" existed between the two factions; underscoring the permanency of the rift during the first few months of the commission's activities, he added: "It can *never be bridged.*"[74]

As the calendar turned to summer, the weather in Beaufort became oppressive: temperatures there often top 85°F, with high humidity. Both Smith and Wording became ill, and all three members of the commission appear to have spent at least part of the summer of 1863 in the North. Smith's illness may or may not have been connected to excessive alcohol consumption. Wording, for his part, "seemed to be at the point of death for several weeks" before taking a turn for the better.[75] He spent much of his recuperation in New York, with Brisbane at his side for at least part of the time. There, Wording and Brisbane unilaterally dismissed J. C. Alexander from his post as the commission's clerk on the grounds that he was incompetent as a surveyor and replaced him with Thomas Coryell. They wrote to Smith, still in Beaufort, to inform him of this arrangement and to note that the new clerk would begin his work on July 1, at which time the old clerk's position would be terminated.[76]

According to Brisbane, Smith immediately set out for New York. When he arrived, Brisbane "urged him most earnestly" to attend a meeting with Wording, but Smith refused, adding that rather than meeting with the duo, he was leaving for Washington, where, he told Brisbane, "I will show you up." Brisbane believed Smith spent the summer in the capital.[77] (Smith later wrote that he had gone to Washington to "aid in making the necessary arrangements" for the next round of land sales in South Carolina.)[78]

Brisbane and Wording's actions clearly shocked Smith. He returned to Beaufort in September, with the *Free South* newspaper reporting that his health was "much improved" and that his absence was "by no means a pleasure excursion."[79] Back in the Sea Islands, Smith wrote to Washington to complain about the clerk's dismissal without any sort of formal meeting.[80]

Unbeknownst to Smith, however, Brisbane and Wording had been engaging in their own correspondence with Washington, secretly lobbying to have Smith removed from the commission because of his drinking. Near the end of August, Brisbane wrote an informal note to Chase:

> My dear friend, you have no idea how difficult it is to work with Judge Smith. I inclose herewith some letters which will show you the *animus* of the man. Judge Wording will corroborate everything in my letter to Judge Smith. I have been hoping that he would finally show a better spirit, but I feel at last compelled to let you see something of what we have to trouble us. I do not make this an official communication, because I sincerely desire to keep from the public eye what may damage Judge Smith in the estimation of those who do not personally know his habits. I have earnestly desired to get along with him in as friendly a way as possible. But he is too overbearing & insulting. Judge Wording & myself can get along most harmoniously; but neither of us can get on comfortably with Judge Smith.[81]

Yet Brisbane could not have been too worried about keeping the issue from the public eye: only nine days later, on September 5, he and Wording lodged a formal complaint with Chase:

> It is with extreme reluctance we obtain our own consent to complain of our colleague Hon. A. D. Smith. We have patiently borne with him thus far in the cherished hope that his own course or other circumstances might render such a communication as this unnecessary. But we feel that we owe it to the country in general, and to our own Commission in particular to now say to you that the frequent inebriation of our said colleague unfits him for the proper duties of the Commission; and that the difficulty of conducting the business with him is such, as to force upon us the duty of respectfully asking

the Government through you, to take such action in the premises as may be considered best for the credit of the Commission and the interests of the country.[82]

Was Smith indeed drinking too much? And "too much" by whose standards? Drinking levels in the decade before the Civil War had dropped to the lowest rates in American history, and as political debates had become more and more focused on slavery, prohibition had "all but collapsed as a major public issue," according to Mark Lender and James Martin.[83] Nevertheless, Brisbane was a Baptist, and members of that faith ardently advocated abstaining from alcohol. There is no way to know just how much Smith drank, and any amount, no matter how small, might have offended his teetotaler colleagues.

Whatever the case, the secretary of the treasury apparently had more pressing matters than the Sea Islands to attend to in late 1863, and Smith was not removed from his post. Nor does he appear to have received any sort of warning from Washington that he was on probation.

That fall, the Port Royal Experiment seemed to be progressing as it should. Edward Pierce, a Boston lawyer who acted as a special agent for the Treasury Department, wrote in the September 1863 *Atlantic Monthly* that the exercise, "begun in doubt, is no longer a bare hope or possibility. It is a fruition and consummation. The negroes will work for a living. They will fight for their freedom. They are adapted to civil society."[84]

But all was not well among the members of the Direct Tax Commission, who were, in the words of one observer, "as amicably disposed towards each other as cat and dog."[85] The acrimony intensified after the president ordered a new sale of forty thousand acres of Sea Island land, about half of it in twenty-acre plots reserved for former slaves at a price of $1.25 per acre.[86] Smith, Saxton, and French felt that too little land was being set aside for the number of freedmen who might like to purchase plots and disagreed with the stipulation that the former slaves could bid only on those specific plots; if they preferred different pieces of land, they would have to compete for it against northern investors, who had far more resources.[87]

General Saxton began what Willie Lee Rose has called a campaign that had "all the earmarks of deliberate obfuscation in a worthy cause."[88] Saxton told the freedmen to begin staking claims on whatever government land they pleased and to bring money and a description of the land they wished to purchase to his office.[89] Doing so, he believed, had a good chance of forcing the commissioners to have the instructions changed to suit the status quo. In this way, he suggested, *all* the land would eventually fall into the hands of the people who had earned it through years of enslaved labor.⁹⁰

Rev. French traveled to Washington to lobby Chase yet again for widespread preemption. On his return to Beaufort, French informed General Saxton and the commissioners that the rules had changed, but according to Brisbane kept the new rules "in profound secrecy from the majority of the Board."⁹¹ When the official orders dated December 31 finally arrived, they were not good news for Brisbane and Wording: Lincoln now directed the commission to allow "any loyal resident of Helena Parish (black or white)" to preempt between twenty and forty acres at $1.25 an acre.⁹² In a final act of subterfuge, French deliberately withheld the orders from Brisbane and Wording until after the steamer *Arago* had left the dock, preventing them from sending an immediate protest to Washington.⁹³

William F. Allen, a Wisconsin man who spent 1863–1864 teaching former slaves in the Sea Islands, noted that Lincoln's new orders were "clear, concise and judicious"—and a victory for Smith.⁹⁴ And according to Smith himself, the new regulations generated much happiness in the Sea Islands: "The people hailed the instructions of the 31st December as almost a second deliverance—they gave scope to their awakened aspirations—their promulgation was a great joy—second only to their freedom." (Then, in what could be interpreted as an obsequious move, Smith crossed out "their freedom" and replaced it with "Proclamation of the President.")⁹⁵

That happiness, not surprisingly, did not extend to Brisbane and Wording. They were livid. Determined to be heard, Brisbane immediately marched off to General Saxton and "entreated him to delay publication" of the new orders until the two commissioners had conferred with Washington. Saxton refused. Brisbane then asked the general for a week to think about the new orders. Again, Saxton refused. Now desperate, Brisbane asked for twenty-four hours. This time Saxton agreed. In a January 16, 1864, letter to Joseph Lewis, commissioner of internal revenue, Brisbane implied that Saxton either had been drinking or had lost his temper, making him "unfit" to hear their side of the story: "It was utterly impossible to get him to listen to a connected argument, or to give the slightest indication of a disposition to grant the request for delay until we could confer with the department. He has issued his orders to his agent to go immediately forward and divide up the lands."⁹⁶

Brisbane wrote angrily in his diary on January 15, 1864, "Oh! That man French does mean mischief by his meddlesome spirit than his head is worth; and General Saxton seems to be a crazy man about the division of these lands. Much, much trouble is ahead, and I fear my colleague Judge

Wording will resign and if he does I could not long remain with any satisfaction here."[97]

When the tax commission met again in mid-January, Smith apparently tried to convince Brisbane and Wording to obey Lincoln, but they would have none of it: "Judge Smith tried to get us to begin to carry out the new instructions but he was drunk and Judge Wording and myself were not disposed to make fools of ourselves by trying to do what we knew could not legally be done."[98] Brisbane learned that a mass meeting was to take place at the Brick Baptist Church on nearby St. Helena Island on January 17 and concluded that under the guise of religious worship, Saxton, French, and by implication Smith were set to foment excitement about the new policy. Powerless to stop the gathering, Brisbane lamented, "The negroes will be confused beyond measure, and while they will be wondering what it all means, keen-sighted white men will be travelling over the Islands to see where to locate their pre-emptions."[99]

Much to Brisbane's disgust, the meeting went ahead as planned, with dozens cramming inside the Brick Church (still standing today amid spiky palmettos and weather-beaten gravestones) to hear Saxton, French, and Smith hold court. French must have taken considerable delight in reading Lincoln's new instructions aloud and then leading the assembled group through a religious service.[100] When it was Smith's turn to speak, he did so with great emotion—and incoherence. Spitting tobacco and possibly inebriated, Smith walked to the front of the church to face the crowd. Recalled William Allen, who was in attendance,

> Judge Smith ascended the pulpit, and, looking around at the audience, asked why—why—when hearts were bursting with joy, heads were bent and tongues silent, and manly faces bathed in tears. As everybody was looking straight at him, and nobody was shedding any tears except himself (he occasionally wiped his eyes with a dirty pocket-handkerchief) there didn't seem to be any occasion to answer the question, so nobody did. He then relieved himself of a very large mouthful of tobacco, wiped the tears from his eyes, and went on to say that there were two kinds of joy, and this was t'other kind.[101]

Allen also wrote that the growing rift on the commission was apparent to anyone who had occasion to observe the acrimonious trio: "There has been a chronic quarrel in the board of Tax Commissioners, between Dr. Brisbane and Judge Smith. The third member, Worden [sic] is a man of straw, who has sided with Brisbane and given him the majority."[102]

Despite Smith's wobbly appearance, the meeting indeed spurred droves of property claims by freedmen.[103] Brisbane and Wording, however, refused to acknowledge the claims. Brisbane told Lewis, "If all of this be law, I as a Commissioner and my truly honest and upright colleague Judge Wording will carry it out in its letter and spirit so long as we remain in office. But to our view to make these new instructions law, will require an Act of Congress.... Under the law there is no authority whatsoever for the pre-emption of improved lands.... [A]s the instructions therefore are inconsistent with the law, how can we give a valid title under them?"[104]

Saxton, angered by Brisbane's and Wording's noncompliance, wrote to Chase on January 22 to complain that the two commissioners were failing to carry out the "wise and human orders" of the president.[105] "The delay, at this critical period of year, when all these thousands of homeless ones should be preparing their land for the next season's crop, will be exceedingly disastrous," the general warned, "and cause many who, otherwise, would be able to provide for themselves, to become a tax upon the bounty of the government."[106] About a dozen residents of Beaufort signed the document. In a separate letter to Chase written later the same day, Saxton noted that Smith had given the new instructions "his cordial and hearty support" but "most respectfully" suggested that either Brisbane or Wording "be displaced and another appointed [to the commission] whose head and heart are more in sympathy with your enlightened policy."[107]

Saxton told Brisbane not to concern himself with the legality of matters—that was President Lincoln's responsibility.[108] This advice further outraged the already near-apoplectic Brisbane. It was preposterous to think that Lincoln had time to examine the fine details of the land sales, Brisbane wrote to Lewis, and furthermore, that was precisely the commission's job. The president and Chase had "a right to expect of us that they be informed correctly and truly in all matters for which they are to be held responsible by their sanction," he continued. "Can we under the shelter of the President's responsibility violate the law that we are sworn to carry out and expect that he himself whose name has been the synonym of honesty would justify us in using *his* name" to implement a flawed and fraudulent plan of pre-emption?[109]

In the days after the meeting at the Brick Church, Brisbane set about articulating his argument more formally and again put pen to paper, sending an eight-page screed to Joseph Lewis on January 21 that detailed what Brisbane saw as the insanity and illegality of the new orders:

> Without any consultation, without any word of inquiry with the majority of the Commissioners, Mr. M. French proceeds to Washington and returns to Beaufort with new instructions for the Board of Commissioners.... [W]hat

> do these new instructions do? We are told by gentlemen who are particularly interested in promising them or in advocating them that they were designed for the benefit of the negroes. What? Is it for *their* benefit that twenty thousand acres of land which had been appropriated to them exclusively is taken away from them again and opened to the adroit, skillful and ready witted and educated white man to get ahead of them to pre-empt? Never were a poor ignorant people more terribly wronged by their enemies than the people have in this case been wronged by their friends. I can scarcely keep from weeping, my dear sir.[110]

Brisbane also expressed concern that Wording might quit over the debacle: "I do sincerely hope that if he tenders his resignation it may not be accepted. I too feel a longing for my home and to be with my children; but I must while there is a plank to stand upon or a hope to cling to, look to this interest until I can feel assured that the future for this, my native state, has a bright and glorious pathway."[111]

The correspondence clearly illustrates that both Brisbane and Smith believed that the freedmen needed to be able to own land in the area where they had been born and raised. But the two men simply could not agree on the best way to achieve this goal. Smith seems to have maintained his silence at this juncture, but his reasons are unknown. He may have felt that the best course of action was to keep any smug satisfaction with French's intervention to himself. Or he may have been drinking more heavily.

And even as Brisbane and Wording complained bitterly about their colleague, the Smith-Saxton alliance was receiving very public accolades in the press. The *New York Tribune* suggested "the resignation of Messrs Wording and Brisbane is contemplated" and that "the announcement that such a resignation was accepted by the Treasury Department would be received by [the Sea Islands] community with fortitude."[112] The *Tribune* went on to invoke Smith's record in Wisconsin as "the first incumbent of a bench in a Supreme Court who declared the 'Fugitive-Slave Law' to be unconstitutional" and extolled his contribution to the lives of the freedmen.

> As a sound lawyer, Judge Smith has won fame equal to that which is gaining in this department as a fearless advocate of equal rights before the law for all human beings. Gen. Saxton has no more earnest supporter, no abler adviser, than is this excellent gentleman, in all that relates to the elevation of the people from the debasement and dependence of Slavery to the dignity and independence of Liberty. Wisconsin may remember, with proper pride, the elevation of such a man to the highest judicial position in her Commonwealth. In [South Carolina] the name of A. D. Smith will ever be associated with

that of Gen. Saxton and the good work of planting civilization in a moral and intellectual wilderness, and saving the land itself from becoming a desert.[113]

As the battle over preemption heated up, Smith and his allies had considerable support, but it was mitigated by the charges of alcoholism that plagued Smith. Willie Lee Rose has noted that "while Brisbane and Wording may have been, as was freely charged, more solicitous of the United States Treasury than of the freedmen's security, they at least had no outstanding personal vices to discredit their influence. Even the missionaries who supported him knew that *their* man on the Commission was a heavy drinker."[114] Worse, Smith's drinking apparently had begun interfering with his ability to carry out his work on the commission, as he arrived late for meetings after sleeping in. "If you catch him before ten, you will find him sober and clear; but then he doesn't get up till quarter of ten," admitted William Allen—and he was one of Smith's supporters.[115]

As the preemption debate continued to simmer, Brisbane filed a report of the commission's activities on February 2, affirming that the two-man "majority" was "unwilling to proceed" until further instructions came from Lewis's office.[116] Brisbane noted that an extremely wet January had caused the surveyors to fall behind, delaying the commission's work, as had the expropriation of some of their horses and wagons by the U.S. military. Beneath his signature, Brisbane added, "Commissioner Smith requests that I add that he dissents from the above and will forward a minority report."[117]

Indeed, Smith said he was "compelled" to dissent and filed a separate report to Lewis five days later.[118] According to Smith, Brisbane had not shown him the report until 6:00 on the evening of February 1, thus forcing him to cobble together his response on short notice: "The delay of progress on our surveys is, in my opinion, inexcusable," he wrote. "I am credibly informed that the season has not been unusually wet or otherwise prejudicial to the operations of the survey. If there be a fault in this respect, it must consist in the fact that they were not begun earlier in the season.[119]

Smith also countered Brisbane's assertion that the commissioners' transportation had been disrupted by the military's confiscation of horses and wagons, noting that General Saxton had always paid prompt attention to their requirements and that animals and vehicles had not been seized until the past few days. Any delays, Smith suggested, stemmed from the refusal of some commission members to comply with their most recent instructions. Smith asserted that Brisbane had no justification for raising alarm: "I have been unable to discover, after careful examination and collation of all the laws, regulations and instructions, any point in which the President, the

Secretary or the Commissioner of Internal Revenue have forgotten the law of the land. I see no difficulty with willing minds in carrying them out to their full intent and purpose."[120]

As Smith forwarded his learned opinion to higher powers, others were writing letters that would cause irreparable damage to his reputation. Initially, most of these missives were crafted by Brisbane, but even Smith's erstwhile allies such as Senator Doolittle, who had secured the judge's appointment to the commission, began to turn against him. Writing to Chase on February 6, 1864, Doolittle declared,

> I have the most unwavering confidence in the integrity, good judgment, sobriety and humanity of Dr. Brisbane and Judge Wording. I know them well. I had great confidence in Judge Smith, but for causes which give me great pain when I think of them, my confidence in him is broken down. I venture to give my opinion in decided terms. I would either remove Judge Smith immediately or I would direct that all the proceedings there should be under the [illegible] of a majority of the Board. The former is probably the wiser course, as matters stand.... I have much more faith in Dr. Brisbane's real friendship for the colored man than in the utopian ideas of the [Reverend] French. As I was mainly responsible for the appointment of these gentlemen, and I find that in Judge Smith in spite of all his promises to me of abstinence from intoxicating drinks or drugs I have been so greatly disappointed in my hopes, I am willing to bear my full share of responsibility for his removal.[121]

That same day, Chase reversed the preemption orders. When news of the reversal reached Beaufort on February 12, Smith must have felt terribly betrayed. By Brisbane's account, Smith was "very much disappointed" and Wording "very much elated." Brisbane described himself as taking the news "quietly," but he must have been just as pleased as Wording was.[122] After weeks of suffering through the self-righteousness of Smith, Saxton, and French, Brisbane could not "but rejoice that the order of the Secretary of the date of the 6th instant restores matters to their former position and prevents a hopeless confusion," he wrote to Lewis. Nevertheless, Brisbane expressed concern that Smith and his cohort were working behind the scenes to undermine the latest order: "It pains me to have to say that Judge Smith seems determined if he possibly can to get the people to believe that their applications for preemption, although never entertained by the Board, are themselves valid preemptions; and on Saturday brought forward resolutions to that effect." Worse, French had used a funeral oration to "excite a spirit of resistance to the disposition of the lands as under the old instructions. Under these circumstances we may yet have a vast amount of trouble."[123]

In his diary, Brisbane plainly recorded his amazement at the "obtuseness of General Saxton," his disgust "with Judge Smith's inebriations," and his indignation at "the intriguing character and cant of French." Brisbane apparently believed these behaviors went beyond character flaws: "My hope is in God that he will yet bring to light the hidden things of darkness, overturn the machinations of malice & cunning, & yet save from ruinous confusion this interest so important to the country & so absolutely essential to the welfare of the poor colored people."[124]

Back in Washington, Chase and Lewis must have found their patience wearing thin with the feuding and the barrage of he said–he said communications arriving from the Sea Islands. The government had issues of far greater importance than the squabbles of Beaufort's tax commissioners. During the same week that Chase reversed the preemption orders, President Lincoln ordered another half million men be drafted into service, General William T. Sherman started the Meridian Campaign in Mississippi, and skirmishes were afflicting Tennessee, Alabama, Virginia, and Missouri.[125]

And despite his victory in getting the order reversed, Brisbane remained unsatisfied. On February 23, he wrote to Lewis to insist on Smith's removal from the commission:

> My dear Sir, allow me to express myself to you about our troubles with Judge Smith. I must say I think it is cruel to Judge Wording and myself that we should be having to be continually annoyed with his indecorous treatment of us, his want of punctuality at our meetings, his attending to the business of another office which he holds under General Saxton, and his violent speeches to the negroes producing discontent among them & encouraging violent opposition on their part to white proprietors of the lands.[126]

According to Brisbane, he had warned Smith about the plan to seek his removal from his post, but Smith had disdainfully told Brisbane to go ahead: Smith would return "the favor" by asking that Brisbane be removed.[127] Brisbane declared that he preferred "to be on my farm in Wisconsin than to have official association with such a man as" Smith and issued an ultimatum:

> If the Department should deem it best to retain Judge Smith I shall feel that self-respect and the hopelessness of accomplishing any good results by remaining will require me to resign. I am sure I have been faithful to the trust I have had and fear not the most thorough investigation of my official course: I respectfully ask you, Honored Sir, to take this matter into consideration and talk to the Secretary about it. I once asked the Secretary to get Judge Smith appointed to some other position for which he might be better adapted. But

> I would now take that back, as further experience with him really satisfies me that I would do wrong to advise his appointment to any Governmental Office. Whatever he once was he is not now adapted to a responsible public position in my judgment.[128]

Two days after Brisbane's letter, Wording, previously an infrequent correspondent with Washington, chimed in, writing to Joseph Lewis that Smith was now using "every conceivable means" to prevent bidding in the next round of land sales.[129] On March 5, Brisbane added charges of nepotism to the list of Smith's offenses. Returning to the previous summer's spat, Brisbane asserted that the dismissed clerk, John Candee Alexander, was related to Smith through William Sprague Candee, who had married Smith's second daughter, Maria Cecilia:

> I will also add here how Mr. Alexander himself was appointed. It was done in the city of Milwaukee without my consent, without my knowledge and when I was on my route to Washington by the urgent requirement of the Secretary as communicated by a note from Judge Smith himself. After thus writing me, Judge Smith proceeded to Milwaukee, got Judge Wording to meet him there, urged him to agree to appoint Mr. Alexander whom he highly recommended to him, saying he had no doubt I would agree to it, persuaded him to make the appointment, of all which I knew nothing until I met my colleagues in Washington, having Mr. Alexander with them.[130]

At the time, according to Brisbane, he had not made a fuss about the appointment "for the sake of harmony," though he certainly would have objected if he had known of the family connection, particularly since Brisbane had told his son that he could not work for the commission. Brisbane further asserted that Alexander was still receiving his salary from the commission.[131]

By March 10, even Smith's allies had to concede that the Sea Islands were in chaos. "We are in great affliction," French wrote to Lewis. "Uncertainty hangs over everything. The people turn from man and make their complaints known to God. What a pity that so many men intending good should be left, for lack of harmony, to do much harm."[132]

Though Brisbane, Wording, and French did not know it, Smith's days on the commission were already numbered. Lewis, likely weary to the point of exasperation with the debacle in the Department of the South, had written to Chase on February 5 and recommended Smith's removal:

> I deem harmony among the members of the board of the utmost importance, and that it appears to me that hope of such harmony, constituted as the board now is, is more than vain. Dr. Brisbane and Judge Wording are

certainly laboring faithfully to accomplish the objects of the Commission. I see no evidence of co-operation by Judge Smith with the other members.... I assume the responsibility of recommending that Judge Smith be removed and that the vacancy be filled by some person who can act with other members cordially and with a disposition to do his whole duty. Judge Smith may be useful in some other field of the public service. As tax commissioner for the insurrectionary district of South Carolina he not only does nothing, as I believe, to forward the work in hand, but his influence is exerted to embarrass and annoy his colleagues.[133]

On March 5—the same day he penned the letter accusing Smith of underhandedly finagling a plum government job for his son-in-law's cousin—Brisbane learned through a private letter from Lewis of the "truly agreeable news" that "the President had nominated to the Senate some one to take Judge Smith's place in our Commission."[134]

On March 1, Chase wrote to Brisbane that "The President has thought fit to appoint [Iowa lawyer Dennis N.] Cooley in the place of Judge Smith. The preponderance of statements by those who seem best acquainted with the condition of things in the District, seemed to render this action necessary." But Chase also was saddened that the situation had reached this point:

> I have been, and am greatly perplexed by the differences between yourself and Judge Wordding [*sic*] on one side, and Judge Smith, General Saxton and Mr. French on the other. Both parties seem equally anxious for the welfare of the colored laborers, which in my judgment should be the paramount object.... I know the task of dealing with this situation is difficult, but I can not help thinking that by mutual concessions among those who have the same objects in view, some plan might be agreed upon which would be practically useful.... I regret the necessity [of removing Smith] exceedingly, for I can never forget the early services of Judge Smith to the cause of freedom when, to render them, required great courage and genuine manhood.[135]

Not surprisingly, Brisbane found this development "truly agreeable.... God be thanked for it."[136] Others, however, had different sentiments. Writing in his diary, Rufus Saxton's brother, Willard, described Smith's dismissal as another symptom of the toxic atmosphere in the Sea Islands: "The last mail brought the news of the relief of Judge Smith from the Board of Tax Commissioners," meaning that Brisbane and Wording, "the Jesuit and the Jackass," "are triumphant."[137] Things had become so bad that "Rufus wrote to Mr. Stanton asking to be relieved of his special duties here as Mil. Gov., feeling that he can do the people no farther good.... It would not make me cry to be obliged to leave here entirely."[138]

In his letter, Rufus Saxton also strongly defended himself against rumors regarding his role in the affair:

> I have heard that I am held responsible for Mr. French's mission to Washington—*I am not*. I gave him no permission to go and no instructions to act upon when there, and I also forbade him to use my name in any way. I have heard that I kept the instructions from the Board of Commissioners. *I did not!* I first saw them in the hands of one of them, Hon. A. D. Smith, sent to him for them, had them copied and returned to him within the hour. I refrained from publishing them for twenty-four hours at the earnest solicitation of Dr. W. H. Brisbane.[139]

Chase refused Saxton's resignation and sent a special agent to investigate how things in Beaufort had unraveled so spectacularly.[140] Arriving on April 1, the agent, Austin Smith, found that A. D. Smith was still "acting and recognized as one of the District Tax Commissioners for South Carolina," although he officially terminated his duties on April 15 when his successor arrived.[141] Austin Smith (no relation to A. D. Smith) devoted particular attention to the circumstances surrounding Alexander's replacement by Coryell, ultimately concluding that by refusing to attend the meeting in New York, Judge Smith had waived his right to object to the hiring of a replacement. The agent also concluded that Alexander and Coryell had acted in good faith and that both were entitled to fair compensation for the work they had completed on behalf of the commission.[142]

Neither A. D. Smith's official departure from the commission nor Austin Smith's report stemmed the bickering, however, as Brisbane and Wording demanded that their former colleague return nearly two hundred items—including stationery, thirteen paperweights, four knives, two erasers, and an armrest—that they alleged he had taken from the commission's office.[143] Upon receiving their letter, Smith immediately replied to ask, "By what authority? Upon what data? The list which you present is utterly without basis in regard to very many articles and erroneous in regard to others." Moreover, he continued, "it is proper for me further to state I was actually gathering up the debris or fragments in my possession when I received your communication. Nothing but press of other duties has prevented an early delivery."[144]

When Smith moved out of his rooms on April 29, 1864, at least a few people were disappointed that he had not prevailed. Shortly after Smith received official word of his dismissal, General Saxton wrote his friend a kind and reassuring letter that implies that Smith's drinking may not have been as serious as his opponents had suggested:

> I can assure you, my dear Judge, that it gives me the greatest pleasure to bear witness to your entire devotion and attention to the arduous duties of your commission. I have visited your office at all hours, and *always* have found you busily employed at your post of duty. The freedmen have ever found in you a wise counselor, an ever ready and sympathetic friend. I sincerely regret to learn that your duties may call you elsewhere, and that I, too, shall be deprived of your much-valued co-operation and advice in my own peculiar and sometimes perplexing duties. Should you leave the Department, you can have the assurance that your name and memory will be cherished by these lowly ones, to whom you have spoken cheering words of hope and encouragement, long after the names of those who have slandered you shall have been forgotten, or remembered not for the good they have done here. I am, with great respect, and esteem, your friend, sincerely.[145]

By mid-May, official government correspondence no longer referred to Smith, and Brisbane stopped writing about his nemesis in his diary. The Saxton brothers also apparently stopped corresponding with Smith. But there is also no indication that he returned to Milwaukee. In all probability, he remained in Beaufort for more than a year after his dismissal, likely continuing his earlier employment as a magistrate in Saxton's office (the "attend[ance] to the business of another office which he holds under General Saxton" about which Brisbane had complained in his February 23, 1864, letter).[146]

So what really prompted Smith's dismissal, and what was the genesis of the cloud of acrimony that hung over the commission? While Smith's ongoing feud with Brisbane and Wording could be categorized as a simple personality clash, evidence suggests a deeper ideological division. Brisbane had been a member of the Liberty Party in the 1840s, making a bid for Congress under its banner and later working with the party's leader, James Birney, to organize its convention in Cincinnati in 1845.[147] In addition, by the time the commissioners arrived in South Carolina, Salmon P. Chase and Brisbane had been friends for nearly two decades, a connection that might have predisposed the secretary to listen more closely to Brisbane's complaints than to Smith's counterarguments.[148]

Brisbane and Chase also shared similar religious views. A Baptist minister, Brisbane identified with the viewpoint that slavery was born of immorality, while the young Chase "had lived for several years with his uncle, the Episcopalian bishop of Ohio. Chase read the Bible and recited psalms every morning before breakfast, attended church regularly, admired chastity and disliked drinking, cursing, and the theatre."[149] Chase had also been a member of the Young Men's Temperance Society in Cincinnati, where he had been "shocked by the proliferation of taverns and the intemperate behavior of many citizens."[150] Chase's loathing of "the monster Intemperance" made it unlikely that he would abide Smith's insobriety.[151]

In addition, Smith's extant letters and speeches say little or nothing about faith. It is obvious that Smith was to at least some extent a man of science—he was a dyed-in-the-wool Democrat, the party that fought for separation of church and state; he had medical training, read Charles Darwin, practiced phrenology, and lectured on "physical immortality."[152] Unlike both Chase and Brisbane, Smith did not tie politics to his religion. He advocated what he believed to be instinctively and inherently moral, not what a specific religion decreed. This separation of politics and religion might well have exacerbated Brisbane's dislike of Smith.

Finally, Chase "combined religious conviction and humorlessness with unquenchable ambition and shrewd political insight."[153] To him, Smith's situation was clear: he was a Democrat at heart who now stood without a party—Republicans had no further obligation to support a drunkard who could not be trusted to toe the party line and was rapidly emerging as yesterday's man. Making matters worse, Smith was "neglectful in promoting the political ambitions of Secretary Chase," and shortly before Smith's dismissal, Brisbane warned his friend, "You will be seriously injured if you sustain Judge Smith."[154] Chase would have seen little political advantage in keeping Smith in a patronage position.

By 1864, then, Smith had alienated both the Democrats (with his decision in the Joshua Glover case) and the Republicans (first with an ultra-states'-rights stand, which made Republicans so anxious that they sent him to enemy territory during the Civil War, and then with some combination of his personality, actions, and drinking as a member of the Direct Tax Commission). The unifying thread that runs through Smith's track record in Wisconsin and particularly in South Carolina is a remarkable racial liberalism that would have made most Americans, even abolitionists, uncomfortable at the very least. This adherence to a belief in racial equality would have put him in conflict with the most powerful men in both parties. As Jean H. Baker documents, "intense racism" was rampant within the Democratic Party, as was typified by the party's northern leader, Stephen Douglas: "Along with most nineteenth-century Democrats, Douglas's views on slavery were interwoven with his conception of race; having come to accept polygenetic theory, he believed Negroes irredeemably inferior to whites.

Neither their individual achievements nor their oppression in the United States shook this idea, and his comments on blacks were invariably harsh in tone, biological in metaphor, and popular in idiom."[155]

Despite the party's antislavery foundations, Republicans, too, were "guilty of more than a little racism," and most believed that radicals of Smith's ilk would only cause problems.[156] As historian Kenneth Stampp points out, promoting the party as a haven for whites constituted simple political pragmatism: "Given the racial attitudes of the 1850s, no party—not even one appealing primarily to northern voters—could have adopted a platform advocating equal political and legal rights for blacks without suffering total defeat. As an Indiana Republican warned, if his party permitted the Democrats to define the issue between them as 'the equality of the black with the white race we shall be beaten not only in Indiana but in the Union from this time forward.'"[157] Right up until the Civil War, Republicans, dogged by Democratic accusations of pandering to blacks at the expense of industrious whites, "insisted that they, not the Democrats, were the real 'white man's party'" and that barring slavery in the territories was beneficial in part because it would prevent mixing of the races.[158] Even prominent and ardent antislavery Republicans such as William H. Seward and Salmon P. Chase held racist beliefs, and they were not alone for "almost all [Republicans] accepted in some degree the racial stereotypes of their time."[159]

Lincoln himself steered clear of advocating full racial equality. In October 1858, during one of his famous debates with Douglas, Lincoln declared that he had "no purpose to introduce political and social equality between the white and black races":

> There is a physical difference between the two, which, in my judgment, will probably forever forbid their living together upon a footing of perfect equality, and inasmuch as it becomes a necessity that there must be a difference, I, as well as Judge Douglas, am in favor of the race to which I belong having the superior position. . . . I hold that notwithstanding all this, there is no reason in the world why the negro is not entitled to all the natural rights enumerated in the Declaration of Independence—the right to life, liberty, and the pursuit of happiness.[160]

In most political circles—certainly some more than others—the attitude that blacks deserved a measure of political and social rights but remained inferior as a race carried through the Civil War and Reconstruction and beyond. Smith's racial liberalism would have made finding a political home increasingly difficult as he became more outspoken and the war inched toward its conclusion. Smith would not have been able to tolerate the rampant racism of the Democrats; Republicans, even Chase and other radicals, might have had difficulty tolerating Smith, whose vision of defending the disenfranchised and downtrodden included the freedmen—and was potentially dangerous to the welfare of the party as a whole. In fact, Smith repeatedly expressed a firm belief that blacks and whites were *together* entitled to the same freedoms, as he wrote in a March 1863 letter to the Internal Revenue Commission:

> It must be as gratifying to the Department as it certainly is to me, that the cash sales of this small Parish have brought more than enough to defray all the expenses of the Commission for a year, besides vesting in the Gov't a great abundance of lands to settle, support, educate and elevate all the freed people that can in any event come here, and also enough thereon to settle by purchase or demise loyal white citizens who, together with the colored will be able to protect & defend the whole. It has indeed been a difficult and laborious task—but thank God it has been a success. What scarcely anybody believed feasible, what very many ridiculed, is now made a fait accompli and the future is comparatively simple and plain. The lands purchased by Gov't may now be [illegible], or subdivided & sold, furnishing homes to the poor loyal freedmen, to the faithful soldier, to the enterprising citizen of every grade.[161]

Defending Smith in a February 1863 letter to Chase, Mansfield French credited Smith with a biblical dedication to the former slaves and their welfare: "I must say, what you will be rejoiced to hear, that Judge Smith is as true to his trust, and to the freedmen, as were Caleb & Joshua to the charge committed to them by Moses."[162]

Yet Joseph Lewis saw Smith as doing nothing "to forward the work in hand" and as embarrassing and annoying his colleagues.[163] While Brisbane, like Chief Justice Roger Taney, freed the slaves he inherited, it is doubtful that his vision of "citizens of every grade" quite matched that of Smith, whose freethinking attitudes on racial equality would have undoubtedly been an embarrassment for the cranky South Carolinian. Saxton and Smith's preemption plans were, in Brisbane's eyes, outrageous, and he did not hesitate to tell Chase so in February 1864. Brisbane claimed to have "the greatest respect" for Saxton but simply could not support his "squatter system": "The condition of things here under it would be such that no salary or prospect of wealth could tempt me to remain here one year longer. And I told General Saxton that the worst harm I could do him would be to go away & allow his measures full scope. It would ruin his reputation forever. . . . I am sorry for it that General Saxton committed himself to this wild scheme, that out radicals all the radicalism I ever heard of in agrarian history."[164]

In February 1863, Brisbane referred to Saxton derisively as a man "who has a heart too big for his head" (and then added, "although his head doesn't lack").[165] Brisbane believed that he and Wording had earned Saxton's displeasure because "we do not allow more for what he & Mr. French term 'the good of the cause,' which means the advocacy of the interests of the negroe."[166] Saxton, French, and Smith saw only themselves as doing enough to advocate the interests of the freedmen of Port Royal, and Smith's principles cost him his post.

Exactly how the commission's disgraced and discarded third wheel spent his final year in Beaufort or what he told his family about his career setback is not known. In the immediate aftermath of losing his position, Smith seems to have busied himself with efforts to forge "the first integrated delegation sent to a national party convention."[167] According to the *Free South*, Smith was nominated chair of a group to "represent the Union people of South Carolina in the National Convention" in Baltimore on June 7, 1864.[168] The group drafted resolutions "that called for the complete ending of slavery, greater use of colored troops, the equality of pay between black and white soldiers, the removal of all restriction from commercial vessels employing the port of Port Royal, the encouragement by the government of northern emigration to the South, and the reserving of lands as homesteads for soldiers and freedmen."[169] In the end, Smith and fifteen other delegates from South Carolina were chosen to attend the convention but were not permitted to vote because they represented an occupied territory rather than an official state government.[170] It is not clear whether Smith actually traveled to Baltimore or what he did in the months that followed.

On the morning of June 2, 1865, Smith boarded the army steamer *Arago*—"one of the finest ocean steamships in her day"—at Hilton Head and waited for the anchor to be lifted around noon.[171] Brisbane, Wording, and their families were also aboard. It is not clear whether the voyage was meant to be a permanent journey north for anyone or everyone in the Wisconsin party, but Brisbane recorded feelings of great hope in his diary: "I am truly thankful to God for that care he has taken of us, and that he has enabled me to be attentive and successful in the trusts confided to me." His optimistic mood was not sullied in the least when he discovered that his "former colleague Judge A. D. Smith is also on board. He is perfectly broken down and will probably even pass away."[172]

But Smith's name does not appear on the *Arago*'s passenger list for that voyage. According to Brisbane, Smith initially did not even have a room on the ship. Perhaps somewhat surprisingly, despite his seeming cold indifference to Smith's plight, Brisbane went out of his way to look after the ailing man:

> All that his protégé Alexander did was to get him on board and request Mr. Stemson, the Express Agent, to look after him. I saw his situation—that he had no berth and I went to [the] Capt. of the vessel and to the purser to give him a suitable place.... I got him a good state room and being next to mine I can pay him some attention.... I then helped him to his room and saw that a waiter should attend upon him. Today he has seemed to be getting worse and there is some question whether he will hold out through the voyage.[173]

At 6:00 on the morning of Sunday, June 4, darkness still enveloped the *Arago* as it pushed through the waves off the Eastern Seaboard and made its way north toward New York. The boat carried an assortment of military personnel; 132 "paroled & escaped" men; numerous bureaucrats, their wives, and their children; and the corpse of Abram Daniel Smith.[174] Only five days shy of his fifty-fourth birthday, Smith had reached the "end of life's journey." As he lay dying, he looked not into the eyes of his friends or family but rather at the shadows of the onboard physician and of a man who had spent much of the preceding two years disparaging and complaining about Smith to anyone who would listen. Brisbane himself appreciated the irony: "It is rather strange it falls upon me to pay him these attentions," he wrote, "there being no friends of his special favor to look after him. They have used him and now they let him go without one to attend upon him."[175] When Smith's heart finally gave out, Brisbane leaned over and closed the dead man's eyes.[176]

In some ways, a death upon the restless ocean waves was a fitting end to the life of A. D. Smith. He died as he lived—in motion. Though he did not live to see the final act, Smith and his colleagues had built the stage on which Reconstruction would play out.

"Smith, along with Wording and Brisbane, had commenced a tremendous transformation," says one history of the Beaufort area during the war. "They oversaw the sea islands' greatest real estate transaction since Charles II deeded the area to the Lord Proprietors. Though the sales did not go the way any of them expected, they did begin the creation of a new community."[177]

CONCLUSION

Act, One and All

> Great events find ready record, but minor doings are often neglected until they become so obscured with the dust of time as to be forever clouded; yet from such humble origin may spring the mightiest results. History is commonly regarded as but the doings of rulers, who have the world for their theater of operations and the fate of empires for their subject. Such grave performances are of necessity remembered, but they are no more, in themselves, worthy of preservation than are the simpler deeds of heroism which pioneers so modestly participated in.... The people are seldom named in history.
>
> —JOHN G. GREGORY, *History of Milwaukee, Wisconsin*

On an early June day in 1865, Mary Augusta Smith was enjoying time with two of her daughters, Marion Augusta and Mary Frances, and her grandchildren, far away from the wave-tossed *Arago*.[1] She went for walks with her eldest granddaughter and namesake, Mary Augusta Huggins, and enjoyed the warmth of a midwestern summer at the Ann Arbor, Michigan, home of Mary Frances and her second husband, Lucius Delison Chapin, a minister whom she had married two days after Christmas 1864. There, in the large yard with a giant oak tree, Mary Augusta's three grandchildren and two step-grandchildren, ranging in age between four and ten, picked fruit and threw buckets of water at one another. The war was over, but for Mary Augusta, those pleasant days in Ann Arbor came to a sudden and devastating end with the news that she was a widow.[2]

It is not clear how or from whom she learned of A. D. Smith's demise or when she had last seen him. According to the memoirs of the Smiths' granddaughter, Mary Augusta Huggins Gamble, Mary Augusta Smith and her youngest daughter, Marion (known affectionately as Dattie, apparently a variation on Dutty, the term of endearment Smith used for his wife) "went suddenly to Milwaukee one day when word came that Grandpa Smith (who was one of the judges of the Supreme Court of Wisconsin) had died on the boat as he was coming home from his work in Beaufort, South Carolina, where he had been sent by President Lincoln to help in some government work (reconstruction?)."[3]

Even before Smith's body had reached Milwaukee, the city's bar met and drafted a series of resolutions that demonstrated the deep regard in which his fellow attorneys held him:

- Resolved, that we have learned with regret the melancholy intelligence of the death of Hon. A. D. Smith, a member of this Bar and later one of the justices of the Supreme Court of Wisconsin.
- Resolved, that we recall with pleasure the many good qualities of the deceased as a man, a lawyer and a judge, and we mourn his death as that of an eminent man in Wisconsin, whose name will fill a prominent place in the history of the State.
- Resolved, that in case of the removal of the remains of the deceased to this city for burial, we will receive them with the usual marks of respect and will attend his funeral in a body.
- Resolved, that a copy of these resolutions be transmitted to the family of the deceased with the assurance of the condolence and sympathy of the Bar.[4]

Smith's remains arrived in Milwaukee on Saturday, June 10, and were taken to the family home on Spring Street.[5] The funeral took place the following day. At about half past noon on that summer afternoon, the Freemasons of Wisconsin Lodge no. 13 made their way through the streets of Milwaukee, trudging in a dark procession to the Smith house.[6] They made their way inside the home, likely to the parlor, where many nineteenth-century funerals were held. Smith's widow would have been clad in the long black mourning dress that was the fashion and was supported by at least two of her children: Maria Cecilia, now married and about five months pregnant with her first child, and fourteen-year-old Marion Augusta. Both Maria Cecilia and Marion Augusta lived in Milwaukee.

It is not known whether Mary Frances accompanied her mother and sister back to Milwaukee, but given her role as mother to five very young children, it is quite likely that she did not. Her story is a sidelight to that of her father, but it speaks to the wider cultural shifts that resulted from the prevalence of death in Civil War–era U.S. society. As Drew Gilpin Faust writes, death and how Americans coped with its aftermath shaped not only the nineteenth-century world but also the times that followed it:

> In the twenty-first century Americans considering the impact of death regularly invoke the notion of "closure," the hope and anticipation of an end to the disruption of loss. Civil War Americans expected no such relief. For hundreds of thousands, the unknown fate of missing kin left a "dread void of uncertainty" that knowledge would never fill. Even for those who had detailed information or, better still, the consolation of a body and a grave, mourning had no easy or finite end. Many bereaved spent the rest of their lives waiting for the promised heavenly reunion with those who had gone before. Wives, parents, children, and siblings struggled with the new identities—widows, orphans, the childless—that now defined their lives. And they carried their losses into the acts of memory that both fed on and nurtured the widely shared grief well into the next century.[7]

Mary Augusta Smith's younger sister, Martha, and her husband, Alexander Mitchell, the wealthiest man in Milwaukee, were no doubt present at the funeral. Mitchell was an executor of Smith's will, as was William Sprague Candee, Maria Cecelia's husband. Also gathered at the house would have been a veritable who's who of Milwaukee society, including several lawyers and judges. At 2:00, a somber hush fell over the room and the funeral service began.[8]

Smith's death probably came as a sad surprise to everyone assembled. Though there are no records indicating when or if Mary Augusta and A. D. Smith had seen each other after he left Wisconsin in the summer of 1862, the existing evidence indicates that their marriage was a happy one, and it seems likely that he eventually intended to return to Milwaukee, even if that was not his immediate destination when he left Hilton Head. He might have hoped to find work in New York or to obtain another federal posting: he surely would have coveted a position with the newly created Bureau for the Relief of Freedmen and Refugees (better known as the Freedmen's Bureau). It is also possible that he was leaving Beaufort in June 1865 simply to escape the oppressive summer heat and risk of malaria, as was customary for the wealthy Carolina whites whose rice plantations dotted the Low Country.[9] Or he might have hoped to become a "carpetbagger"—one of the northern men who took advantage of economic and political change in the South for personal advancement. Smith's brother-in-law, Harrison Reed, followed that path. After serving on the Direct Tax Commission in Florida, Reed returned there after the war and in 1868 became the state's governor.[10]

Smith's demise came at a time when the country had grown weary of death, finding its presence all too common during the Civil War. The president himself had been murdered less than two months earlier, his funeral train winding its way through the north under clouds of uncertainty. The assassination plunged the entire country, and particularly northerners, who had looked to their Republican president for guidance regarding the rebirth of the Union, into greater darkness. Smith's family and friends must have found the day of his funeral dreadfully bleak.

It is not clear whether those gathered at the funeral still believed Smith to be working on the tax commission at the time of his death. Smith's obituaries imply that he was, even though he had been dismissed from that position more than a year before. The memoirs of Smith's granddaughter, Mary Augusta Huggins Gamble, suggest the family had no reason to believe that the family patriarch was near death or that he was no longer working as a tax commissioner in Beaufort.

It is possible that not even Mary Augusta Smith was aware of her husband's activities in the months preceding his death. When attorney Jonathan Arnold, who had worked with Smith, announced his death to the Wisconsin Supreme Court on July 25, 1865, he declared, "Very little is known to me of the circumstances of his last illness and death. I have learned from one of his family that some weeks before he left South Carolina, his health had become impaired by severe labors in his official duties. . . . [H]e had no particular disease, but his powers of life seemed to be gradually sinking."[11]

Of Smith's three daughters, his death had the most profound impact on Marion. Sometime after the funeral, she and her mother became boarders at a house on Van Buren Street. Mary Augusta's health began to fail, and she died on April 26, 1866, and was buried next to her husband at Forest Home Cemetery, his grave marked by a towering obelisk and hers by a small stone. Next to her grave, an even smaller stone marks the final resting place of their son, Marius.[12] At age sixteen, Marion was an orphan. She went to live with her sister, Maria Cecelia, and her family. In September 1872, the *Milwaukee Sentinel* noted Marion's marriage to Charles Elkanah Andrews, who had established a dry goods empire known for its Pearl Baking Powder. According to the paper, "The church was beautifully decorated with flowers, and the services were very impressive being participated in by five clergymen. There was a very large attendance of invited guests."[13]

In the month following his death, the Wisconsin Supreme Court acknowledged Judge Smith's contributions, with colleagues speaking of him in glowing terms. Orsamus Cole, who had shared the bench with Smith for four years, declared that his former colleague had an original and vigorous mind that was enhanced by his love of reading and learning. Smith's home library, listed in his will, indicates that his collection was extensive and included not only the day's most controversial scientific works, among them Darwin's *On the Origin of Species*, but also volumes of poetry.[14] Cole also noted that Smith was motivated in all things by a desire to help the downtrodden and to right the wrongs of the world:

> He had an abiding love for and devotion to the great principles of civil liberty and natural justice; and I believe it was the strongest desire of his soul that every human being, however degraded, should enjoy his natural rights. And if for the purpose of securing these rights to the downtrodden and oppressed, Judge Smith ever advanced from the bench constitutional views which some deem unsound, it is sufficient to say that the great mass of the loyal people of the country have adopted his views in regard to the particular law which called them forth, overlooking his errors, if he fell into any, and freely pardoning something of the spirit of liberty by which he was actuated. Furthermore, he was fearless and independent in all his judgments, following no authority which did not seem to be founded on principle and reason.[15]

According to Arnold, even those who disagreed with Smith had to concede that his opinions were the work of a pioneer: "Whether they were true or false, right or wrong, he was the leading spirit that originated and taught them. He lived to see them become the settled law and policy of the state.... He is identified with them as their author, and will go down with them for the praise or censure of posterity."[16]

Posterity.

Over and over again, in all facets of Smith's life, he and the people who interacted with him assumed that the activities, decisions, and events with which he was involved and associated would make him be remembered. This recurring element defined his life: his contemporaries saw him as someone worthy of the American collective memory.

But that was not the case.

A. D. Smith quickly faded away, and a century and a half after his death, few people have heard of him. Even more striking is how little can be known about his life—at least until more information is discovered in a long-forgotten manuscript file or untended attic. So much of his life remains a question mark. Yet his story of passion and eccentricity and even failure emerges as a chronicle worth knowing, worth subjecting to historical interpretation. If not a representation of his times, his life story constitutes an articulation of moments within an era that can be tied together by common themes that illuminate life in the nineteenth century. As historian Jill Lepore notes,

> If the subjects of microhistories, however extraordinary, are not valued for their unique contributions to history, they are often people whose incompletely documented lives point historians toward a single question shrouded in mystery.... Traditional biographers seek to profile an individual and recapitulate a life story, but microhistorians, tracing their elusive subjects through slender records, tend to address themselves to solving small mysteries, in the process of which a microhistorian may recapitulate the subject's entire life story, though that is not his primary purpose. The life story, like the mystery, is merely the means to an end—and that end is always explaining the culture.[17]

What, then, can the life of A. D. Smith, shrouded in mystery as it is, tell us about American history and culture? He pursued ideas and actions that are woven through decades to form the fabric of a half century, falling in and out of favor and at times, like Smith, disappearing forever or becoming a mere footnote to other more salient or fashionable theories of a time and people. His adult life spanned the 1830s, 1840s, 1850s, and the turbulent Civil War years, providing a window into the thoughts and fears of an antebellum generation. Most strikingly, he stands as something of an example of the diversity that existed within the political and social subgroups of his time. Nineteenth-century U.S. history fairly invites readers to see a world defined by sweeping categorization of black and white, Republican and Democrat, North and South.

Smith's life illustrates that assumptions based on such oversimplification cannot stand. His involvement with Locofocoism, for example, would suggest that Smith belonged to the blue-collar class of the Cleveland society in which he lived, but he was also a doctor and lawyer, meaning that he was an exception within the movement if not an anomaly. Later, in Wisconsin, he was a dedicated Democrat, a status that does not accord with accusations that he was a nativist who hated Catholics; those views suggest that he might have been better suited to the Whig Party. Finally, Smith is on record as an advocate of temperance, speaking about its merits publicly while privately engaging in heavy drinking. In all of these things, he stands out as the exception to expectations regarding his time and serves as a reminder of the decidedly heterogeneous nature of the people of his time—and ours.

Smith's life is much more, though, than an example of being mindful of history's square pegs or of one man's abject failure to attain the long-lasting fame predicted by his friends and colleagues. At its heart, Smith's life story speaks to a greater part of the meaning of being an American in the nineteenth century. For all the ways Smith was exceptional—or at the very least different from his countrymen in the states in which he lived or the political bandwagons on which he jumped—in one central way he was very much a man of his time. For it was not the individual chapters of his life that made him emblematic of his era but rather the collective narrative they tell about antebellum America. That narrative was—like the new nation—dynamic.

"Fortunes, ideas and laws are constantly altering," said Alexis de Tocqueville. "Unchanging nature herself appears to change, so greatly is she transformed by the hand of man."[18] Tocqueville detected something in the American psyche, a mood or a propensity that made Americans reluctant to remain idle for very long. "Everyone is in a state of agitation," he wrote, "some to attain power; others to grab wealth."[19] Yale historian George W. Pierson documents numerous examples of this peculiarly American trait: Americans, he notes, "don't seem anchored to place. Our families are all scattered about. Our loyalties are to abstractions and constitutions, not to birthplace or homestead or inherited associations. We share an extraordinary freedom to move again and again. No locality can claim us long."[20]

Countless other antebellum nomads, like Smith, spent much of their lives in transition from one location to the next. Though Smith and William Henry Brisbane, his colleague on the tax commission, clashed repeatedly in Beaufort, the two men were kindred spirits as wanderers and careerists. A South Carolinian by birth, Brisbane moved from Ohio to Wisconsin before taking to the road as an army chaplain in the Civil War, returning to his native state to work in Port Royal, and later journeying back to Wisconsin. Though most of Smith's brothers-in-law eventually settled permanently in Wisconsin, they, too, were prone to wandering. Harrison Reed, for example, moved from Vermont to New York to Wisconsin to Florida.

Among the more prominent nineteenth-century men who journeyed from state to state in search of a better cities and prospects was Ulysses S. Grant. His family, though American "in all its branches, direct and collateral," had wandered to numerous small towns through Massachusetts, Connecticut, Pennsylvania, and Ohio, where he was born in Clermont County.[21] "As a boy—indeed, all his life, Grant was restless," writes Grant biographer William S. McFeely.[22] "He liked to get out and away from home often, and his competence with horses provided the means of doing so."[23] As Grant wrote in his *Personal Memoirs*,

> While still quite young I had visited Cincinnati, forty-five miles away, several times, alone; also Maysville, Kentucky, often, and once Louisville. The journey to Louisville was a big one for a boy of that day. I had also gone once with a two-horse carriage to Chilicothe, about seventy miles, with a neighbor's family, who were removing to Toledo, Ohio, and returned alone; and had gone once, in like manner, to Flat Rock, Kentucky, about seventy miles away. On this latter occasion I was fifteen years of age.[24]

As a young adult, Grant traveled to West Point; after a stint in the Mexican War, he found himself posted in California and Oregon before settling in Missouri and later in Galena, Illinois. His Civil War career took him across the United States, and when the conflict ended, he traveled the world before settling in New York. According to Mark Perry, Grant and his friend Samuel Clemens (Mark Twain) "had the same dream, of traveling on the big steamboats of the Mississippi to make their fortunes."[25] Clemens, of course, was one of the nineteenth century's great wanderers, using the rivers of his beloved America to travel and to reflect: "For him, rivers were the highways of America's first decades of economic growth and, therefore, a symbol of the nation's freedoms. Rivers brought settlers to the West, transported their harvests to market, conveyed finished goods from the cities, and served as a province and temporary home to that most romantic of all nineteenth-century figures, the riverboat captain."[26] Clemens became a riverboat pilot and indulged his passion for traveling the waterways through his employment.[27] Though his hometown was Hannibal, Missouri, Clemens lived for periods of time in Louisiana, California, Nevada, New York, and Connecticut and traveled extensively in Europe, the Middle East, South Africa, India, and Australia.[28] One of Clemens's many biographers, Ron Powers, cites a letter Clemens wrote to his mother while waiting for a ship's departure: "All I do know or feel, is, that I am wild with impatience to move—move—*Move!* . . . Curse the endless delays! They always kill me—they make me neglect every duty & then I have a conscience that tears me like a wild beast. I wish I never had to stop *any*where a month."[29]

Like Grant and Clemens, William Tecumseh Sherman felt he, too, was "cursed to live a vagabond life."[30] Motivated to succeed, Sherman had broken away from his hometown of Lancaster, Ohio, and joined the army, seeing action, like Grant, in the Mexican War. After a posting in St. Louis, Sherman left military life to pursue a banking career in California. Biographer James M. Merrill notes that "Sherman's letters from San Francisco at this time showed his eager imagination and a restlessness which had been growing since his Lancaster days."[31] Sherman subsequently worked as a lawyer in Kansas, returned briefly to Ohio, and spent time as superintendent of a Louisiana military institute.[32] All this travel, often marked by long separations from his family, wore thin on Sherman's wife, Ellen, who angrily wrote to her husband that she had "wandered enough" with her young family.[33] With the country on the brink of Civil War, Sherman realized his hopes of having his family join him in the South were unlikely to be realized, as he confided in an 1860 letter to his daughter: "What I have been planning so long and patiently, and thought we were on the point of realizing the dream and hope of my life, that we could all be together once more in a home of our own, with peace and quiet and plenty around us all, I fear is about to vanish, and again I fear I must be a wanderer, leaving you all to grow up at Lancaster without your Papa."[34] Sherman then relocated to St. Louis before rejoining the military.[35] Ellen Sherman, like many other nineteenth-century wives, never really understood why her husband could not be satisfied with a life in the town where they had both grown up.[36]

But it was not just the military leaders and the writers and poets who were possessed by this wanderlust. Tradesmen, miners, and farmers like pioneer Charles Ingalls, best known as "Pa" in his daughter's beloved *Little House* books, were also crisscrossing the country. Ingalls "would always be a wanderer, propelled by hopes of a better future farther on," leading the family on an epic journey that touched Wisconsin, Iowa, Minnesota, Kansas, and Dakota Territory—some more than once.[37] "It's just that my wandering foot gets to itching," Laura Ingalls Wilder quoted her father as saying to her exasperated mother.[38]

As Caroline Fraser notes in her Pulitzer Prize–winning work about the family, the Ingallses were neither powerful nor wealthy. "Generation after generation, they traveled light, leaving things behind. . . . As far as we can tell, from the moment they arrived on this continent they were poor, restless, struggling, constantly moving from one place to another in an attempt to find greater security from hunger and want. And as they moved, the traces of their existence were scattered and lost. Sometimes their lives vanish from view, as if in a puff of smoke."[39]

And members of all classes sought greener grass beyond the more familiar turf of home, uprooting and moving in search of better opportunities, of a place where they could make their mark.

In *Country of Exiles: The Destruction of Place in American Life*, author William Leach concludes that from the late eighteenth century on, "indifference to place has been a hallmark of American life":

> Whole populations swarmed across the continent, enticed by fantasies of paradise; by hopes of freedom and individual liberation; by great reserves of mostly unoccupied public lands; by government policies (subsidies to railroads, homestead laws, eviction of Indians from their homelands) that made it easy for people to move; by the treatment of land as property to sell and speculate on rather than as a community to live in; and, most of all, by prospects of unlimited wealth.[40]

This trait set Americans very much apart from Europeans, Leach argues, and forged an identity that left an indelible imprint on the consciousness of the country:

> Such was the American way. Unlike most Europeans, who rarely moved far from where they were born (unless, of course, they were forced by economic change to migrate to cities or to emigrate . . .), Americans often decided to migrate whenever prospects elsewhere were brighter. The very size of the country, of course, with its untapped resources, dictated much of this mobility. But after 1850, as the country grew more urbanized and seemed to invite more settlement, Americans still displayed the same propensity to move, to get out.[41]

Even non-Americans saw Americans in this way, depicting them as incurable movers who were never content to remain idle for very long. On his 1842 tour of the United States, Charles Dickens noted that Americans were fickle and "so given to change, that your inconsistency has passed into a proverb."[42]

Domingo Faustino Sarmiento, an Argentine statesman born in 1811, the same year as A. D. Smith, traveled across the United States five years after Dickens and described American roads and rivers as scenes of constant activity, with "thousands of steamboats . . . dispersing themselves in every direction" along the Mississippi and "traffic jams" along the Hudson, where "steamboats cross each other's paths like shooting stars."[43] The American man, said Sarmiento, always carried a watch and a "geographic map" in his pocket while seeking new opportunities to own land: "He talks of nothing else but going out to occupy and settle new lands. His evenings are spent over the map, computing the stages of the journey, tracing a route for his wagon."[44]

In her 1857–1858 diary, Englishwoman Barbara Leigh Smith Bodichon noted that the constant, reckless transportation of Americans was hazardous to their health: she spoke with a doctor "about the American rashness and the number of accidents in carriage, rails and steamboats."[45] Two Norwegians who studied living conditions on the Illinois-Wisconsin border in 1839 were struck by what they considered an American indifference to substandard housing that stemmed: "We do not know, and can only guess, the reason for this poor method of building, but we think it comes from the American's bent and necessity to move from one place to another. When a person has got a piece of new land cultivated enough so that he can earn a little from it, he sells it and begins on a new piece. It sometimes happens that for one reason or another he is obliged to move yet again, without the slightest compensation for his house or the cultivation of his land."[46]

Canadian Thomas Chandler Haliburton also noted this impulse among his American neighbors. Haliburton's *The Clockmaker* was first published as a serial in 1835 and went on to become Canada's first international best seller. It chronicles the adventures of a Yankee, Sam Slick of Slicksville, who travels around Nova Scotia and opines on matters of politics and society with those he meets along the road. Sam's repeated exasperation with the Nova Scotians' more relaxed pace of life is a recurring theme in the book, which stresses Sam's perspective as a wholly American view of the world. When asked what could possibly be done about the sloth of the Nova Scotians, Sam is quick with an answer: "They must recede before our free and enlightened citizens like the Indians; our folks will buy them out, and they must give place to a more intelligent and ac-*tive* people."[47] He continues, by pointing out that in the United States, "the maxim is, 'Youth is the time for improvement; a new country is never too young for exertion; push on—keep movin—go ahead."[48] While Sam Slick was a fictional character, his persona speaks to something that Canadians recognized about Americans and their way of life in Smith's era. Simply put, there was nothing worse in American eyes than remaining immobile, because immobility causes the loss of chances and fortunes.

American literature and poetry also reflect this inherent need to move, to seek and to explore beyond the horizon in the quest for the new and the better. As Walt Whitman wrote in *On Journeys through the States*, published as part of *Leaves of Grass* in 1855,

> On journeys through the States we start,
> (Ay through the world, urged by these songs,

> Sailing henceforth to every land, to every sea,)
> We willing learners of all, teachers of all, and lovers of all.
> We have watch'd the seasons dispensing themselves and passing on,
> And have said, Why should not a man or woman do as much as the seasons, and effuse as much?
> We dwell a while in every city and town,
> We pass through Kanada, the North-east, the vast valley of the Mississippi, and the Southern States,
> We confer on equal terms with each of the States,
> We make trial of ourselves and invite men and women to hear,
> We say to ourselves, Remember, fear not, be candid, promulge the body and the soul,
> Dwell a while and pass on, be copious, temperate, chaste, magnetic,
> And what you effuse may then return as the seasons return,
> And may be just as much as the seasons.[49]

A decade later, Whitman wrote admiringly of the pioneers as a "resistless, restless race" that would not halt no matter how weary, that would "take up the task eternal, and the burden and the lesson," finally "conquering, holding, daring, venturing as we go the unknown ways."[50]

Commenting on life in New York, Clemens also appreciated Americans' need to remain in a constant state of agitation:

> There is something about this ceaseless buzz, and hurry, and bustle, that keeps a stranger in a state of unwholesome excitement all the time, and makes him restless and uneasy, and saps from him all capacity to enjoy anything or take a strong interest in any matter whatever—a something which impels him to try to do everything, and yet permits him to do nothing. He is a boy in a candy-shop—could choose quickly if there were but one kind of candy, but is hopelessly undetermined in the midst of a hundred kinds. A stranger feels unsatisfied, here, a good part of the time.[51]

There is perhaps no better example of the American fear of immobility than Washington Irving's beloved tale of Rip Van Winkle, who awakens from a lengthy slumber to find his familiar, languid world changed:

> There was, as usual, a crowd of folks about the door, but none that Rip recollected. The very character of the people seemed changed. There was a busy, bustling, disputatious tone about it, instead of the accustomed phlegm and drowsy tranquillity. He looked in vain for the sage Nicholas Vedder . . . or Van Bummel, the schoolmaster. . . . In place of these a lean, bilious-looking fellow, with his pockets full of handbills, was haranguing vehemently about rights

of citizens—elections—members of congress—liberty—Bunker's Hill—heroes of seventy-six—and other words, which were a perfect Babylonish jargon to the bewildered Van Winkle.[52]

A. D. Smith thus embodied a very American state of lifelong agitation, a characteristic to which at least part of his failure to become a memorable historical character can be attributed. He rarely remained in any one place long enough to become a monument to a particular movement or political venture. His family is difficult to trace not only because of his surname but also because he moved repeatedly, and his parents likely did, too. Moreover, his three surviving children did the same, settling in Indiana, Illinois, and Michigan. And their descendants are now scattered across the United States.

What pushed him, and others of his time, to engage in this constant shifting and turning? What pulled at them to leave their recently built homes and settle in new places, only to pack their bags and do the same thing again? Seeking answers to these questions, Tocqueville suggests that in some ways this incessant motion in fact harmed Americans' development: "Amid this widespread upheaval, this repeated grating of opposed interests, men's unremitting progress toward wealth, where could we find the tranquility needed for deep intellectual investigations? How could the mind dwell upon one point, if everything around it was in constant movement and every day man himself is dragged along like flotsam in the raging torrent which carries all before it?"[53]

Smith's story shows him to be something of a magpie—his eye always caught by the latest, shiniest idea. He likely left New York for the promise inherent in moving west to the frontier of Ohio. In the face of a devastating financial depression and the collapse of the Hunters' Lodge, its secrets and its plots, Smith headed farther west to Wisconsin, which had not yet attained statehood. After a landmark legal case that was hailed around the nation and with a domestic life that, if not perfect, was certainly stable and perhaps even enviable by the standards of the day, Smith might have been expected to remain in Milwaukee; instead, personal scandal and a rift with his political party prompted Smith yet again to seek new environs. In Beaufort, South Carolina, Smith was at odds with his surroundings and his colleagues, and his time there did not end well. With the conclusion of the Civil War, he felt inclined to move yet again, boarding the *Arago* on a journey whose intended destination has been lost but that ultimately took him to his death. Only then did he return to the place of his past.

As Tocqueville wrote, an antebellum life like Smith's was a life of constant activity, and one that rarely produced lasting achievement: "At the heart of these [democratic] nations resides a small, awkward movement, where incessant rumblings put men against each other; this disturbs and distracts their minds without stimulating or improving them. Men living in democratic societies not only have difficulty with meditation but they entertain a naturally low regard for it. The state of society and the democratic institutions include the majority of men to a constantly active life."[54]

This constant motion or "jostling," Tocqueville argued, meant that Americans could rarely achieve their goals. This need for motion was simply not conducive to deep thought or to the completion of a task. It is impossible, he theorized, to carry through on anything when there is a constant need to uproot, to relocate and to redefine oneself:

> The man of action is frequently forced to accept compromise because he would never reach the fruition of his plans if he wished to achieve perfection in every detail. He has to rely endlessly upon ideas which he has not had the time to test thoroughly, for he is aided much more by the opportunity of an idea he is adopting than its strict accuracy.... In ages when almost every man is engaged in action, an excessive value is generally placed upon those rapid flights and superficial ideas of the intellect while its slower and deeper efforts are considerably undervalued.[55]

Was this true of A. D. Smith? He rarely met a trend he did not like, particularly if it were of the radical kind. He appears to have abandoned ideas as quickly as he sought new ones, many of them ill conceived. The Hunters, though fervent in their sense of duty, fraternity, and republicanism, failed miserably in gauging the pulse of Upper Canadians. Rather than picking up weapons to assist their "liberators," the Canadians withdrew in bewilderment, demonstrating the stark divergence in Canadian and American appetites for revolution and overthrow of government. Few if any outsiders seem to have been aware of Smith's involvement in the group, possibly because the "president of Canada" left "office" even before the invasion designed to inaugurate him. He practiced the emerging "science" of phrenology when it was at the forefront of social trends but dropped it, too, in later years. His landmark legal decision in Wisconsin put him at the center of the debate over states' rights, but he necessarily set this philosophy aside as he hastened to champion South Carolina's former slaves.

Like his changes of location, Smith's changing of causes was clearly related to ambition. He sought to occupy a place of public importance and a position of power and presumably to achieve status and wealth. Tocqueville saw this tendency, too, in the character of nineteenth-century Americans: "Apart from the possessions he already has, he continually thinks of the thousand others which death will stop him enjoying if he does not hasten. This thought floods his mind with agitation, fear, and regret; it holds his soul in a sort of ceaseless nervousness which leads him perpetually to change plans and location.... [O]ften death is less feared than the persistent efforts needed to achieve the same ambition."[56]

The constant movement of Americans created what historian George W. Pierson calls a "nation of joiners," keen to find some self-identification within social groups that created a sense of belonging in the absence of attachment to geographical place.[57] Consequently, membership in various groups swelled, with Americans joining Masonic groups, anti-Masonic groups, benevolent societies, and reform groups. In this respect, Smith was typical in his avid embrace of Freemasonry, the Hunters' Lodge, and reform movements such as temperance and education for women. Smith evidently loved participating in political dialogue, in the movements that defined his age; he was, as Clemens described, compelled to try everything he could but ultimately achieved less than he desired in all of those ventures.

A. D. Smith was one of the "peripatetic self-reinventors" historian Walter McDougall describes in his analysis of Herman Melville's protagonist in *The Confidence Man*: "They are also hustlers in the positive sense: builders, doers, go-getters, dreamers, hard workers, investors, organizers, engineers and a people supremely generous. Needless to say those qualities, not their baser ones, were what justified Americans' faith in themselves, their nation and their nation's destiny among nations."[58]

Most of these descriptors apply to Smith: he was involved in the shaping of frontier cities, was seen by his peers as a doer and an organizer, was a go-getter no matter where he had to go to get, a hard worker who invested in radical ideas, and a republican dreamer who believed wholeheartedly in liberty and equality to free the white working class from the tyranny of banks, African Americans from the tyranny of slavery, Canadians from the tyranny of monarchy, and women from the tyranny of ignorance and the inability to own property.

So was Smith the real-life version of Melville's imaginary confidence man? Historian Karen Halttunen describes how antebellum advice manuals were full of references to this shadowy archetype, cautioning young men in particular to avoid being duped and corrupted by these worldly yet dishonest and deceitful charlatans.[59] A confidence man, Halttunen writes, was seen as "a man without principle, a man whose art it is to deceive others through false appearances."[60] He was something of a drifting opportunist, always on the lookout for the next great scam—or victim ripe for scamming. His mobility, alongside that of all Americans as well as increased urbanization, generated great anxiety:

> The writers of antebellum advice literature expressed a deep disenchantment with the direction of historical change in early nineteenth-century America. In the figure of the urban associate, they cast their fears of the major social forces transforming American society: a high rate of geographical mobility and particularly of migration to the city, the decline of social deference and a loosening of ties between family generations, the breakdown of traditional restraints over single workingmen, and in general a replacement of traditional hierarchical social relations with modern peer relations.[61]

Though not above using people or politics to suit his own purposes, Smith thus seems to fall short of being the type of confidence man described by Halttunen and conjured by Melville. There is no evidence that he fancied himself any sort of thief (although he did accept a bribe) or that he intended to hoodwink others. He was certainly a roving opportunist, but he seems to have been motivated by sincere beliefs about what was right not only for himself but for others. That Smith was guilty of self-righteousness and moral conceit on a grand scale is obvious, but his actions appear to have been motivated by a desire to contribute to a greater good. Whereas the traditional confidence man attempted to lure his victims to a darker side of humanity, Smith seems to have been guided by an earnest belief that he was leading people to the path that was just and true. There was no dark pessimism attached to his schemes to free Canadians or women or slaves. Rather, he was a perpetual optimist, believing wholeheartedly in a more perfect republic. And these principles led him to move from city to city, join secret societies, and apparently to abandon his family.

At heart, Smith was a very American optimist. As Pierson writes,

> Migration was not only the Destroyer, Distorter, Conservator, Atomizer and Energizer of western society, but its most effective "Optimizer." First of all, out of the welter of old-world classes and temperaments it selected the up-and-coming and the hopeful. Pessimists didn't bother; you had to be an optimist to move. Next it required sacrifice and waiting, and so captured many believers, the men of faith. Finally, it rewarded the successful—and those who weren't lucky were given a second try. America the golden was the land of the second chance. And from failure it offered a full timetable of escapes.[62]

The mid-nineteenth-century United States was an optimistic place, and with good reason. The period from roughly 1830 to 1860 saw spectacular economic growth and urbanization. In the twenty years prior to the Civil War, for example, manufacturing increased 350 percent nationwide.[63] After 1845, the arrival of a staggering three million immigrants brought the largest-ever proportionate increase in foreign-born Americans. Their labor improved the country's infrastructure and expanded the nation ever farther westward.[64] According to historian James M. McPherson, the population doubled every twenty-three years, the gross national product doubled every fifteen years, and a "transportation revolution" was moving Americans from one end of the continent to the other and deep into the interior faster than ever before.[65]

Smith's life story is one of optimistic escape, over and over and over again. He repeatedly re-created himself—lawyer, phrenologist, doctor, radical, politician, president, reformer, judge, tax commissioner, defender of freedmen. He was a nineteenth-century chameleon, but each time he reinvented himself, he hoped that his actions were contributing to a greater good and to a Jeffersonian "empire for liberty."[66]

Pierson posits that A. D. Smith and others like him saw their constant movements not as lateral but as vertical.[67] Further, the likelihood that a move would bring power or success depended on the mover's ability to arrive at his destination before his competitors: "On the margins of empire, in the frontier areas, in the sprawling new cities, class barriers broke down, society became atomic, the enterprising and the aggressive could rise. Especially if you got there first."[68] Smith arrived in Ohio when the Western Reserve was first opening to settlement, and he departed for Wisconsin when opportunity beckoned there. He was also among the first of the "carpetbagging" northerners to journey to the occupied South, abandoning Wisconsin when it was clear that his upward mobility had been compromised by his position on states' rights and his involvement in the railway scandal. Smith's moves only once catapulted him upward in society—to a judgeship in Wisconsin. But he may have sold that one opportunity for a stack of railroad bonds.

As historian Peter S. Onuf writes, Thomas Jefferson, whom Smith was known to quote, saw the sort of civic involvement and consciousness in which Smith engaged as the ideal: "A republican people, fully conscious of itself, would be enlightened enough to sustain consensual union and strong enough to resist coercion by any enemy. Union was predicated on shared commitment to 'federal and republican principles' that in turn depended on reciprocal recognition and identification among citizens in an inclusive national community."[69] Smith's beliefs in American democracy and in republicanism informed his interpretation of his responsibilities to his country and propelled his actions. But it was not enough that he be personally committed—he also saw it as his duty to inspire others.

And indeed, in his last fully documented speech on the eve of the Civil War, Smith shouted a rallying call to the people, urging them to rise up as defenders of states' rights: "There is the only hope. Trust no longer in politicians. If Rome is saved, Romans must rush to the rescue. Fretting, scolding, denunciation will do no good. Action! Action!! Action!!! United, vigorous, determined Action alone will suffice. Arouse, one and all. Act, one and all, and together. Salvation is yet for us ... millions of hearts will leap for joy, and all the people will shout AMEN!"[70]

EPILOGUE

Lost and Found

> I'll only hope we may be found able to tread in the path you have opened. You have more than the thanks, the blessing of all who love liberty or our institutions. Believe me.
>
> —WENDELL PHILLIPS to A. D. Smith, July 27, 1854

Sometimes, the information we seek is found at the bottom of a box of old papers in a historical society. Sometimes, it is found in a book that had been overlooked, on a tombstone just discovered, or in an online database that has been updated since the last time we looked. Sometimes, we have to sift through documents that are falling apart or soiled by dust or dirt—or even by animals: "We recently received a box full of papers for the town of Lowville—mostly 1830–1870s—but there was one or two going back to 1807. . . . I will let you know if I come across a Smith," read one email message I received from a historical society. "PPS—We received them drenched in cat urine—long story—they still smell, but they are dried out and can be handled."[1]

I had checked for evidence of Smith in basements, libraries, archives, private clubs, and historical societies large and small. In some cases, I had checked more than once—more times than I could remember or would care to count. *"It's been eight years since I checked this library. Maybe there is something new."*

I would find myself doing things like going back to a list of some of the original settlers in Lowville, New York, staring again at the various Smiths, from John to Thaddeus.

Was one of those men A. D. Smith's father? Had I checked those names before? I must have, all those years ago in the probate records of the Lowville courthouse. I went back to my notes but saw nothing. Had I overlooked them? I plugged their names into genealogy databases.

But as I spent more hours poring over my notes and sources, neither Thaddeus nor John seemed to fit the Smith I had come to know more than a decade ago. And so, year after year, I traveled in circles, retracing my steps, second-guessing my ability to overturn every archival stone. The fact that I could not find what I was looking for was evidence that I had not looked hard enough, not tried hard enough. I could not accept that the information I sought was simply not there to be found.

Journalists face tight deadlines and must go with whatever is available. (Or, as I recall reading on a homemade sign in one newsroom, "Schlock before deadline is better than art after deadline.") But for historians, the luxury of time breeds a tenacity that often leads to a reluctance to believe that their story is ever done.

It had always seemed to me that the information was out there somewhere. The scraps of detail I sought—the identity of A. D. Smith's parents, the cause of his death, the fate of his descendants—had to exist. And if they existed, they could be found.

Slowly, reluctantly, I have had to admit that perhaps that is not the case. I continue to search for Smith's parents, and I still believe I will eventually find them. But other pieces of the puzzle I have had to set aside—I have decided that if Smith kept journals, they no longer exist, perhaps tossed away by a relative who did not know their value.

But some pieces of the puzzle are still surfacing, often in unlikely places. Like, say, a cupboard in Pasadena, California. Out of the blue in June 2013 I received an email with the subject line, "Amazing Discovery re Smith." I held my breath as I read the note from the curator of the Gamble House, which had once been the home of Mary Augusta Huggins Gamble, daughter of A. D. Smith's eldest child, Mary Frances, and her husband, David Gamble:

> I've made quite an amazing find related to Abram Smith. Don't ask me how it had lain for so long undiscovered (possibly 40–50 years, and no one recalls seeing them previously), but I have found an album of typed copies of family genealogy and correspondence, which looks to have been assembled by David Gamble. It contains papers relating to his own family as well as Mary's, and included among these are about 30 pages of letters from Smith to his wife, as well as a copy of his will, his commission from Lincoln, and an amazing letter written August 29, 1862 from Washington, D.C., on the eve of the second battle of Bull Run. I know you will appreciate these letters more than anyone else, so wanted to share with you asap.[2]

I downloaded the documents and my eyes raced over the pages for information. The thing I wanted most was the names of A. D. Smith's parents, but on that front, it was another dead end.

The cache of letters proved fruitful in other ways, however. Until this discovery, I had never known much about Smith's relationship with his wife. Other than the fact that she was referred to as his beloved in his will (probably a not-uncommon endearment in such circumstances), I had never been able to find any evidence of affection between the two, much less any indication of Mary Augusta Smith's feelings about her husband's colorful exploits across various states. But this correspondence clearly showed that Abram Daniel Smith adored his wife.

"Oh! Dutty how happy I am, in having a sweet, good, intelligent wife, to whom I can unbosom my whole heart," he wrote in 1853. "Oh! *How I do love you! Dear, Dear Dutty.* So good, so generous, so loving. My own, my sweet Dutty."[3]

Sweet Dutty? The find might have contributed little to an understanding of Smith's views on constitutional law, but it was exceptional in terms of understanding his personal life (not to mention highly amusing for someone who had only ever encountered Serious Smith). The strength of Smith's convictions shone through the forceful yet very formal prose in the primary sources I had seen before; here, however, he was reduced to a puddle of lovesick ramblings. In another 1853 letter, Smith wrote to his wife from Madison that he was unable to sleep at 1:00 a.m. and had been lying in bed "in a delightful retrospect of the sweetness of my dear Dutty":

> As I lay thinking of you, trying to urge my way along towards the land of dreams, the past twenty years, swept by me for review, and all along its course was the prospect rendered both grateful and delightful by the view of your constancy of affection, forbearance of temper and gentleness of manner towards your wayward boy. These things are pleasant to remember, My Dear, because they add intensity to love and awaken gratitude in the heart, which is always a source of joy to the good man. We have trotted along life's pathway, thus far together, Dutty, making now and then a stumble, as is common to human nature, the future as we have progressed, heretofore promising us but little, though never entirely without hope, until at last, if life and health be spared us, we may well be thankful to Him who shapes our destinies, for the promises which now beam upon and around us. We have great joy in our children. Dear Sweet, affectionate Darlings. We have a good home, all our own, and a fair station in the council and authority of our government. Oh! How sweet indeed is the honor of this world, when they are sanctified by your love, and your goodness.[4]

In a February 1856 letter, Smith is even more effusive, imploring God to make him worthy of his wife.

> May he also make me a better man, a better father & a better husband. Oh! My Dear, if I can only make you as happy as you ought & deserve to be, and so use all my efforts & powers, as to gladden your precious heart, and atone in some measure for my many past, grievous wrongs, & short comings, and soothe & heal the many wounds I have inflicted upon you, I shall be so thankful, so happy. Oh! Dear Dutty, accept my love—deep—intense—& my assurance, that in you and you alone I am supremely happy. Kiss, Kiss, Kiss, A. D.[5]

The letters provide no clues about what Smith's past transgressions might have been. Was he referring to his struggles with alcohol? Perhaps. But his reference three years earlier to her "wayward boy" and his closing line—"in you and you alone I am supremely happy"—may indicate that Mary Augusta required assurances that the shadow of a third party had not fallen over the marriage. Smith's extensive travels would have offered him ample opportunities for secret affairs, but I have found no other evidence indicating that this was the case.

His references to "grievous wrongs" and "many wounds" suggest repeated and serious blows to the marriage, but without further context or detail, it is difficult to determine if we are reading too much into a letter written at a time when such florid language was common.

Though such details remain murky, Smith clearly valued his wife's opinion on political and legal matters. While staying at New York's Union Place Hotel in 1857, Smith wrote to Mary Augusta, "Oh! Dearest Duttie, I have never felt the want of you as I do now—your advice. But it will be over, day after tomorrow, when I shall leave for my dear, dear home."[6]

And later that same year, Smith wrote from Milwaukee to his wife, who appears to have been visiting Mary Frances in Michigan: "How lonely do you think my bedroom is at night?" he asked. "How strange the whole house without its mistress! Oh! What a Queen is a good wife of a husband having a homestead however humble!!! What a power! What an influence! How vast! How enduring! How incessant! Did you ever!"[7]

As for what Mary Augusta Smith thought, we may never know. The woman at the center of Smith's world remains, like so many women in history, without a voice. I move forward without knowing what she thought or felt but still convinced that the evidence about her is lurking somewhere, just another archive or Google search away. Could I find that one, yellowed diary of Mary Augusta Smith? Could I locate the one letter she wrote in response to her husband's "grievous wrongs?" And if I did, what would they tell me about her? What would they tell me about Smith? At what point does the historian stop trying to tie up every loose end and amass every last document, no matter how peripheral?

In his presidential address at the 2013 annual meeting of the American Historical Society in New Orleans, William Cronon spoke of historians' slavish dedication to documents as evidence:

> For us, the deepest challenge of our discipline—the maddening constraint that is also the wellspring of our creativity—is that we are not permitted to argue or narrate beyond the limits of our evidence. We cannot even begin to imagine a story without first having spent enormous amounts of time answering the question that arguably defines our discipline more deeply than any other, a question so seemingly simple that few who are not historians recognize its profundity: *"What are the documents?"* It is our devotion to documents, our awareness that without them the past lies forever beyond the reach of our inquiry, that supplies the epistemological foundation on which all our professional practice is built.[8]

At the end of my road with A. D. Smith, I was still missing documents. It came to a point where it was impossible for me to think of my subject without thinking of what I was missing. I could tell so much more of his story, I thought, if I could just find more documents. Letters. Diaries. Newspaper clippings. Old books.

I was not fussy—I just had to find *more*. But this dedication to the documents became debilitating, for it shut down the impulse to write what I did know and piece together the evidence I had found. My worst fear has always been that the story of A. D. Smith would remain untold, yet my unwillingness to wave the white flag of surrender was the single biggest threat that story now faced.

Cronon quoted filmmaker Steven Spielberg on the differences between history and historical fiction. Spielberg argued, in a speech that might make pioneering German historian Leopold von Ranke roll over in his grave, that sometimes we must let go of the documents to give life to historical characters:

> History forces us to acknowledge the limits of memory. It keeps track of memory's victories, it keeps track of memory's defeats. It tells us that memory is imperfect, that no matter how much of the past we've recovered, much that once was or has been now is lost to us. It's simply not the job—and in fact, I believe it's the betrayal of the job—of the historian to promise perfect and complete recall of the past.... One of the jobs of art is to go to the impossible

places that other disciplines like history must avoid. Through art we enlist the imagination to bring what's lost back to us, to bring the dead back to life. This resurrection is of course just an illusion, it's a fantasy, and it's a dream, but dreams matter somehow to us.[9]

I, however, am more inclined to think of words often attributed to Spielberg's colleague and creative partner, George Lucas: "A movie is never finished, only abandoned."

And so I have abandoned the unfinished story of A. D. Smith. There are a thousand leads I have left unchased, a dozen archives that remain unchecked, and untold manuscripts that remain unopened in their banker's boxes. There are church session minutes that have yet to be read, libraries that have not been visited, and microfilms that have not been spun through their spools.

But at what point can we be satisfied that we have done all that we can do to paint the most accurate picture possible? For the filmmaker, it is when the production deadline looms. For the prosecutor building a case, it is when the trial starts. And for the journalist today, it is immediate, as social media causes stories to break incrementally, each new tweet building on the last.

But for the historian, there is often no set time to let go and no internal compulsion to do so—in fact, for many historians, quite the opposite is true as we scramble to unearth one more document that will reveal all. In doing so, we fool ourselves into believing that we can reveal all. *No matter how much of the past we've recovered, much that once was or has been now is lost to us.*

Lost, but always with the promise, the hope, of being found. Smith was certain that his story would be found, that his deeds and decisions—indeed, his life—would live on in the pages of history. Dormant for more than a century, Smith's life has been found, even if all his letters, diaries, and family ties have not. But perhaps as much as anyone, Smith had to come to terms with his own unfinished business—a presidency that never was, a legal argument that was brushed aside, and a death before his time. Smith spent a lifetime trying to finish his own story, for it was never good enough the way it was.

But sometimes, even Smith acknowledged it was time to call it a day.

Writing to his dear Dutty on a cold January night in Madison in 1853, he realized with reluctance that he had to stop writing, even though he still had so much more to say: "It will put an end to my writing to you, but my Dear, it will not put an end to my thinking of you," he wrote. "Now I must put aside the paper and old hat & let the remainder go in thinking. A thousand kisses, good night . . . I'll finish this off in the morning."[10]

NOTES

INTRODUCTION In Search of a Man Named Smith

1. Ambrose, interview.
2. Wayne, *Death of an Overseer*, 185.
3. Lowenthal, *Past Is a Foreign Country*.
4. *Oxford Dictionary of Quotations*, 96.
5. Van Deusen, *Jacksonian Era*, 138.
6. Backscheider, *Reflections on Biography*, 71.
7. Kinchen, *Rise and Fall*, 38–39. Kinchen cites several sources for the paragraph that contains this piece of information, but it is unclear which citation refers to Smith, and those that I have checked do not substantiate the claim that he was Canadian. Kinchen, a Tennessean, was a historian with an avid interest in Canadian and Confederate history. See Kinchen, *Confederate Operations*.
8. MacCabe, *Cleveland Directory*, 93.
9. U.S. Census, Cleveland, Ohio, 1840.
10. William Ganson Rose, *Cleveland*, 155.
11. A. D. Smith, coded letter of appointment of Lucius V. Bierce, [August 18, 1838], Bierce Papers, Container 1, Folder 4, Western Reserve Historical Society.
12. Records of the Rebellions of 1837–1838, Library and Archives Canada.
13. Justice of the Peace Docket, Cleveland Township, Cuyahoga County Archives.
14. Winslow, *Story of a Great Court*, 41; Bryant, biography.
15. Correspondence and telephone conversations with Sheila Lowe of Sheila Lowe and Associates, spring 2003. Lowe is a U.S.-based handwriting expert who has been certified by the American Handwriting Analysis Foundation and the Society of Handwriting Analysts. In 2012, she became president of the American Handwriting Analysis Foundation.
16. Cockshut, *Truth to Life*, 13. For the account of a biographer who felt the same way about her subject, see Lepore, "Historians Who Love Too Much," 129.
17. A. D. Smith, Last Will and Testament, recorded October 8, 1856, Probate Collection, Milwaukee County Historical Society.
18. *Milwaukee Sentinel*, July 25–27, 1848, February 23, 1858, October 26, 1842.
19. Strouse, "Semiprivate Lives," 115.
20. Ibid.

21. *Milwaukee Sentinel*, May 2, 1859.

22. The Salem witch trials have provided endless fodder for historians playing detective. See Norton, *In the Devil's Snare*; Karlsen, *Devil in the Shape*. Other mysteries that continue to fascinate historians and readers include the Boston Massacre (see Zobel's definitive work, *Boston Massacre*) and the tragic tale of rape and lynching in Oney, *And the Dead Shall Rise*. For a deeper look at questions of crime and the mysteries of the law, see Friedman, *Crime and Punishment*, which examines enduring courtroom mysteries such as the Salem witch trials, the Lindbergh kidnapping, and the infamous Lizzie Borden.

23. Crane, *Killed Strangely*, 6–7.

24. Ibid., 2.

25. Wayne, *Death of an Overseer*, 3–4.

26. Ball, *Slaves in the Family*, 8.

27. Ibid., 15.

28. Reynolds, *John Brown*, 9.

29. Meyers, *Jacksonian Persuasion*, examines the inner conflict of the Jacksonians, looking at how they dealt with old ideals in a new age.

30. Schlesinger, *Age of Jackson*, 8, 7.

31. Feller, *Jacksonian Promise*, 12–13

32. Whitney Cross, *Burned-Over District*; Harry L. Watson, *Liberty and Power*, 7–8.

33. Harry L. Watson, *Liberty and Power*, 8. See also Alice Felt Tyler, *Freedom's Ferment*, which examines the optimism of the era and analyzes the impact of the Second Great Awakening on nineteenth-century life. For a look at the impact of revivals in one Upstate town and a cultural examination of Rochester in the context of the Burned-Over District, see Paul E. Johnson, *Shopkeeper's Millennium*.

34. Wilentz, *Rise of American Democracy*, 513.

35. Huston, *Calculating the Value*, 200.

36. Pessen, *Jacksonian America*, 296.

37. Degler, "Inquiry into the Locofoco Party," 97.

38. Ibid.

39. Pessen, *Jacksonian America*, 296.

40. There are several explanations of how the Barnburner name came to be, though this particular version is by far the most prevalent. In *Safire's New Political Dictionary*, William Safire notes that the phrase may go as far back as 1629, when Thomas Adams wrote, "The empiric to cure the fever, destroys the patient; so the wise man, to burn the mice, set fire to his barn" (45).

41. Rayback, *Free Soil*, 60–61.

42. Safire, *Safire's New Political Dictionary*, 45.

43. William Henry Brisbane to Chase, February 15, 1864, in Chase, *Salmon P. Chase Papers* (hereafter *Chase Papers*).

44. See Burns, *American Idea of Mission*. For a more recent and less dated exploration of such ideas, see Mandelbaum, *Case for Goliath*.

45. Backscheider, *Reflections on Biography*, 61.
46. Morley, "Secret of the Ebony Cabinet," 89.
47. Backscheider, *Reflections on Biography*, 80.
48. Ibid., 81.
49. Wayne, *Death of an Overseer*, 185.
50. McFeely, *Grant*, xiii.
51. McFeely, "Why Biography?" ix.
52. McFeely, *Grant*, xiii.
53. McFeely, "Why Biography?" xiii.

CHAPTER 1 New York, Vermont, Ohio

1. *Ottawa Citizen*, July 4, 2003.
2. Wood, *Radicalism of the American Revolution*, 358.
3. Nellie Rice Molyneux, "Genealogy Western New York," copy in possession of Kathleen Candee.
4. "The Eaton Families Association," http://www.eatongenealogy.com/guest_features/molyneux_critique.php.
5. For more on Lowville, see Hough, *History of Lewis County*, 152.
6. Whitney Cross, *Burned-Over District*, 6.
7. Ibid., 4.
8. Ibid., 5.
9. Fischer, *Albion's Seed*, 93–97.
10. Daniel Scott Smith as quoted in ibid., 93.
11. Marriage certificate for A. D. Smith and Mary Augusta Reed, September 21, 1832, Vermont, Vital Records, 1720–1908 [database online], Ancestry.com; Conard, *History of Milwaukee*, 262; *Wisconsin Argus*, April 1, 1845.
12. Katy Thornblade, "Re: Abram Smith," email to author, February 23, 2015.
13. Whitney Cross, *Burned-Over District*, 8–9.
14. McKivigan, *War against Proslavery Religion*, 24, 172.
15. Fischer, *Albion's Seed*, 796.
16. Ibid., 796.
17. Perry Miller, "Garden of Eden," 114.
18. Patricia Homer, "Re: What I've Found," email to author, March 6, 2015.
19. A. D. Smith, Last Will and Testament, recorded October 8, 1856, Probate Collection, Milwaukee County Historical Society.
20. Patricia Homer, "Re: What I've Found," email to author, March 6, 2015.
21. Bryant, biography.
22. Graves, *Guns across the River*, 31.
23. Bryant, biography.
24. Wood, *Creation of the American Republic*, 12.
25. Bailyn, *Ideological Origins*, 330.
26. Pocock, *Machiavellian Moment*, 507–508.

27. Bailyn, *Ideological Origins*, 56.
28. Elkins and McKitrick, *Age of Federalism*, 22.
29. Wood, *Creation of the American Republic*, 68.
30. Ibid.
31. Ibid., 427.
32. Ibid.
33. Patrick Henry, "Give Me Liberty or Give me Death," March 23, 1775, http://avalon.law.yale.edu/18th_century/patrick.asp.
34. Bailyn, *Ideological Origins*, 25–26.
35. A. D. Smith, Last Will and Testament, recorded October 8, 1856, Probate Collection, Milwaukee County Historical Society, Milwaukee.
36. Wood, *Radicalism of the American Revolution*, 369.
37. Waite, *History of the First Medical College*, 114.
38. Donald Wickman, "Vermont Academy of Medicine," in Duffy, Hand, and Orth, *Vermont Encyclopedia*, 300.
39. Ibid., 102–103.
40. William Ganson Rose, *Cleveland*, 118.
41. Catalogue of the Officers and Students of the Vermont Academy of Medicine: Castleton, 1830, U.S. College Student Lists, 1763–1924 [database online], Ancestry.com.
42. Catalogue of the Officers and Students of the Vermont Academy of Medicine: Castleton, 1831, in ibid.
43. *Documents of the Assembly*, 8:425–426.
44. *Executive Documents*, 89–90.
45. Harrison Reed Papers, Wisconsin Historical Society (hereafter WHS).
46. For background on the Reed family, see John G. Gregory, "Early Wisconsin Editors," 460; Current, *Three Carpetbag Governors*, 7.
47. *Milwaukee Journal*, February 14, 1902.
48. Troy City Directory, 1832–1833, 61, Rensselaer County Historical Society.
49. Vermont, Vital Records, 1760–1954 [database online], FamilySearch.org; Marriage certificate for A. D. Smith and Mary Augusta Reed, September 21, 1832, Vermont, Vital Records, 1720–1908 [database online], Ancestry.com.
50. Marriage certificate for A. D. Smith and Mary Augusta Reed, September 21, 1832, Vermont, Vital Records, 1720–1908 [database online], Ancestry.com; Steele, *Annual Thanksgiving of the State*, 1–11.
51. Mary Frances Smith was very likely born on this date, though various records offer conflicting information. See FindaGrave Index, 1600s–Current [database online], Ancestry.com.
52. A. D. Smith to J. C. Fairchild, April 30, 1852, 1, Fairchild Papers, WHS; A. D. Smith, Last Will and Testament, recorded October 8, 1856, Probate Collection, Milwaukee County Historical Society.
53. Buley, *Old Northwest*, 3.
54. Ibid., 43–44, 100–101.

55. Ibid., 48.
56. William Ganson Rose, *Cleveland*, 119.
57. *Cleveland Herald and Gazette*, November 4, 1837.
58. Annals of Cleveland [newspaper index], 1838, Abstract 1415, Cleveland Public Library.
59. *Cleveland Herald and Gazette*, February 10, 1837.
60. MacCabe, *Cleveland Directory*, 93.
61. Annals of Cleveland [newspaper index], 1837, Abstract 2203, Cleveland Public Library.
62. Weisenburger, *Passing of the Frontier*, 370. Local antislavery societies had begun to appear before the American Revolution, and by 1838, the United States had about 1,350 such groups (Kennicott, "Black Persuaders," 6).
63. Feller, *Jacksonian Promise*, 115.
64. Prothero, *American Jesus*, 168. For a recent biography of Finney that has academic and popular appeal, see Hambrick-Stowe, *Charles G. Finney*. For an examination of Finney's life and theology, see Hardman, *Charles Grandison Finney*.
65. Paul Johnson, *History of Christianity*, 429.
66. Wood, *Radicalism of the American Revolution*, 354.
67. Weisenburger, *Passing of the Frontier*, 162.
68. Ibid., 163.
69. Lender and Martin, *Drinking in America*, 66.
70. Rorabaugh, *Alcoholic Republic*, 190.
71. William Ganson Rose, *Cleveland*, 155.
72. Gerring, "Chapter in the History," 760–761.
73. Peterson, *Jefferson Image*, 71.
74. Ibid., 68, 69.
75. Annals of Cleveland: Officeholder Series, Historical Record of Public Officeholders in Cuyahoga County, Register of Public Officeholders in Cleveland, 1802–1891, 1:118, Cleveland Public Library.
76. Harry L. Watson, *Liberty and Power*, 192. There are many versions of this episode, which has passed into American political legend.
77. Van Deusen, *Jacksonian Era*, 95.
78. Weisenburger, *Passing of the Frontier*, 311.
79. Van Deusen, *Jacksonian Era*, 95.
80. Degler, "Locofocos," 322.
81. Ibid., 329.
82. Ibid., 330.
83. *Cleveland Herald and Gazette*, August 11, 1837.
84. *Cleveland Daily Advertiser*, August 5, 1837.
85. Ibid., August 4, 1837.
86. Schlesinger, *Age of Jackson*, 149.
87. Hugins, *Jacksonian Democracy*, 11.
88. Wilentz, *Chants Democratic*, 172–173, 175.

89. Ibid., 76.
90. Schlesinger, *Age of Jackson*, 205.
91. Ibid., 208.
92. Van Deusen, *Jacksonian Era*, 95.
93. Feller, *Jacksonian Promise*, 172.
94. Ibid., 190.
95. Weisenburger, *Passing of the Frontier*, 339.
96. Some records of Maria Cecilia's birth indicate that she was born in 1839, while others simply say "around 1840." The records agree that she was born in Ohio, however, so she was certainly a part of the Smith family before they moved to Wisconsin.
97. Kinchen, *Rise and Fall*, 11–12.
98. Creighton, *John A. Macdonald: The Young Politician*, 52.
99. Bellasis, *Rise, Canadians!*, 77.
100. For a full account of the debacle at Montgomery's Tavern, see Guillet, *Lives and Times*, 15–28. Estimates of the number of participants vary widely. Library and Archives Canada estimates that Mackenzie's eight hundred men faced about one thousand militia and volunteers ("Upper Canada, 1837–1838," Rebellions of 1837 and 1838, *From Colony to Country: A Reader's Guide to Canadian Military History*, www.collectionscanada.ca/military/025002-3000-e.html).
101. Quoted in Guillet, *Lives and Times*, 72n.
102. Ibid., 79; Kinchen, *Rise and Fall*, 15.
103. Guillet, *Lives and Times*, 80.
104. Shortridge, "Canadian-American Frontier," 15.
105. Samuel Watson, "United States Army Officers," 492.
106. See Carroll, "Passionate Canadians"; Carroll, *Good and Wise Measure*.
107. Martin Van Buren, inaugural address, March 4, 1837, http://avalon.law.yale.edu/19th_century/vanburen.asp
108. Guillet, *Lives and Times*, 80.
109. *Cleveland Weekly Herald and Gazette*, November 3, 1837.
110. Kinchen, *Rise and Fall*, 31.
111. Ibid., 56–57.
112. Iding, *Forward Freemasonry*, 283. Smith was initiated into the Masons in Cleveland and was a member and a master of Milwaukee Lodge No. 3 and later of Tracy Lodge No. 13. He served as grand master in 1846, 1847, 1848, and 1851, overseeing the settling of "questions of territorial jurisdiction between the Grand Lodge of Wisconsin and the Grand Lodges of Illinois and Iowa." See also the *Wisconsin Masonic Journal*, December 2000, which indicates that Smith was initiated in 1841, just before he arrived in Milwaukee.
113. Kinchen, *Rise and Fall*, 52.
114. Ibid., 54.
115. Ibid.
116. Ibid., 49.

117. Allan Smith, "American Culture and the Concept of Mission in 19th Century English Canada," in Bumsted, *Canadian History before Confederation*, 488.
118. Kilbourn, *Firebrand*, 238; J. E. Rea, "William Lyon Mackenzie—Jacksonian?" in Bumsted, *Canadian History before Confederation*, 383.
119. Kilbourn, *Firebrand*, 100.
120. S. F. Wise and Brown, *Canada Views the United States*, 32, 36.
121. Ibid., 37–38.
122. Kinchen, *Rise and Fall*, 122.
123. Ibid., 5; Shortridge, "Canadian-American Frontier," 20.
124. Graves, *Guns across the River*, 53.
125. Weisenburger, *Passing of the Frontier*, 359.
126. *Cleveland Daily Advertiser*, January 4, 1838.
127. Ibid.
128. *Freeman's Advocate*, November 30, 1838. The *Freeman's Advocate*, edited by James Mackenzie, William Lyon Mackenzie's son, began publication in September 1838 and ceased publication in March 1839. The newspaper can be found at Library and Archives Canada. See Amicus No. 27104190.
129. Wiltse, *New Nation*, 82.
130. Graves, *Guns across the River*, 53.
131. Kinchen, *Rise and Fall*, 40; Graves, *Guns across the River*, 53.
132. John Mittleberger to Sir George Arthur, October 1838, Records of the Rebellions of 1837–1838, Library and Archives Canada; Graves, *Guns across the River*, 54.
133. Records of the Rebellions of 1837–1838, Library and Archives Canada, Ottawa.
134. Graves, *Guns across the River*, 54.
135. Lindsey, *William Lyon Mackenzie*, 440–441.
136. Bierce Papers, Western Reserve Historical Society.
137. Bonthius, "Patriot War," 31.
138. Ibid.
139. Blau, *Social Theories of Jacksonian Democracy*, xxviii.
140. Sharp, *Jacksonians versus the Banks*, 6.
141. William Jones, sworn deposition, Records of the Rebellions of 1837–1838, Library and Archives Canada.
142. Graves, *Guns across the River*, 11. Graves's work is the most recent to tackle the story of the Hunters and is the definitive book on the Battle of the Windmill. My account of the battle is based on his work.
143. Graves, *Guns across the River*, 81.
144. Ibid., 84–87.
145. Ibid., 88–89.
146. Ibid., 91, 92.
147. Ibid., 101.
148. Cahill, *Forgotten Patriots*, 62.

149. Graves, *Guns across the River*, 125, 136.
150. Ibid., 134.
151. Kinchen, *Rise and Fall*, 76–77.
152. Graves, *Guns across the River*, 163.
153. DeCelles, *MacKenzie, Papineau*, 444. For an examination of the fates of the men sent to the penal colonies, see Cahill, *Forgotten Patriots*.
154. The definitive biography of Macdonald's life is Creighton, *John A. Macdonald: The Young Politician*. See also Creighton, *John A. Macdonald: The Old Chieftain*. For a more recent biography, see Gwyn, *John A.*
155. Guillet, *Lives and Times*, 133, 143.
156. Kinchen, *Rise and Fall*, 81; for a description of the battle, see 79–82. See also Guillet, *Lives and Times*, 143–152.
157. Kinchen, *Rise and Fall*, 82.
158. Ibid., 82.
159. Ibid., 82–83.
160. S. F. Wise and Brown, *Canada Views the United States*, 43.
161. Kinchen, *Rise and Fall*, 101.
162. For a discussion of the Durham Report in the context of liberalism, see Ajzenstat, "Liberalism and Nationality."
163. John Tyler, "Proclamation 46A—Warning against Lawless Incursions into Canada," September 25, 1841, www.presidency.ucsb.edu/ws/index.php?pid=67555.
164. Van Deusen, *Jacksonian Era*, 172.
165. Ibid., 173.
166. For an examination of the McLeod case, see Jennings, "Caroline and McLeod Cases."
167. Van Deusen, *Jacksonian Era*, 139.
168. Ibid., 173.
169. Ibid.
170. McLaughlin, *Patriot War*, 175.
171. Kilbourn, *Firebrand*, 219–220.
172. Kinchen, *Rise and Fall*, 20.
173. Guillet, *Lives and Times*, 132.
174. If, indeed, he was born in the United States, as records suggest. The ambiguity regarding Smith's birthplace leaves open the possibility that was born in Upper Canada or that his parents were Canadian emigrants to the United States.
175. Kinchen, *Rise and Fall*, 63.
176. Ibid., 54–55.
177. Kinchen, *Rise and Fall*, 20. Bierce, for example, seemed more interested in "bombastic addresses and proclamations" than in taking part in any sort of combat (Guillet, *Lives and Times*, 143).
178. Kinchen, *Rise and Fall*, 43, 54.
179. Hugins, *Jacksonian Democracy*, 148.
180. Ibid., 148.

181. *Freeman's Advocate*, December 28, 1838.
182. Ibid., November 23, 1838.
183. Ibid., February 1, 1839.
184. Gerring, *Party Ideologies in America*, 183.

CHAPTER 2 Wisconsin

1. Buck, *Pioneer History of Milwaukee*, 2:123.
2. Winslow, *Story of a Great Court*, 40.
3. John Nondorf, "Re: A. D. Smith," email to author, April 22, 2009.
4. Marshall, "Samuel Marsden Brookes," 51; Draper, *Collections of the State Historical Society of Wisconsin*, 41.
5. John G. Gregory, *History of Milwaukee, Wisconsin*, 922.
6. Foner and Garraty, *Reader's Companion to American History*, 1.
7. Almost all genealogical information has been gleaned from online searches at www.familysearch.org and www.ancestry.com.
8. Quaife, *Convention of 1846*, 788.
9. Current, *Those Terrible Carpetbaggers*.
10. *Milwaukee Sentinel*, December 2, 1857; Newspaper clipping, Reed Papers, WHS.
11. *Dictionary of Wisconsin Biography*, 299.
12. Reed Papers, WHS; *Milwaukee Sentinel*, February 6, 1838.
13. Alice E. Smith, *History of Wisconsin*, 162–163.
14. Still, *Milwaukee*, 70–71.
15. Alice E. Smith, *History of Wisconsin*, 75.
16. Ibid., 73.
17. Ibid., 80.
18. Wheeler, *Chronicles of Milwaukee*, 120–122.
19. Ibid., 125.
20. H. Robert Baker, "Rescue of Joshua Glover," chapter 2, p. 1.
21. John G. Gregory, *History of Milwaukee, Wisconsin*, 922.
22. *Milwaukee Sentinel*, October 26, 1842, March 30, 1844.
23. A. D. Smith, *Message of His Excellency*, 4.
24. Alice E. Smith, *History of Wisconsin*, 648; Ranney, *Trusting Nothing to Providence*, 47.
25. Ranney, *Trusting Nothing to Providence*, 48.
26. Alice E. Smith, *History of Wisconsin*, 655.
27. Ranney, *Trusting Nothing to Providence*, 50.
28. Alice E. Smith, *History of Wisconsin*, 655.
29. Quaife, *Struggle over Ratification*, 388.
30. Ibid., 564–587.
31. Ranney, *Trusting Nothing to Providence*, 58.
32. Alice E. Smith, *History of Wisconsin*, 664.

33. Quaife, *Struggle over Ratification*, 568.
34. Ibid., 570–571.
35. Ranney, *Trusting Nothing to Providence*, 57; Quaife, *Struggle over Ratification*, 577.
36. Ranney, *Trusting Nothing to Providence*, 52–53.
37. Quaife, *Struggle over Ratification*, 584.
38. Ibid., 587.
39. *Milwaukee Sentinel*, January 25, 1847.
40. Ibid., February 23, 1847.
41. Harry L. Watson, *Liberty and Power*, 194.
42. Quaife, *Struggle over Ratification*, 578.
43. Alice E. Smith, *History of Wisconsin*, 665.
44. Ranney, *Trusting Nothing to Providence*, 67. Wisconsin was admitted to the Union on May 29, 1848.
45. Winslow, *Story of a Great Court*, 41.
46. *Milwaukee Sentinel*, July 26, 1848.
47. Ibid.
48. Ibid.
49. Ibid., August 2, 1848.
50. Flower, *History of Milwaukee, Wisconsin*, 75; *Milwaukee Sentinel*, August 2, 1848.
51. *Milwaukee Sentinel*, August 5, 1848.
52. *Milwaukee Daily Free Democrat*, December 7, 1850.
53. *Milwaukee Sentinel*, May 19, 21, 1851.
54. John G. Gregory, *History of Milwaukee, Wisconsin*, 999.
55. Berryman, *History of the Bench*, 47.
56. Conard, *History of Milwaukee*, 200.
57. Ibid., 214.
58. Winslow, *Story of a Great Court*, 38
59. Holt, *Rise and Fall*, 956, 764.
60. Buck, *Pioneer History of Milwaukee*, 4:297.
61. Fairchild Papers, WHS; Flower, *History of Milwaukee, Wisconsin*, 990.
62. Fairchild Papers, WHS.
63. Ibid.
64. Winslow, *Story of a Great Court*, 32.
65. *Report of the Proceedings*, 124.
66. *Resolutions of the Wisconsin Legislature*, 3; A. D. Smith to Mary Augusta Smith, January 23, 1853, Gamble Family Record Book, Box 187b, Greene and Greene Collection, Greene and Greene Archives, Gamble House, University of Southern California (hereafter GFRB).
67. *Journal of the Assembly of Wisconsin*, 968.
68. Jackson and McDonald, *Finding Freedom*, 27.
69. H. Robert Baker, *Prigg v. Pennsylvania*, 47.
70. Lubet, *Fugitive Justice*, 6
71. Ibid.

72. Butler, "Public Life and Private Affairs," 175.
73. Finkelman and Kennon, *Congress and the Crisis*, 38.
74. Ranney, "Suffering the Agonies," 86.
75. Ranney, "World in Which Nothing," 17.
76. McKivigan and Harrold, *Antislavery Violence*, 19; Thoreau as quoted in Bordewich, *Bound for Canaan*, 323.
77. Fehrenbacher, *Dred Scott Case*, 177.
78. Foner, *Free Soil, Free Labor*, 134.
79. Horton, "Kidnapping and Resistance," 159.
80. McKivigan and Harold, *Antislavery Violence*, 3.
81. Carol Wilson, "Active Vigilance Is the Price of Liberty: Black Self Defense against Fugitive Recapture and Kidnapping of Free Blacks," in ibid., 123.
82. Wilentz, *Rise of American Democracy*, 646.
83. Ibid.
84. McPherson, *Battle Cry of Freedom*, 76; Wilentz, *Rise of American Democracy*, 646.
85. Bordewich, *Bound for Canaan*, 321.
86. Ibid., 340; Wilentz, *Rise of American Democracy*, 647.
87. Bordewich, *Bound for Canaan*, 325.
88. Ibid., 330.
89. McPherson, *Battle Cry of Freedom*, 85.
90. Ibid., 85.
91. Horton, "Kidnapping and Resistance," 168; Bordewich, *Bound for Canaan*, 337. Some histories of the case refer to Jerry's surname as McHenry; others use the surname Henry.
92. Bordewich, *Bound for Canaan*, 339.
93. Horton, "Kidnapping and Resistance," 166; Wilentz, *Rise of American Democracy*, 648.
94. As quoted in Bordewich, *Bound for Canaan*, 340.
95. Ranney, "Suffering the Agonies," 86.
96. Ibid.
97. A. D. Smith to Mary Augusta Smith, January 23, 1853, GFRB.
98. *Milwaukee Sentinel*, March 13, 1854.
99. John G. Gregory, *History of Milwaukee, Wisconsin*, 746. For the most recent and thorough scholarly account of Glover's story, see H. Robert Baker, *Rescue of Joshua Glover*. For a more popular account, see Jackson and McDonald, *Finding Freedom*.
100. Butler, "Public Life and Private Affairs," 175; H. Robert Baker, *Rescue of Joshua Glover*, 2.
101. John G. Gregory, *History of Milwaukee, Wisconsin*, 747.
102. Butler, "Public Life and Private Affairs," 176.
103. Ibid., 169.
104. Ibid., 174.

105. Holmes, *Badger Saints and Sinners*, 195. Booth later denied having shouted these words, but whatever his exact message, he unquestionably gathered a crowd (H. Robert Baker, *Rescue of Joshua Glover*, 10).

106. Holmes, *Badger Saints and Sinners*, 196; Butler, "Public Life and Private Affairs," 178.

107. John G. Gregory, *History of Milwaukee, Wisconsin*, 751.

108. *Milwaukee Daily Free Democrat*, March 15, 1854.

109. Ranney, *Trusting Nothing to Providence*, 98.

110. *Milwaukee Daily Free Democrat*, May 27, 1854.

111. Ranney, *Trusting Nothing to Providence*, 98–99.

112. *Milwaukee Daily Free Democrat*, June 6, 1854.

113. Maltz, *Slavery and the Supreme Court*, 198.

114. H. Robert Baker, *Rescue of Joshua Glover*, 114.

115. *Milwaukee Daily Free Democrat*, June 8, 1854.

116. Ibid.

117. Ellis, *Union at Risk*, 1, 4.

118. Wilentz, *Rise of American Democracy*, 533–534.

119. McManus, *Political Abolitionism in Wisconsin*, 137.

120. Schmitt, "Rethinking *Ableman v. Booth*," 1329.

121. Ibid.

122. *Milwaukee Daily Free Democrat*, June 8, 1854.

123. Ibid.

124. Ibid.

125. Schmitt, "Rethinking *Ableman v. Booth*," 1334.

126. Ibid.

127. *Milwaukee Sentinel*, July 20, 1854.

128. Ranney, "Suffering the Agonies," 94.

129. Ibid.

130. Schmitt, "Rethinking *Ableman v. Booth*," 1335.

131. Ibid., 1326.

132. Wert, *Habeas Corpus in America*, 30.

133. Schmitt, "Rethinking *Ableman v. Booth*, 1334–1335."

134. *Milwaukee Daily Free Democrat*, June 8, 1854.

135. Ranney, "Suffering the Agonies," 91.

136. *Milwaukee Daily Free Democrat*, June 10, 1854.

137. *Milwaukee Sentinel*, June 12, 1854.

138. Ibid.

139. *Milwaukee Daily Free Democrat*, June 12, 1854.

140. Mason, "Fugitive Slave Law in Wisconsin," 138.

141. *Milwaukee Sentinel*, June 19, 1854.

142. Ibid., July 17, 1854.

143. *Frederick Douglass' Paper*, June 23, 1854.

144. Butler, "Public Life and Private Affairs," 184.

145. *Milwaukee Daily Free Democrat*, August 4, 1854.
146. *Milwaukee Sentinel*, August 5, 1854.
147. *Milwaukee Daily Free Democrat*, August 4, 1854.
148. Holmes, *Badger Saints and Sinners*, 197; Butler, "Public Life and Private Affairs," 184.
149. H. Robert Baker, *Rescue of Joshua Glover*, 131.
150. *Milwaukee Sentinel*, July 14, 1856.
151. Ibid., May 7, 1855.
152. Ibid., April 16, 1857.
153. *Milwaukee Daily Free Democrat*, February 7, 1860.
154. A. D. Smith to Mary Augusta Smith, February 9, 1856, GFRB.
155. Ibid., February 25, 1856.
156. Marriage certificate for William S. Huggins and Mary Frances Smith, October 5, 1854, Wisconsin Marriages, 1836–1930 [database online], FamilySearch.org; for birth and death information for Mary Augusta Huggins Gamble, see https://www.findagrave.com/memorial/42521575/gam.
157. Ericson, *Slavery in the American Republic*, 91.
158. Huebner, *Taney Court*, 32; Young, *Landmark Constitutional Law Decisions*, 41.
159. Steiner, *Life of Roger Brooke Taney*, 182; Huebner, *Taney Court*, 32.
160. Huebner, *Taney Court*, 34.
161. Steiner, *Life of Roger Brooke Taney*, 55; Huebner, *Taney Court*, 34.
162. Huebner, *Taney Court*, 42, 41.
163. Fehrenbacher, *Dred Scott Case*, 560.
164. Foner and Garraty, *Reader's Companion to American History*, 831.
165. Finkelman, "Prigg v. Pennsylvania," 161.
166. Ibid.
167. Huebner, *Taney Court*, 42, 158–159. This condensed version of Margaret Morgan's story is based on Huebner's work, but my synopsis has also been informed by Fehrenbacher, *Dred Scott Case*, 40–47.
168. McPherson, *Battle Cry of Freedom*, 79.
169. Finkelman, "Prigg v. Pennsylvania," 163.
170. Huebner, *Taney Court*, 161, 160.
171. Fehrenbacher, *Dred Scott Case*, 45.
172. Huebner, *Taney Court*, 161.
173. Wiecek, "Slavery and Abolition," 557; Urofsky, *Documents*, 389.
174. Wiecek, "Slavery and Abolition," 557.
175. Urofsky, *Documents*, 390.
176. Ibid.
177. Huebner, *Taney Court*, 163.
178. Ibid.
179. Ibid.
180. Ibid., 163–164.

181. Young, *Landmark Constitutional Law Decisions*, 65. Young provides a concise synopsis of the well-documented case. For more a more detailed evaluation, the standard has been set by Fehrenbacher's Pulitzer Prize–winning *Dred Scott Case*. For more recent scholarship on *Dred Scott v. Sandford*, see also Graber, *Dred Scott and the Problem*; Allen, *Origins*. The Sanford name was apparently recorded incorrectly in the original legal documents.

182. Fehrenbacher, *Dred Scott Case*, 275.

183. Kutler, *Supreme Court and the Constitution*, 150.

184. Fehrenbacher, *Dred Scott Case*, 2; *Dred Scott v. Sandford* (1857) as cited in Urofsky, *Documents*, 425.

185. Ibid., 428–429.

186. Simon, *Lincoln and Chief Justice Taney*, 129.

187. Holt, *Fate of Their Country*, 119.

188. Stampp, *America in 1857*, 105–106.

189. Foner, *Free Soil, Free Labor*, 293.

190. Freehling, *Road to Disunion*, 2:121.

191. Fehrenbacher, *Dred Scott Case*, 455.

192. Holzer, *Lincoln-Douglas Debates*, 106.

193. Potter, *Impending Crisis*, 326–329.

194. Wendell Phillips, speech to New York Anti-Slavery Society, *The Liberator*, May 29, 1857.

195. A. D. Smith to Mary Augusta Smith, May 27, 1857, GFRB.

196. Kutler, *Supreme Court and the Constitution*, 110.

197. Ranney, "Suffering the Agonies," 104; *Ableman v. Booth*, Justia, http://supreme.justia.com/us/62/506/case.html.

198. *Ableman v. Booth*.

199. Ibid.

200. Mason, "Fugitive Slave Law in Wisconsin," 299.

201. *Milwaukee Daily Free Democrat*, March 11, 1859.

202. Simon, *Lincoln and Chief Justice Taney*, 163.

203. Ranney, "Imperia in Imperiis," 2.

204. *Dictionary of Wisconsin Biography*, 256.

205. Buck, *Pioneer History of Milwaukee*, 2:125.

206. *Milwaukee Sentinel*, May 29, 1858.

207. Ibid.

208. Ibid., May 15, 29, 1858.

209. Winslow, *Story of a Great Court*, 116.

210. Holt, *Rise and Fall*, 532.

211. Wilentz, *Rise of American Democracy*, 643.

212. A. D. Smith as quoted in Ranney, *Trusting Nothing to Providence*, 100.

213. S. S. Gregory, "Historic Judicial Controversy," 192.

214. McManus, *Political Abolitionism in Wisconsin*, 175.

215. Current, *History of Wisconsin*, 224–230.

216. McManus, *Political Abolitionism in Wisconsin*, 175.
217. Ibid.
218. Current, *History of Wisconsin*, 236.
219. Winslow, *Story of a Great Court*, 116.
220. McManus, *Political Abolitionism in Wisconsin*, 175.
221. Ibid.
222. Winslow, *Story of a Great Court*, 116; *Milwaukee Daily Free Democrat*, March 11, 1859.
223. Mason, "Fugitive Slave Law in Wisconsin," 297.
224. *Milwaukee Sentinel*, March 17, 1859.
225. Ibid., March 19, 1859.
226. Winslow, *Story of a Great Court*, 118.
227. *Milwaukee Sentinel*, May 2, 1859, January 14, 1860.
228. Winslow, *Story of a Great Court*, 122; Ranney, "Suffering the Agonies," 108–109; *Milwaukee Sentinel*, February 7, 1860.
229. *Milwaukee Sentinel*, January 17, 1860.
230. *Milwaukee Daily Free Democrat*, January 21, 1860.
231. A. D. Smith, *State Rights*, 5.
232. Ranney, "Suffering the Agonies," 109. For a more dated examination of states' rights in Wisconsin, see Sellers, "Republicanism and State Rights."
233. *Milwaukee Sentinel*, April 16, 1857.
234. Sellers, "Republicanism and State Rights," 217–218.
235. Ibid.
236. Current, *History of Wisconsin*, 283.
237. Morris, *Free Men All*, 200.
238. A. D. Smith, *State Rights*, 11–12.
239. Finkelman, *Imperfect Union*, 336; Foner, *Free Soil, Free Labor*, 135.
240. Potter, *Impending Crisis*, 296.
241. Bradley and Ranney, "Tradition of Independence," 44.
242. Ranney, "Suffering the Agonies," 111.
243. The *Milwaukee Daily Free Democrat* had changed hands several times over the preceding two years. By the spring of 1859, in addition to his legal battle in *Ableman v. Booth*, Booth was fighting charges that he had seduced a fourteen-year-old girl (Butler, "Public Life and Private Affairs," 190). In March of that year, Booth sold the newspaper to Sholes & Crounse, which became Crounse & Thomson the following day. In February 1860, the firm became Crounse & Fitch, and by May 1860, the paper was bought by C. C. Olin and G. W. Tenney. Smith purchased the paper on December 3, 1860 (Flower, *History of Milwaukee, Wisconsin*, 627).
244. *Milwaukee Daily Sentinel*, December 13, 1860; Current, *History of Wisconsin*, 274.
245. U.S. Census, Kalamazoo, Michigan, 1860.
246. There is no concrete evidence that Smith and his wife had additional children, though such long periods of infertility are unusual for mid-nineteenth-

century families. In the 1850 census, the Smith household includes twelve-year-old Ohio-born Sylvester Smith. His relationship (if any) to the rest of the Smith family is not indicated. I have been unable to locate further records for Sylvester Smith: he is not buried with the family and is not listed in the 1860 census.

247. U.S. Census, Milwaukee, Wisconsin, 1850.

248. Gamble, "Story," 6. The Candees went on to have six children: Mary Augusta, Henry, Alexander Mitchell, Charles Lucius, Robert, and William Leavitt.

249. A. D. Smith to William Sprague Candee, November 1, 1861, GFRB.

250. Ibid.

251. Berlin et al., *Wartime Genesis of Free Labor*, 35.

252. Doolittle attended Geneva (later Hobart) College in Upstate New York. The school has no record of Smith. See Sellers, "James R. Doolittle." For a concise biography of Doolittle, see "Doolittle, James Rood, (1815–1897)," Biographical Directory of the United States Congress, http://bioguide.congress.gov/scripts/biodisplay.pl?index=D000428.

253. A. D. Smith to William Sprague Candee, November 1, 1861, GFRB.

254. *Milwaukee Sentinel*, January 28, 1862.

CHAPTER 3 South Carolina

1. Garrison, *Letters of William Lloyd Garrison*, 120–121.
2. Long and Long, *Civil War Day by Day*, 276.
3. Garrison, *Letters of William Lloyd Garrison*, 120–121.
4. Ibid., 120. A. D. Smith attended medical school in Castleton, Vermont, about one hundred miles south of Ryegate, though I have found no evidence to link him to that town.
5. Eva Garcelon-Hart, "Re: Research Request," email to author, November 22, 2012.
6. A. D. Smith to Chase, Report of the Commission, January 1, 1863, Records of the Internal Revenue Service, Direct Tax Commissions in Southern States, South Carolina, General Correspondence, 1862–1893, RG 58, National Archives, College Park (hereafter RDTC).
7. Willie Lee Rose, *Rehearsal for Reconstruction*.
8. McPherson, *Battle Cry of Freedom*, 369.
9. Ibid., 371; Willie Lee Rose, *Rehearsal for Reconstruction*, 106.
10. Willie Lee Rose, *Rehearsal for Reconstruction*, 107.
11. Ibid.
12. Freehling, *Road to Disunion*, 1:216; McPherson, *Negro's Civil War*, 57. For more about the freedmen's lives before the occupation and their reaction to their newfound freedom, see Report of the Commission, January 1, 1863, 55–60, RDTC.
13. Berlin et al., *Wartime Genesis of Free Labor*, 227.
14. Metzger and Coogan, *Oxford Companion to the Bible*, 253; Ochiai, "Port Royal Experiment Revisited," 94.

15. Guelzo, *Fateful Lightning*, 182.
16. Alice E. Smith, *History of Wisconsin*, 475.
17. Hoffman, "From Slavery to Self-Reliance," 10.
18. Berlin et al., *Wartime Genesis of Free Labor*, 227.
19. Ibid., 36.
20. Foner, *Free Soil, Free Labor*, 149–150.
21. Ibid., 180.
22. Goodwin, *Team of Rivals*.
23. Overy, "Wisconsin Carpetbagger."
24. Berlin et al., *Wartime Genesis of Free Labor*, 227.
25. *Milwaukee Sentinel*, July 19, 1862.
26. Connecticut, Hale Collection of Cemetery Inscriptions and Newspaper Notices, 1629–1934 [database online], Ancestry.com. For more on William Huggins's life and death, see Haskell and Huggins, *Three Sermons to Young Men*.
27. *Milwaukee Sentinel*, August 16, 1862.
28. Gamble, "Story," 3.
29. A. D. Smith to Chase, August 6, 1862, RDTC.
30. Doolittle to Chase, February 6, 1864, in ibid.
31. Courtwright, "Opiate Addiction as a Consequence," 110–111.
32. A. D. Smith to Mary Augusta Smith, August 20, 1862, GFRB.
33. Ibid.
34. Willie Lee Rose, *Rehearsal for Reconstruction*, 7.
35. C. Vann Woodward, introduction to ibid., xv; A. D. Smith to Chase, January 1, 1863, RDTC.
36. Sandage, *Born Losers*, 136.
37. Ibid., 134.
38. Ibid., 138–139.
39. Brisbane to Reed, Reed Papers, WHS.
40. *Milwaukee Sentinel*, March 12, 1862.
41. Ibid., December 2, 1857; Futch, "Salmon P. Chase," 170.
42. Willie Lee Rose, *Rehearsal for Reconstruction*, 202.
43. Stephen R. Wise, Rowland, and Spieler, *Rebellion, Reconstruction, and Redemption*, 158.
44. For more on the Saxton brothers, see Saxton Papers, Yale University.
45. Berlin et al., *Wartime Genesis of Free Labor*, 227.
46. Ibid.
47. A. D. Smith to George Boutwell, November 2, 1862, RDTC.
48. A. D. Smith to Chase, October 30, 1862, in ibid.
49. Ibid., January 1, 1863.
50. Ibid.
51. Ibid.
52. Ibid.
53. Ibid.

54. Ochiai, "Port Royal Experiment Revisited," 100.
55. A. D. Smith to Chase, January 1, 1863, RDTC
56. Ibid.
57. Berlin et al., *Wartime Genesis of Free Labor*, 108.
58. Wood, *Radicalism of the American Revolution*, 179.
59. Foner, *Story of American Freedom*, 9, 20–21.
60. McPherson, *Battle Cry of Freedom*, 840.
61. Ibid., 841–842. I have found no evidence to suggest that Smith was involved with these efforts, though it is possible. There is no indication that he returned to Milwaukee when he was relieved of his duties on the tax commission.
62. Foner, *Story of American Freedom*, 113.
63. Foner, *Reconstruction*, 235.
64. Woodley, *Great Leveler*, 352–353, 360.
65. Foner, *Reconstruction*, 236.
66. Ochiai, "Port Royal Experiment Revisited," 98; Berlin et al., *Wartime Genesis of Free Labor*, 102.
67. Mansfield French to Chase, January 6, 1863, in *Chase Papers*.
68. Berlin et al., *Wartime Genesis of Free Labor*, 228.
69. Ibid., 103.
70. A. D. Smith, "A Semi-Official Report," March 12, 1863, RDTC.
71. Stephen R. Wise, Rowland, and Spieler, *Rebellion, Reconstruction, and Redemption*, 260.
72. Berlin et al., *Wartime Genesis of Free Labor*, 108.
73. Willie Lee Rose, *Rehearsal for Reconstruction*, 196–197.
74. Mansfield French to Chase, February 7, 1863, in *Chase Papers*.
75. Brisbane and Wording to Joseph Lewis, November 2, 1863, RDTC.
76. Ibid.
77. Brisbane to Joseph Lewis, March 5, 1864, Brisbane and Wording to Joseph Lewis, November 2, 1863, both in ibid.
78. A. D. Smith to Joseph Lewis, December 5, 1863, in ibid.
79. *Free South*, September 26, 1863.
80. Smith to Chase, October 2, 1863, in *Chase Papers*.
81. Brisbane to Chase, August 27, 1863, in ibid. The enclosures Brisbane mentions could not be found in either the *Chase Papers* or in the records of the Direct Tax Commission.
82. Wording and Brisbane to Chase, September 5, 1863, RDTC.
83. Lender and Martin, *Drinking in America*, 84, 85–86.
84. Pierce, "Freedmen at Port Royal."
85. Pearson, *Letters from Port Royal*, 231.
86. Ochiai, "Port Royal Experiment Revisited," 100.
87. Berlin et al., *Wartime Genesis of Free Labor*, 106–107.
88. Willie Lee Rose, *Rehearsal for Reconstruction*, 275.
89. Ibid., 274.

90. Ibid., 275.
91. Brisbane to Joseph Lewis, January 21, 1864, RDTC.
92. Ibid.; Berlin et al., *Wartime Genesis of Free Labor*, 107.
93. Brisbane to Joseph Lewis, January 16, 1864, RDTC.
94. William F. Allen diary, January 17, 1864, Allen Family Papers, WHS.
95. A. D. Smith to Joseph Lewis, February 7, 1864, RDTC.
96. Brisbane to Joseph Lewis, January 16, 1864, in ibid.
97. William Henry Brisbane diary, January 15, 1864, Brisbane Papers, WHS.
98. Ibid., January 16, 1864.
99. Ibid.
100. Willie Lee Rose, *Rehearsal for Reconstruction*, 285–286.
101. William F. Allen diary, January 17, 1864, Allen Family Papers, WHS.
102. Ibid.
103. Willie Lee Rose, *Rehearsal for Reconstruction*, 286–287.
104. Brisbane to Joseph Lewis, January 16, 1864, RDTC.
105. Saxton to Chase, January 22, 1864, in ibid.
106. Ibid.
107. Saxton to Chase, January 22, 1864, in *Chase Papers*.
108. Brisbane to Joseph Lewis, January 16, 1864, RDTC.
109. Ibid.
110. Ibid., January 21, 1864.
111. Ibid.
112. *New York Tribune*, January 27, 1864.
113. Ibid.
114. Willie Lee Rose, *Rehearsal for Reconstruction*, 291.
115. William F. Allen diary, Allen Family Papers, WHS.
116. Brisbane to Joseph Lewis, February 2, 1864, RDTC.
117. Ibid.
118. A. D. Smith to Joseph Lewis, February 7, 1864, in ibid.
119. Ibid.
120. Ibid.
121. Doolittle to Chase, February 6, 1864, in ibid.
122. William Henry Brisbane diary, February 12, 1864, Brisbane Papers, WHS.
123. Brisbane to Joseph Lewis, February 15, 1864, RDTC.
124. William Henry Brisbane diary, January 18, 1864, Brisbane Papers, WHS.
125. Long and Long, *Civil War Day by Day*, 459–560.
126. Brisbane to Joseph Lewis, February 23, 1864, RDTC.
127. Ibid.
128. Ibid.
129. Wording to Joseph Lewis, February 25, 1864, in ibid.
130. Brisbane to Joseph Lewis, March 5, 1864, RDTC. According to Baldwin, *Candee Genealogy*, Alexander and Candee were cousins.
131. Brisbane to Joseph Lewis, March 5, 1864, RDTC.

132. French to Lewis, March 10, 1864, ibid.
133. Joseph Lewis to Chase, February 5, 1864, in *Chase Papers*.
134. William Henry Brisbane diary, March 5, 1864, Brisbane Papers, WHS.
135. Chase to Brisbane, March 1, 1864, in *Chase Papers*.
136. William Henry Brisbane diary, March 5, 1864, Brisbane Papers, WHS.
137. S. Willard Saxton diary, March 9, 1864, Saxton Papers, Yale University. It is not clear why Willard Saxton referred to Brisbane as a Jesuit since he was a Baptist, not a Catholic. Rufus Saxton was a freemason, and Willard, too, likely was a member of the order. Masons of the time saw Jesuits as nefarious operators who "sought to convert [Masonry's] pure philanthropy and toleration into political intrigue and religious bigotry" (Mackey and McClenachan, *Encyclopedia of Freemasonry*, 368).
138. S. Willard Saxton diary, March 9, 1864, Saxton Papers, Yale University.
139. Rufus Saxton to Chase, March 9, 1864, in ibid.
140. Ibid., March 28, 1864.
141. Austin Smith to Chase, May 27, 1864, RDTC.
142. Austin Smith, report, May 26, 1864, in ibid.
143. T. D. Coryell to A. D. Smith, May 27, 1864, in ibid.
144. A. D. Smith to Direct Tax Commission, May 28, 1864, in ibid.
145. Rufus Saxton to A. D. Smith, April 18, 1864, Saxton Papers, Yale University.
146. Coryell to Joseph Lewis, June 6, 1864, RDTC.
147. McNulty, "William Henry Brisbane," 5–6.
148. The two men had met through their ties to the Liberty Party, and Brisbane's letters to Chase frequently addressed him as "dear friend." See *Chase Papers*.
149. Foner, *Free Soil, Free Labor*, 78.
150. Blue, *Salmon P. Chase*, 16.
151. Ibid.
152. *Milwaukee Sentinel*, December 7, 1860.
153. McPherson, *Battle Cry of Freedom*, 61.
154. Overy, "Wisconsin Carpetbagger," 22n.
155. Jean H. Baker, *Affairs of Party*, 177.
156. Stampp, *America in 1857*, 106.
157. Ibid., 133.
158. Foner, *Free Soil, Free Labor*, 265, 266.
159. Ibid., 295.
160. Holzer, *Lincoln-Douglas Debates*, 285.
161. A. D. Smith to George S. Boutwell, May 28, 1864, RDTC.
162. Mansfield French to Chase, February 7, 1863, in *Chase Papers*.
163. Joseph Lewis to Chase, February 5, 1864, in ibid.
164. Brisbane to Chase, February 15, 1864, in ibid.
165. Ibid., February 10, 1863.
166. Ibid.

167. Stephen R. Wise, Rowland, and Spieler, *Rebellion, Reconstruction, and Redemption*, 281.

168. *Free South*, May 21, 1864.

169. Stephen R. Wise, Rowland, and Spieler, *Rebellion, Reconstruction, and Redemption*, 280.

170. *Daily National Republican*, June 8, 1864; Stephen R. Wise, Rowland, and Spieler, *Rebellion, Reconstruction, and Redemption*, 281.

171. William Henry Brisbane diary, June 2, 1865, Brisbane Papers, WHS; Eldredge Collection notebooks, Mariners' Museum and Archives, Box 3, File 27.

172. William Henry Brisbane diary, June 2, 1865, Brisbane Papers, WHS.

173. Ibid., June 3, 1865.

174. Passenger list of the *Arago*, RG 92, entry 1403, Preliminary Inventory of the Textual Records of the Office of the Quartermaster General (RG 92): Charters, Bills of Lading, Claims Papers, Plans and Correspondence Relating to Vessels, 1834–1900, National Archives, Washington, D.C.

175. William Henry Brisbane diary, June 3, 1865, Brisbane Papers, WHS.

176. Ibid., June 4, 1865.

177. Stephen R. Wise, Rowland, and Spieler, *Rebellion, Reconstruction, and Redemption*, 274.

CONCLUSION Act, One and All

1. Gamble, "Story," 8. This account of the Chapin home in Ann Arbor and of the day Mary Augusta Smith learned of her husband's demise draws exclusively from this document.

2. Ibid.

3. Ibid.

4. *Daily Wisconsin*, June 7, 1865.

5. Gamble, "Story," 8; *Daily Wisconsin*, June 10, 1865.

6. *Milwaukee Sentinel*, June 10, 1865.

7. Faust, *This Republic of Suffering*, 170.

8. If Mary Frances was in attendance, the service might have been conducted by Chapin, her new husband, who had been the minister at Milwaukee's Presbyterian Church in the 1840s.

9. Freehling, *Road to Disunion*, 1:29.

10. Current, *Three Carpetbag Governors*, 3–35. Reed had a stormy tenure as governor. After only five months in office, he faced a mutiny in the legislature. Though he survived three impeachment attempts, his enemies ousted him on their fourth try. Reed and his wife, the Syracuse-born Chloe Merrick Reed, subsequently remained in Florida.

11. "Remarks of Jonathan E. Arnold," in Conover, *Reports*, x.

12. *Milwaukee Sentinel*, April 28, 1866. The register of burials at Milwaukee's Forest Home Cemetery lists no cause of death for Mary Augusta Smith. Although

the Smith family plot contains six graves, only the bodies of A. D., Mary Augusta, and Marius are buried there.

13. *Milwaukee Sentinel*, September 4, 1872. Marion gave birth to two children—a daughter, also named Marion, and a son, Lawrence. Her daughter later achieved some prominence as manager of the Marion Andrews Concert Bureau, which promoted operas and concerts in Milwaukee (Wascher, *Who's Who in Music*, 15).

14. A. D. Smith, Last Will and Testament, recorded October 8, 1856, Probate Collection, Milwaukee County Historical Society, Milwaukee.

15. Berryman, *History of the Bench*, 112.

16. Ibid., 111.

17. Lepore, "Historians Who Love Too Much," 133.

18. Tocqueville, *Democracy in America*, 712.

19. Ibid., 531.

20. Pierson, *Moving American*, 32.

21. Ulysses S. Grant, *Personal Memoirs*, 15–20.

22. McFeely, *Grant*, 11.

23. Ibid., 11.

24. Ulysses S. Grant, *Personal Memoirs*, 9.

25. Perry, *Grant and Twain*, 36.

26. Ibid.

27. Ibid.

28. For a recent biography of Clemens, see Powers, *Mark Twain*.

29. Ibid., 195.

30. Merrill, *William Tecumseh Sherman*, 104.

31. Ibid., 103.

32. Ibid., 123–133.

33. Ibid., 123.

34. Ibid., 148–149.

35. Sherman, *Memoirs*, 157.

36. Fellman, *Citizen Sherman*, 43.

37. Fraser, *Prairie Fires*, 29.

38. Wilder, *These Happy Golden Years*, 139.

39. Fraser, *Prairie Fires*, 29.

40. Leach, *Country of Exiles*, 9.

41. Ibid., 10.

42. Dickens, *Works of Charles Dickens*, 464.

43. Sarmiento, *Travels in the United States*, 306, 219.

44. Ibid., 151, 176, 166.

45. Bodichon, *American Diary*, 92,

46. Alice E. Smith, *History of Wisconsin*, 476.

47. Haliburton, *Clockmaker*, 37.

48. Ibid., 42.

49. Walt Whitman, "On Journeys through the States," in *Leaves of Grass*, 12.
50. Walt Whitman, "Pioneers! O Pioneers!" in ibid., 217–221.
51. Samuel Clemens to *San Francisco Alta California*, June 5, 1867, www.twainquotes.com/New_York.html.
52. Irving, *Rip Van Winkle*, 22–23.
53. Tocqueville, *Democracy in America*, 531.
54. Ibid., 531–532.
55. Ibid., 532.
56. Ibid., 624.
57. Pierson, *Moving American*, 18.
58. McDougall, *Freedom Just around the Corner*, 7.
59. Halttunen, *Confidence Men and Painted Women*, 1–32.
60. Ibid., 2.
61. Ibid., 20.
62. Pierson, "M-Factor in American History," 285.
63. Levine, *Half Slave and Half Free*, 57.
64. McPherson, *Battle Cry of Freedom*, 32.
65. Ibid., 11, 10.
66. Onuf, *Jefferson's Empire*, 56.
67. Pierson, *Moving American*, 12.
68. Ibid.
69. Onuf, *Jefferson's Empire*, 13.
70. A. D. Smith, *State Rights*, 13.

EPILOGUE Lost and Found

1. Lewis County Historical Society, "Re: A Lowville Mystery," email to author, February 27, 2013.
2. Anne Malek, "Amazing Discovery re Smith," email to author, June 28, 2013. David Gamble was the son of James Gamble, an Irish-born soap maker who in 1837 joined forces with English-born candlemaker William Procter, forming what is now a multinational consumer-products company.
3. A. D. Smith to Mary Augusta Smith, January 23, 1853, GFRB.
4. Ibid., January 14, 1853.
5. Ibid., February 25, 1856.
6. Ibid., March 16, 1857.
7. Ibid., May 27, 1857.
8. William Cronon, "Storytelling" (address, annual meeting of the American Historical Association, New Orleans, January 4, 2013).
9. Ibid.
10. A. D. Smith to Mary Augusta Smith, January 14, 1853, GFRB.

BIBLIOGRAPHY

Primary Sources
ARCHIVAL COLLECTIONS

Cleveland Public Library, Cleveland

Annals of Cleveland, 1818–1876, 1933–1938 [newspaper index]
Annals of Cleveland: Officeholder Series, Historical Record of Public Officeholders in Cuyahoga County, Register of Public Officeholders in Cleveland, 1802–1891

Cuyahoga County Archives, Cleveland

Justice of the Peace Docket, Cleveland Township, 1837–1842

Gamble House, Pasadena, California

Gamble, Mary Augusta Huggins, "The Story of Mary Augusta Huggins Gamble"

Library and Archives Canada, Ottawa

Records of the Rebellions of 1837–1838, R5201-0-6-E (formerly MG24-B97), Upper Canada Collection

Mariners' Museum and Archives, Newport News, Virginia

Eldredge Collection Notebooks

Milwaukee County Historical Society, Milwaukee

Probate Collection

National Archives, College Park, Maryland

Records of the Internal Revenue Service, Direct Tax Commissions in Southern States, South Carolina, General Correspondence, 1862–1893, RG 58

National Archives, Washington, D.C.

Preliminary Inventory of the Textual Records of the Office of the Quartermaster General (RG 92): Charters, Bills of Lading, Claims Papers, Plans and Correspondence Relating to Vessels, 1834–1900

Rensselaer County Historical Society, Troy, New York

Troy City Directory, 1832–33

Western Reserve Historical Society, Cleveland

Bierce, Lucius Verus, Papers, 1801–1876

Wisconsin Historical Society, Madison

Allen, William F., Family Papers, 1830–1889
Brisbane, William Henry, Papers, 1829–1913
Doolittle, James R., Papers, 1831–1935
Fairchild, Lucius, Papers
Reed, Harrison, Papers, 1838–1940

Yale University, New Haven

Saxton, Rufus, and S. Willard Saxton, Papers

NEWSPAPERS

Bald Eagle (Ohio)
Cleveland Gazette
Frederick Douglass' Paper (formerly *The North Star*)
Freeman's Advocate (Lockport, New York)
Free South (Beaufort, South Carolina)
Milwaukee Daily Wisconsin
Milwaukee Sentinel
Milwaukee Free Democrat
New South (Beaufort, South Carolina)

PUBLISHED WORKS

Ambrose, Stephen E. Interview, Academy of Achievement, May 22, 1998. https://web.archive.org/web/20101212023732/http://achievement.org/autodoc/printmember/amboint-1.

Chase, Salmon P. *Salmon P. Chase Papers*. Edited by John Niven. 43 reels. Frederick, Md.: University Publications of America, 1988.

Documents of the Assembly of the State of New York. Albany: Weed, Parsons, 1875.

Draper, Lyman Copeland, ed. *Collections of the State Historical Society of Wisconsin*. Vol. 2. 1856. Madison: State Historical Society of Wisconsin, 1903. http://content.wisconsinhistory.org/cdm/compoundobject/collection/whc/id/4415/rec/2.

Executive Documents, Printed by Order of the House of Representatives during the Second Session of the Thirty-Eighth Congress, 1864–'65. Washington, D.C.: U.S. Government Printing Office, 1865.

Journal of the Assembly of Wisconsin. Madison: State Printer, 1853.

Report of the Proceedings of the Meetings of the State Bar Association of Wisconsin for the Years 1878, 1881, and 1885. Madison: Taylor and Gleason, 1905.
Resolutions of the Wisconsin Legislature on the Subject of Slavery, with the Speech of Samuel D. Hastings, in the Assembly, Madison, January 27, 1849. New York: Harned, 1849.
Smith, A. D. *Message of His Excellency, A. D. Smith, Governor of the People, Delivered at the Capitol, Jan. 20, 1846.* Madison: Tenney, 1846.
———. *State Rights: Speech of Hon. Abram D. Smith, Delivered in the Assembly Hall, at Madison, March 22, 1860.* Madison: Atwood, Rublee, and Reed, 1860.
Steele, Josephy. *The Annual Thanksgiving of the State of Vermont, in the Congregational Church at Castleton.* Castleton, Vt.: White and Fairfield, 1834.

Secondary Sources

Abbott, Martin. *The Freedmen's Bureau in South Carolina.* Chapel Hill: University of North Carolina Press, 1967.
Ajzenstat, Janet. "Liberalism and Nationality." *Canadian Journal of Political Science/Revue Canadienne de Science Politique* 14 (September 1981): 587–609.
Allen, Austin. *Origins of the Dred Scott Case: Jacksonian Jurisprudence and the Supreme Court, 1837–1857.* Athens: University of Georgia Press, 2006.
Anbinder, Tyler. *Nativism and Slavery: The Northern Know Nothings and the Politics of the 1850s.* New York: Oxford University Press, 1992.
Appleby, Joyce. *Inheriting the Revolution: The First Generation of Americans.* Cambridge: Belknap Press of Harvard University Press, 2000.
———. *A Restless Past: History and the American Public.* New York: Rowman and Littlefield, 2005.
Backscheider, Paula. *Reflections on Biography.* London: Oxford University Press, 1999.
Bailyn, Bernard. *Ideological Origins of the American Revolution.* Cambridge: Harvard University Press, 1967.
Baker, H. Robert. *Prigg v. Pennsylvania: Slavery, the Supreme Court, and the Ambivalent Constitution.* Lawrence: University Press of Kansas, 2012.
———. *The Rescue of Joshua Glover: A Fugitive Slave, the Constitution, and the Coming of the Civil War.* Athens: Ohio University Press, 2006.
———. "The Rescue of Joshua Glover: Lawyers, Popular Constitutionalism, and the Fugitive Slave Law in Wisconsin." PhD diss., University of California, Los Angeles, 2004.
Baker, Jean. *Affairs of Party: The Political Culture of Northern Democrats in the Mid-Nineteenth Century.* Ithaca: Cornell University Press, 1983.
———. "From Belief into Culture: Republicanism in the Antebellum North." *American Quarterly* 37 (Autumn 1985): 532–550.
Baldwin, Charles Candee. *The Candee Genealogy: With Notices of Allied Families of Allyn, Catlin, Cooke, Mallery, Newell, Norton, Pynchon, and Wadsworth.* Cleveland: Leader, 1882.
Ball, Edward. *Slaves in the Family.* New York: Ballantine, 1999.

———. *The Sweet Hell Inside: A Family History*. New York: Harper Collins, 2001.
Bellasis, M. *Rise, Canadians!* London: Hollis and Carter, 1955.
Berlin, Ira, Thavolia Glymph, Steven F. Miller, Joseph P. Reidy, Leslie S. Rowland, and Julie Saville. *The Wartime Genesis of Free Labor: The Lower South*. Ser. 1, vol. 3 of *Freedom: A Documentary History of Emancipation, 1861–1867*. New York: Cambridge University Press, 1990.
Berryman, John R. *The History of the Bench and Bar of Wisconsin*. Vol. 1. Chicago: Cooper, 1898.
Bierce, Ambrose. *The Devil's Dictionary*. 1911. New York: Dover, 1993.
Blau, Joseph L. *Social Theories of Jacksonian Democracy: Representative Writings of the Period 1825–1850*. New York: Liberal Arts Press, 1954.
Blight, David, ed. *Passages to Freedom: The Underground Railroad in History and Memory*. Washington, D.C.: Smithsonian Books, 2004.
Blue, Frederick J. *The Free Soilers: Third Party Politics, 1848–1854*. Urbana: University of Illinois Press, 1973.
———. *Salmon P. Chase: A Life in Politics*. Kent, Ohio: Kent State University Press, 1987.
Bode, Carl, ed. *Mid-Century America: Life in the 1850s*. Carbondale: Southern Illinois University Press, 1972.
Bodichon, Barbara Leigh Smith. *An American Diary: 1857–8*. Edited by Joseph W. Reed Jr. London: Routledge and Kegan Paul, 1972.
Bonthius, Andrew. "The Patriot War of 1837–1838: Locofocoism with a Gun?" *Labour/Le Travail* 52 (Fall 2003): 9–43.
Bordewich, Fergus. *Bound for Canaan: The Underground Railroad and the War for the Soul of America*. New York: Harper Collins, 2005.
Bradley, Ann Walsh, and Joseph A. Ranney. "A Tradition of Independence: The Wisconsin Supreme Court's First 150 Years." *Wisconsin Magazine of History* 86 (Winter 2002–2003): 43–48.
Bryant, Edwin E. [Biography of A. D. Smith.] *The Green Bag* 9 (1897).
Buck, James S. *Pioneer History of Milwaukee: From the First American Settlement in 1833 to 1846*. 4 vols. Milwaukee: Swain, 1881–1890.
Buley, R. Carlyle. *The Old Northwest: Pioneer Period, 1815–1840*. Bloomington: Indiana University Press, 1962.
Bumsted, J. M., ed. *Canadian History before Confederation: Essays and Interpretations*. Georgetown, Ont.: Irwin-Dorsey, 1979.
Burns, Edward McNall. *The American Idea of Mission: Concepts of National Purpose and Destiny*. New Brunswick, N.J.: Rutgers University Press, 1957.
Butler, Diane S. "The Public Life and Private Affairs of Sherman M. Booth." *Wisconsin Magazine of History* 82 (Spring 1999): 167–197.
Cahill, Jack. *Forgotten Patriots: Canadian Rebels on Australia's Convict Shores*. Toronto: Brass, 1998.
Callahan, James Morton. *American Foreign Policy in Canadian Relations*. New York: Cooper Square, 1967.

Campbell, Stanley W. *The Slavecatchers: Enforcement of the Fugitive Slave Law, 1850–1860.* Chapel Hill: University of North Carolina Press, 1970.
Carroll, Francis M. *A Good and Wise Measure: The Search for the Canadian-American Boundary, 1783–1842.* Toronto: University of Toronto Press, 2001.
———. "The Passionate Canadians: The Historical Debate about the Eastern Canadian-American Boundary." *New England Quarterly* 70 (March 1997): 83–101.
Coates, William R. *A History of Cuyahoga County and the City of Cleveland.* Chicago: American Historical Society, 1924.
Cockshut, A. O. J. *Truth to Life: The Art of Biography in the Nineteenth Century.* London: Collins, 1974.
Cole, John Y. *Biography and Books.* Washington, D.C.: Library of Congress, 1986.
Conard, Howard Louis, ed. *History of Milwaukee from Its First Settlement to the Year 1895.* Chicago: American Biographical, 1895.
Conover, O. M. *Reports of Cases Argued and Determined in the Supreme Court of the State of Wisconsin.* Vol. 18. Madison: Atwood and Rublee, 1865.
Corey, Albert B. *The Crisis of 1830–1842 in Canadian-American Relations.* Toronto: Ryerson, 1941.
Courtwright, David T. "Opiate Addiction as a Consequence of the Civil War." *Civil War History* 24 (June 1978): 101–111.
Crane, Elaine Forman. *Killed Strangely: The Death of Rebecca Cornell.* Ithaca: Cornell University Press, 2002.
Creighton, Donald. *John A. Macdonald: The Old Chieftain.* Toronto: Macmillan, 1955.
———. *John A. Macdonald: The Young Politician.* Toronto: Macmillan, 1952.
Cross, D. W. "The Canadian Rebellion of 1837." *Magazine of Western History* 8 (February 1888): 359–370.
Cross, Whitney. *The Burned-Over District: The Social and Intellectual History of Enthusiastic Religion in Western New York, 1800–1850.* New York: Harper and Row, 1965.
Current, Richard N. *History of Wisconsin.* Vol. 2, *The Civil War Era, 1848–1873.* Madison: State Historical Society of Wisconsin, 1976.
———. *Those Terrible Carpetbaggers.* New York: Oxford University Press, 1988.
———. *Three Carpetbag Governors.* Baton Rouge: Louisiana State University Press, 1967.
———. *Wisconsin: A Bicentennial History.* New York: Norton, 1977.
Curti, Merle. *The Roots of American Loyalty.* New York: Russell and Russell, 1946.
Davenport, David Paul. "Migration to Albany, New York, 1850–1855." *Social Science History* 13 (Summer 1989): 159–185.
Davidson, James West, and Mark Hamilton Lytle. *After the Fact: The Art of Historical Detection.* New York: McGraw-Hill, 2005.
Davis, David Brion. *Antebellum American Culture: An Interpretive Anthology.* University Park: Pennsylvania State University Press, 1979.
DeCelles, Alfred D. *MacKenzie, Papineau.* Vol. 10 of *The Makers of Canada.* Toronto: Morang, 1909.

Degler, Carl N. "An Inquiry into the Locofoco Party." Master's thesis, Columbia University, 1947.

———. "The Locofocos: Urban 'Agrarians.'" *Journal of Economic History* 16 (September 1956): 322–333.

Dickens, Charles. *The Works of Charles Dickens*. Vol. 1. New York: Crowell, n.d.

Dictionary of Wisconsin Biography. Madison: State Historical Society of Wisconsin, 1960.

Duffy, John J., Samuel B. Hand, and Ralph H. Orth, eds. *The Vermont Encyclopedia*. Burlington: University of Vermont Press; Hanover: University Press of New England, 2003.

Eastman, Elizabeth C'de Baca. "Old and New Political Science: Motion in Tocqueville's Democracy in America." Paper presented at the annual meeting of the American Political Science Association, Philadelphia, August 28–31, 2003.

Elkins, Stanley, and Eric McKitrick. *The Age of Federalism*. New York: Oxford University Press, 1993.

Ellis, Richard E. *The Union at Risk: Jacksonian Democracy, States' Rights, and the Nullification Crisis*. New York: Oxford University Press, 1987.

Ericson, David F. *Slavery in the American Republic: Developing the Federal Government, 1791–1861*. Lawrence: University Press of Kansas, 2011.

Errington, Jane. *The Lion, the Eagle, and Upper Canada: A Developing Colonial Ideology*. Kingston, Ont.: McGill–Queens University Press, 1987.

Faust, Drew Gilpin. *This Republic of Suffering: Death and the American Civil War*. Toronto: Random House, 2008.

Fehrenbacher, Don E. *The Dred Scott Case: Its Significance in American Law and Politics*. New York: Oxford University Press, 1978.

Feller, Daniel. *The Jacksonian Promise: America, 1815–1840*. Baltimore: Johns Hopkins University Press, 1995.

Fellman, Michael. *Citizen Sherman: A Life of William Tecumseh Sherman*. New York: Random House, 1995.

Ferrell, Robert H., ed. *Foundations of American Diplomacy, 1775–1872*. New York: Harper and Row, 1968.

Filler, Louis. *The Crusade against Slavery, 1830–1860*. New York: Harper and Row, 1960.

Finkelman, Paul. *An Imperfect Union: Slavery, Federalism and Comity*. Chapel Hill: University of North Carolina Press, 1981.

———, ed. *Law, the Constitution, and Slavery*. Vol. II of *Articles on American Slavery*. New York: Garland, 1989.

———. "Prigg v. Pennsylvania and Northern State Courts: Anti-Slavery Use of a Pro-Slavery Decision." In *The Law of American Slavery: Major Historical Interpretations*, ed. Kermit L. Hall. New York: Garland, 1987.

———, ed. *Slavery, Race and the American Legal System: 1700–1872*. 16 vols. New York: Garland, 1988.

Finkelman, Paul, and Donald R. Kennon, eds. *Congress and the Crisis of the 1850s*. Athens: Ohio University Press, 2012.

Fischer, David Hackett. *Albion's Seed: Four British Folkways in America*. New York: Oxford University Press, 1989.

———. *Historians' Fallacies: Toward a Logic of Historical Thought*. New York: Harper and Row, 1970.

Fishlow, Albert. *American Railroads and the Transformation of the Antebellum Economy*. Cambridge: Harvard University Press, 1965.

Flower, Frank A., ed. *History of Milwaukee, Wisconsin*. Chicago: Western Historical, 1881.

Folts, James D. "The Fanatic and the Prophetess: Religious Perfectionism in Western New York." *New York History* 72 (October 1991): 357–387.

Foner, Eric. *Free Soil, Free Labor, Free Men: The Ideology of the Republican Party before the Civil War*. New York: Oxford University Press, 1970.

———. *Reconstruction: America's Unfinished Revolution, 1863–1877*. New York: Harper Collins, 1988.

———. *The Story of American Freedom*. New York: Norton, 1998.

Foner, Eric, and John A. Garraty, eds. *The Reader's Companion to American History*. Boston: Houghton Mifflin, 1991.

Foster, Sarah Whitmer, and John T. Foster Jr. "Chloe Merrick Reed: Freedom's First Lady." *Florida Historical Quarterly* 71 (January 1993): 279–299.

Fox, Stephen C. *The Group Bases of Ohio Political Behavior, 1803–1848*. New York: Garland, 1989.

Fraser, Caroline. *Prairie Fires: The American Dreams of Laura Ingalls Wilder*. New York: Metropolitan, 2017.

Freehling, William W. *The Road to Disunion*. Vol. 1, *Secessionists at Bay, 1776–1854*. New York: Oxford University Press, 1990.

———. *The Road to Disunion*. Vol. 2, *Seccesionists Triumphant, 1854–1861*. New York: Oxford University Press, 2007.

Friedman, Lawrence. *Crime and Punishment in American History*. New York: Basic Books, 1993.

Futch, Ovid L. "Salmon P. Chase and Civil War Politics in Florida." *Florida Historical Quarterly* 32 (January 1954): 163–188.

Garrison, William Lloyd. *The Letters of William Lloyd Garrison*. Vol. 5, *Let the Oppressed Go Free, 1861–1867*. Edited by Walter M. Merrill. Cambridge: Belknap Press of Harvard University Press, 1979.

Garvey, T. Gregory. *Creating the Culture of Reform in Antebellum America*. Athens: University of Georgia Press, 2006.

Gerring, John. "A Chapter in the History of American Party Ideology: The Nineteenth-Century Democratic Party (1828–1892)." *Polity* 26 (Summer 1994): 729–768.

———. *Party Ideologies in America, 1828–1996*. Cambridge: Cambridge University Press, 1998.

Gerteis, Louis S. "Salmon P. Chase, Radicalism, and the Politics of Emancipation, 1861–1864." *Journal of American History* 60 (June 1973): 42–62.

Gienapp, William E. *The Origins of the Republican Party, 1852–1856*. New York: Oxford University Press, 1987.

Goetzmann, William H. *When the Eagle Screamed: The Romantic Horizon in American Diplomacy, 1800–1860*. New York: Wiley, 1966.

Goodwin, Doris Kearns. *Team of Rivals: The Political Genius of Abraham Lincoln*. New York: Simon and Schuster, 2005.

Graber, Mark A. *Dred Scott and Problem of Constitutional Evil*. Cambridge: Cambridge University Press, 2006.

Grant, Marilyn. "Judge Levi Hubbell: A Man Impeached." *Wisconsin Magazine of History* 64 (Autumn 1980): 28–39.

Grant, Ulysses S. *Personal Memoirs*. New York: Konecky and Konecky, n.d.

Graves, Donald E. *Guns across the River: The Battle of the Windmill, 1838*. Prescott, Ont.: Friends of Windmill Point, 2001.

Green, Robert P., Jr., ed. *Equal Protection and the African American Constitutional Experience: A Documentary History*. Westport, Conn.: Greenwood, 2000.

Gregory, John G. "Early Wisconsin Editors: Harrison Reed." *Wisconsin Magazine of History* 8 (June 1924): 459–472.

———. *History of Milwaukee, Wisconsin*. Vol. 2. Chicago: Clarke, 1931.

Gregory, S. S. "A Historic Judicial Controversy and Some Reflections." *Michigan Law Review* 11 (January 1913): 179–197.

Grey, Charles. *Crisis in the Canadas, 1838–1839: The Grey Journals and Letters*. Edited by William Ormsby. Toronto: Macmillan of Canada, 1964.

Guelzo, Allen C. *Fateful Lightning: A New History of the Civil War and Reconstruction*. New York: Oxford University Press, 2012.

Guillet, Edwin C. *The Lives and Times of the Patriots: An Account of the Rebellion in Upper Canada, 1837–1838, and of the Patriot Agitation in the United States, 1838–1842*. Toronto: University of Toronto Press, 1968.

Gwyn, Richard J. *John A: The Man Who Made Us: The Life and Times of John A. Macdonald*. Toronto: Random House Canada, 2007.

Haliburton, Thomas Chandler. *The Clockmaker*. London: Bentley, 1837. www.Gutenberg.org/dires/etexto5/clckm10a.txt.

Hall, Kermit L., ed. *The Law of American Slavery: Major Historical Interpretations*. New York: Garland, 1987.

Halttunen, Karen. *Confidence Men and Painted Women: A Study of Middle-Class Culture in America, 1830–1870*. New Haven: Yale University Press, 1982.

Hambrick-Stowe, Charles E. *Charles G. Finney and the Spirit of American Evangelicalism*. Grand Rapids, Mich.: Eerdmans, 1996.

Hamilton, Holman. *Prologue to Conflict: The Crisis and Compromise of 1850*. New York: Norton, 1964.

Hardman, Keith J. *Charles Grandison Finney, 1792–1875*. Syracuse: Syracuse University Press, 1987.

Hart, Albert Bushnell. *Salmon Portland Chase*. 1899. New York: Greenwood, 1969.

Haskell, Samuel, and William S. Huggins. *Three Sermons to Young Men Preached by Rev. William S. Huggins of Kalamazoo, Michigan, and a Funeral Discourse by Samuel Haskell*. Philadelphia: Presbyterian Publication Committee, 1862.

Hitsman, J. Mackay. "Alarum on Lake Ontario: Winter 1812–1813." *Military Affairs* 23 (Autumn 1959): 129–138.

Hoffman, Edwin D. "From Slavery to Self-Reliance: The Record of Achievement of the Freedmen of the Sea Island Region." *Journal of Negro History* 41 (January 1956): 8–42.

Hollander, Barnett. *Slavery in America: Its Legal History*. London: Bowes and Bowes, 1962.

Holmes, Fred L. *Badger Saints and Sinners*. Milwaukee: Hale, 1939.

Holt, Michael F. *The Fate of Their Country: Politicians, Slavery Extension, and the Coming of the Civil War*. New York: Hill and Wang, 2004.

———. *The Rise and Fall of the American Whig Party: Jacksonian Politics and the Onset of the Civil War*. New York: Oxford University Press, 1999.

Holzer, Harold, ed. *The Lincoln-Douglas Debates*. New York: Fordham University Press, 2004.

Horton, Lois E. "Kidnapping and Resistance: Antislavery Direct Action in the 1850s." In *Passages to Freedom: The Underground Railroad in History and Memory*, ed. David Blight. Washington, D.C.: Smithsonian Books, 2004.

Hough, Franklin B. *A History of Lewis County in the State of New York from the Beginning of Its Settlement to the Present Time*. Albany, N.Y.: Munsell and Rowland, 1860.

Huebner, Timothy S. *The Taney Court: Justices, Rulings, and Legacy*. Santa Barbara, Calif.: ABC-Clio, 2003.

Hugins, Walter. *Jacksonian Democracy and the Working Class: A Study of the New York Workingman's Movement, 1829–1837*. New York: Oxford University Press, 1984.

Huston, James L. *Calculating the Value of the Union: Slavery, Property Rights, and the Economic Origins of the Civil War*. Chapel Hill: University of North Carolina Press, 2003.

Iding, Allan E., ed. *Forward Freemasonry*. Dousman, Wis.: Grand Lodge F. & A.M. of Wisconsin, 1996.

Irving, Washington. *Rip Van Winkle*. London: Blackie, 1900.

Jackson, Ruby West, and Walter T. McDonald. *Finding Freedom: The Untold Story of Joshua Glover, Runaway Slave*. Madison: Wisconsin Historical Society Press, 2007.

Jennings, R. Y. "The Caroline and McLeod Cases." *American Journal of International Law* 31 (January 1938): 82–99.

Johnson, Crisfield. *History of Cuyahoga County, Ohio*. Cleveland: Ensign, 1879.

Johnson, Paul. *A History of Christianity*. New York: Simon and Schuster, 1976.

Johnson, Paul E. *A Shopkeeper's Millennium: Society and Revivals in Rochester, New York, 1815–1837*. New York: Hill and Wang, 1978.

Karlsen, Carol F. *The Devil in the Shape of a Woman: Witchcraft in Colonial New England.* New York: Norton, 1987.

Kellogg, Louise Phelps. "The Fairchild Papers." *Wisconsin Magazine of History* 10 (March 1927): 259–281.

———. "The Origins of Milwaukee College." *Wisconsin Magazine of History* 9 (July 1926): 385–408.

Kennicott, Patrick C. "Black Persuaders in the Antislavery Movement." *Journal of Black Studies* 1(September 1970): 5–20.

Kilbourn, William. *The Firebrand: William Lyon Mackenzie and the Rebellion in Upper Canada.* Toronto: Clarke, Irwin, 1960.

Kinchen, Oscar. *Confederate Operations in Canada and the North.* North Quincy, Mass.: Christopher, 1970.

———. *The Rise and Fall of the Patriot Hunters.* New York: Bookman, 1956.

Kling, Allan E., ed. *Forward Freemasonry: A History of Freemasonry in Wisconsin.* Madison: Grand Lodge of Free and Accepted Masons of Wisconsin, 1996.

Kutler, Stanley I., ed. *The Supreme Court and the Constitution: Readings in American Constitutional History.* New York: Norton, 1977.

Lakevich, George J., ed. *Milwaukee: A Chronological and Documentary History, 1673–1977.* Dobbs Ferry, N.Y.: Oceana, 1977.

Lamis, Alexander P., ed. *Ohio Politics.* Kent, Ohio: Kent State University Press, 1994.

Leach, William. *Country of Exiles: The Destruction of Place in American Life.* New York: Vintage, 1999.

Lender, Mark Edward, and James Kirby Martin. *Drinking in America: A History.* New York: Free Press, 1982.

Lepore, Jill. "Historians Who Love Too Much: Reflections on Microhistory and Biography." *Journal of American History* 88 (June 2001): 129–144.

Levine, Bruce. *Half Slave and Half Free: The Roots of Civil War.* New York: Hill and Wang, 2005.

Lindsey, Charles. *The Life and Times of William Lyon Mackenzie: With an Account of the Canadian Rebellion of 1837 and the Subsequent Frontier Disturbances, Chiefly from Unpublished Documents.* Toronto: Randall, 1862.

———. *William Lyon Mackenzie.* Vol. 11 of *The Makers of Canada.* Toronto: Morang, 1909.

Long, E. B., and Barbara Long. *The Civil War Day by Day: An Almanac, 1861–1865.* New York: Da Capo, 1971.

Lorenz, Alfred Lawrence. "Harrison Reed: An Editor's Trials on the Wisconsin Frontier." *Journalism Quarterly* 53, no. 3 (1976): 417–422.

Lowenthal, David. *The Past Is a Foreign Country.* New York: Cambridge University Press, 1985.

Lubet, Steven. *Fugitive Justice: Runaways, Rescuers, and Slavery on Trial.* Cambridge: Belknap Press of Harvard University Press, 2010.

MacCabe, Julius P. Bolivar. *Cleveland Directory: A Directory of the Cities of Cleveland and Ohio, for the Years 1837–38.* Cleveland: Sanford and Lott, 1837.

Mackey, Albert G., and Charles T. McClenachan. *Encyclopedia of Freemasonry.* Vol. 1. Chicago: Masonic History, 1921.

Madsen, Deborah L. *American Exceptionalism.* Edinburgh: Edinburgh University Press, 1998.

Maltz, Earl M. *Slavery and the Supreme Court, 1825–1861.* Lawrence: University Press of Kansas, 2009.

Mandelbaum, Michael. *The Case for Goliath: How America Acts as the World's Government in the 21st Century.* New York: Public Affairs, 2006.

Manning, William R. *Diplomatic Correspondence of the United States: Canadian Relations.* Vol. 3, 1784–1860. Millwood, N.Y.: Krauss, 1975.

Marshall, Lucy Agar. "Samuel Marsden Brookes." *Wisconsin Magazine of History* 52 (Autumn 1968): 51–59.

Mason, Vroman. "The Fugitive Slave Law in Wisconsin, with Reference to Nullification Sentiment." In *Fugitive Slaves,* ed. Paul Finkelman. New York: Garland, 1989.

May, Robert E. "Young American Males and Filibustering in the Age of Manifest Destiny: The United States Army as a Cultural Mirror." *Journal of American History* 78 (December 1991): 857–886

Mayfield, John. *Rehearsal for Republicanism: Free Soil and the Politics of Antislavery.* Port Washington, N.Y.: Kennikat, 1979.

McDougall, Walter. *Freedom Just around the Corner: A New American History, 1585–1828.* New York: HarperCollins, 2003.

McFeely, William S. *Grant: A Biography.* New York: Norton, 1981.

———. "Why Biography?" In *The Seductions of Biography,* edited by Mary Rhiel and David Suchoff. New York: Routledge, 1996.

McInerney, Daniel J. *The Fortunate Heirs of Freedom: Abolition and Republican Thought.* Lincoln: University of Nebraska Press, 1994.

McKivigan, John R. *The War against Proslavery Religion: Abolitionism in the Northern Churches, 1830–1865.* Ithaca: Cornell University Press, 1984.

McKivigan, John R., and Stanley Harrold, eds. *Antislavery Violence: Sectional, Racial, and Cultural Conflict in Antebellum America.* Knoxville: University of Tennessee Press, 1999.

McLaren, Angus. "Phrenology: Medium and Message." *Journal of Modern History* 46 (March 1974): 86–97.

McLaughlin, Shaun J. *The Patriot War along the New York–Canada Border: Raiders and Rebels.* Charleston, S.C.: History Press, 2012.

McManus, Michael J. *Political Abolitionism in Wisconsin, 1840–1861.* Kent, Ohio: Kent State University Press, 1998.

McNulty, Blake. "William Henry Brisbane: South Carolina Slaveholder and Abolitionist." Unpublished paper, University of Wisconsin Center–Waukesha County, n.d.

McPherson, James M. *Battle Cry of Freedom: The Civil War Era.* New York: Oxford University Press, 1988.

———. *The Negro's Civil War: How American Blacks Felt and Acted during the War for the Union.* New York: Ballantine, 1965.

Merrill, James M. *William Tecumseh Sherman.* Chicago: Rand McNally, 1971.

Metzger, Bruce M., and Michael D. Coogan, eds. *The Oxford Companion to the Bible.* New York: Oxford University Press, 1993.

Meyers, Marvin. *The Jacksonian Persuasion: Politics and Belief.* Stanford: Stanford University Press, 1957.

Miller, Carol Poh, and Robert Wheeler. *Cleveland: A Concise History, 1796–1990.* Bloomington: Indiana University Press, 1990.

Miller, Linus W. *Notes of an Exile to Van Dieman's Land.* Fredonia, N.Y.: McKinstry, 1846.

Miller, Perry. "The Garden of Eden and the Deacon's Meadow." In *A Sense of History.* New York: Simon and Schuster, 2003.

Morgan, Philip D. "The Ownership of Property by Slaves in the Mid-Nineteenth-Century Low Country." *Journal of Southern History* 49 (August 1983): 399–420.

Morley, Christopher. "The Secret of the Ebony Cabinet: A Search for 'Lost' Manuscripts—From the Preface to Boswell's London Journal (1762–1763)." In *The Historian as Detective: Essays on Evidence*, edited by Robin W. Winks. New York: Harper and Row, 1968.

Morris, Thomas D. *Free Men All: The Personal Liberty Laws of the North, 1780–1861.* Baltimore: Johns Hopkins University Press, 1974.

Moss, Sidney P. *Charles Dickens' Quarrel with America.* Troy, N.Y.: Whitston, 1984.

Moss, Sidney P., and Carolyn J. Moss. *American Episodes Involving Charles Dickens.* Troy, N.Y.: Whitston, 1999.

Nadel, Ira Bruce. *Biography: Fiction, Fact, and Form.* London: Macmillan, 1984.

Norton, Mary Beth. *In the Devil's Snare: The Salem Witchcraft Crisis of 1692.* New York: Knopf, 2002.

Nye, Russel Blaine. *Society and Culture in America, 1830–1860.* New York: Harper and Row, 1974.

Ochiai, Akiko. "The Port Royal Experiment Revisited: Northern Visions of Reconstruction and the Land Question." *New England Quarterly* 74 (March 2001): 94–117.

Oney, Steve. *And the Dead Shall Rise: The Murder of Mary Phagan and the Lynching of Leo Frank.* New York: Random House, 2003.

Onuf, Peter S. *Jefferson's Empire: The Language of American Nationhood.* Charlottesville: University Press of Virginia, 2000.

Overy, David H., Jr. "The Wisconsin Carpetbagger: A Group Portrait." *Wisconsin Magazine of History* 44 (Autumn 1960): 15–49.

Oxford Dictionary of Quotations. London: Oxford University Press, 1979.

Pearson, Elizabeth Ware, ed. *Letters from Port Royal, 1862–1868.* New York: Arno, 1969.

Perry, Mark. *Grant and Twain: The Story of an American Friendship.* New York: Random House, 2004.

Pessen, Edward. *Jacksonian America: Society, Personality, and Politics.* Homewood, Ill.: Dorsey Press, 1969.
Peterson, Merrill D. *The Jefferson Image in the American Mind.* New York: Oxford University Press, 1962.
Pierce, Edward L. "The Freedmen at Port Royal." *Atlantic Monthly,* September 1863, 291–315.
Pierson, George W. "The M-Factor in American History." *American Quarterly* 14 (Summer 1962): 275–289.
———. *The Moving American.* New York: Knopf, 1973.
Pocock, J. G. A. *The Machiavellian Moment: Florentine Political Thought and the Atlantic Republican Tradition.* Princeton: Princeton University Press, 1975.
Potter, David M. *The Impending Crisis, 1848–1861.* Completed and edited by Don E. Fehrenbacher. New York: Harper and Row, 1976.
———. *Lincoln and His Party in the Secession Crisis.* New Haven: Yale University Press, 1942.
Powers, Ron. *Mark Twain: A Life.* New York: Free Press, 2005.
Prothero, Stephen. *American Jesus: How the Son of God Became a National Icon.* New York: Farrar, Straus, and Giroux, 2003.
Prucha, Francis Paul. "Distribution of Regular Army Troops before the Civil War." *Military Affairs* 16 (Winter 1952): 169–173.
Quaife, Milo M., ed. *The Convention of 1846.* Madison: State Historical Society of Wisconsin, 1919.
———, ed. *The Struggle over Ratification.* Madison: State Historical Society of Wisconsin, 1920.
Ranney, Joseph A. "Concepts of Freedom: The Life of Justice Byron Paine." *Wisconsin Lawyer* 75 (November 2002): 1–6.
———. "Imperia in Imperiis: Law and Railroads in Wisconsin, 1847–1910." *Wisconsin Lawyer* 66 (June 1993): 26–30, 57–58.
———. "Suffering the Agonies of their Righteousness: The Rise and Fall of the States Rights' Movement in Wisconsin, 1854–1861." *Wisconsin Magazine of History* 75 (Winter 1991–1992): 82–116.
———. *Trusting Nothing to Providence: History of Wisconsin's Legal System.* Madison: University of Wisconsin Law School, 2000.
———. "A World in Which Nothing Is Perfect: Chief Justice Edward G. Ryan." *Wisconsin Lawyer* 75 (September 2002): 1–3.
Rayback, Joseph G. *Free Soil: The Election of 1848.* Lexington: University Press of Kentucky, 1970.
Reed, David Breakenridge. *The Canadian Rebellion of 1837.* Toronto: Robinson, 1896.
Reed, Parker McCobb. *Reed's Bench and Bar of Wisconsin.* Milwaukee: Reed, 1882.
Reynolds, David S. *John Brown: Abolitionist, the Man Who Killed Slavery, Sparked the Civil War, and Seeded Civil Rights.* New York: Knopf, 2005.
Rezneck, Samuel. "The Social History of an American Depression, 1837–1843." *American Historical Review* 40 (July 1935): 662–687.

Riegel, Robert E. "The Introduction of Phrenology in the United States." *American Historical Review* 39 (October 1933): 73–78

Rorabaugh, W. J. *The Alcoholic Republic: An American Tradition.* New York: Oxford University Press, 1979.

Rose, William Ganson. *Cleveland: The Making of a City.* Kent, Ohio: Kent State University Press, 1990.

Rose, Willie Lee. *Rehearsal for Reconstruction: The Port Royal Experiment.* New York: Oxford University Press, 1976.

Safire, William. *Safire's New Political Dictionary: The Definitive Guide to the New Language of Politics.* New York: Random House, 1993.

Sandage, Scott A. *Born Losers: A History of Failure in America.* Cambridge: Harvard University Press, 2005.

Sarmiento, Domingo Faustino. *Travels in the United States in 1847.* Translated by Michael Aaron Rockland. Princeton: Princeton University Press, 1970.

Schafer, Joseph. "Stormy Days in Court—The Booth Case." *Wisconsin Magazine of History* 20 (September 1936): 89–110.

Schlesinger, Arthur M., Jr. *The Age of Jackson.* Boston: Little, Brown, 1945.

Schmitt, Jeffrey. "Rethinking *Ableman v. Booth* and States' Rights in Wisconsin." *Virginia Law Review* 93 (August 2007): 1315–1354.

Sellers, James L. "James R. Doolittle." *Wisconsin Magazine of History* 17 (December 1933): 168–178.

———. "Republicanism and State Rights in Wisconsin." *Mississippi Valley Historical Review* 17 (September 1930): 213–229.

Sharp, James Roger. *The Jacksonians versus the Banks: Politics in the States after the Panic of 1837.* New York: Columbia University Press, 1970.

Sherman, William Tecumseh. *Memoirs of General W. T. Sherman.* Edited, introduction, and notes by Michael Fellman. 1875. New York: Penguin, 2000.

Shofner, Jerrell H. "A New Jersey Carpetbagger in Reconstruction Florida." *Florida Historical Quarterly* 52 (January 1974): 286–293.

Shortridge, William Porter. "The Canadian-American Frontier during the Rebellion of 1837." *Canadian Historical Review* 7 (March 1926): 13–26.

Silbey, Joel H. *The American Political Nation, 1838–1893.* Stanford: Stanford University Press, 1991.

———. *A Respectable Minority: The Democratic Party in the Civil War Era, 1860–1868.* New York: Norton, 1977.

Simon, James F. *Lincoln and Chief Justice Taney: Slavery, Secession, and the President's War Powers.* New York: Simon and Schuster, 2006.

Smith, Alice E. *The History of Wisconsin: From Exploration to Statehood.* Madison: State Historical Society of Wisconsin, 1973.

Smith, Charles W., Jr. *Roger B. Taney: Jacksonian Jurist.* Chapel Hill: University of North Carolina Press, 1936.

Smith, Donnal V. *Chase and Civil War Politics.* Freeport, N.Y.: Books for Libraries, 1972.

Smith, Theodore Clark. *The Liberty and Free Soil Parties in the Northwest*. 1897. New York: Russell and Russell, 1967.
Stampp, Kenneth M. *America in 1857: A Nation on the Brink*. New York: Oxford University Press, 1990.
Steiner, Bernard C. *Life of Roger Brooke Taney: Chief Justice of the United States Supreme Court*. Baltimore: Williams and Wilkins, 1922.
Stevens, Kenneth R. *Border Diplomacy: The Caroline and McLeod Affairs in Anglo-American-Canadian Relationships, 1837–1842*. Tuscaloosa: University of Alabama Press, 1989.
Stewart, Gordon T. *The American Response to Canada since 1776*. East Lansing: Michigan State University Press, 1992.
Still, Bayrd. *Milwaukee: The History of a City*. Madison: State Historical Society of Wisconsin, 1965.
———. "Patterns of Mid-Nineteenth Century Urbanization in the Middle West." *Mississippi Valley Historical Review* 28 (September 1941): 187–206.
Strouse, Jean. "Semiprivate Lives." In *Studies in Biography*, edited by Daniel Aaron. Cambridge: Harvard University Press, 1978.
Tey, Josephine. *The Daughter of Time*. London: Arrow, 1951.
Thayer, William Roscoe. *The Art of Biography*. New York: Scribner's, 1920.
Tocqueville, Alexis de. *Democracy in America and Two Essays on America*. Translated by Gerald Bevan. London: Penguin, 2003.
Tyler, Alice Felt. *Freedom's Ferment: Phases of American Social History from the Colonial Period to the Outbreak of Civil War*. Minneapolis: University of Minnesota Press, 1944.
Tyler, Samuel. *Memoir of Roger Brooke Taney, LL.D.: Chief Justice of the Supreme Court of the United States*. Baltimore: Murphy, 1872.
Unger, Samuel. "The Hunters' Lodges and the Canadian Rebellion of 1837–1838." Master's thesis, Ohio State University, 1931.
Urofsky, Melvin I., ed. *Documents of American Constitutional and Legal History*. Vol. 1, *From Settlement through Reconstruction*. Philadelphia: Temple University Press, 1989.
Van Deusen, Glyndon. *The Jacksonian Era, 1828–1848*. New York: Harper, 1959.
Wager-Smith, Elizabeth. "Historic Attempts to Annex Canada to the United States." *Journal of American History* 5 (1911): 215–232.
Waite, Frederick Clayton. *The History of the First Medical College in Vermont, Castleton: 1818–1862*. Montpelier: Vermont Historical Society, 1949.
Wascher, Arthur E. *Who's Who in Music and Art in Milwaukee: Music, Painting and Sculpturing, Applied Art, Dramatic, and Dancing*. Milwaukee: Advocate, 1927.
Watson, Harry L. *Liberty and Power: The Politics of Jacksonian America*. New York: Hill and Wang, 1990.
Watson, Samuel. "United States Army Officers Fight the 'Patriot War': Responses to Filibustering on the Canadian Border, 1837–1839." *Journal of the Early Republic* 18 (Autumn 1998): 485–519.

Wayne, Michael. *Death of an Overseer: Reopening a Murder Investigation from the Plantation South*. New York: Oxford University Press, 2001.

Weisenburger, Francis P. *The Passing of the Frontier, 1825–1850*. Vol. 3 of *The History of the State of Ohio*, edited by Carl Wittke. Columbus: Ohio State Archaeological and Historical Society, 1941.

Welch, Cheryl. *De Tocqueville*. New York: Oxford University Press, 2001.

Wellman, Judith. *Grass Roots Reform in the Burned-Over District of Upstate New York: Religion, Abolitionism and Democracy*. New York: Garland, 2000.

Wert, Justin J. *Habeas Corpus in America: The Politics of Individual Rights*. Lawrence: University Press of Kansas, 2011.

Wheeler, A. C. *The Chronicles of Milwaukee: Being a Narrative History of the Town from its Earliest Period to the Present*. Bowie, Md.: Heritage, 1990.

Whitman, Walt. *Leaves of Grass*. 1855. Franklin Center, Pa.: Franklin Library, 1979.

Wilder, Laura Ingalls. *These Happy Golden Years*. (New York: HarperCollins, 1971.

Wilentz, Sean. *Chants Democratic: New York City and the Rise of the American Working Class, 1788–1850*. New York: Oxford University Press, 1984.

———. "On Class and Politics in Jacksonian America." *Reviews in American History* 10 (December 1982): 45–63.

———. *The Rise of American Democracy: Jefferson to Lincoln*. New York: Norton, 2005.

Wiltse, Charles M. *The New Nation, 1800–1845*. New York: Hill and Wang, 1964.

Winslow, John B. *The Story of a Great Court*. Chicago: Flood, 1912.

Wise, S. F., and Robert Craig Brown. *Canada Views the United States: Nineteenth-Century Political Attitudes*. Seattle: University of Washington Press, 1967.

Wise, Stephen R., Lawrence S. Rowland, and Gerhard Spieler. *The History of Beaufort County, South Carolina*. Vol. 2, *Rebellion, Reconstruction, and Redemption, 1861–1893*. Columbia: University of South Carolina Press, 2015.

Wittke, Carl. "Ohioans and the Canadian-American Crisis of 1837–38." *Ohio Archeological and Historical Quarterly* 58 (January 1949): 26–37.

Wood, Gordon S. *The Creation of the American Republic, 1776–1787*. Chapel Hill: University of North Carolina Press, 1969.

———. *The Radicalism of the American Revolution*. New York: Knopf, 1992.

Woodley, Thomas Frederick. *Great Leveler: The Life of Thaddeus Stevens*. Freeport, N.Y.: Books for Libraries, 1937.

Young, James V. *Landmark Constitutional Law Decisions: Briefs and Analyses*. Lanham, Md.: University Press of America, 1993.

Zobel, Hiller B. *The Boston Massacre*. New York: Norton, 1970.

INDEX

Ableman, Stephen, 60, 66
Ableman v. Booth, 14–15, 20, 76; Chief Justice Taney and, 73–74; implications for A. D. Smith, 82, 85, 92–93; Supreme Court verdict in, 79–80, 134; in Wisconsin history, 52–53
Adams, John Quincy, 65
Alabama, 111
Alexander, John Candee, 102, 112, 114, 120
Allen, William F., 105–106, 109
Ambrose, Stephen, 1, 11, 18
American Freedmen's Inquiry Commission, 97
American Missionary Association, 101
American Revolution, 19, 21, 26–27; anti-British sentiment and, 25; connection to Canadian Rebellions, 36–38, 40–41; reform and, 31–32
Andrews, Charles Elkanah (son-in-law), 124
Arago, 105, 119–121, 133
Arnold, Jonathan, 124–125
Aroostook War, 38
Arthur, George, 42

Backscheider, Paula, 16–17
Baker, Jean H., 116
Bald Eagle, 42
Ball, Edward, 11–12
Baltimore, Md., 119
Bank Wars, 35
Baring, Alexander, 46
Barnburners, 15, 32–33, 65
Barstow, William, 83
Bashford, Coles, 81, 83
Battle of Christiana, 63–64
Battle of the Windmill, 43–44, 49
Beaufort, S.C., 19, 20, 122–124, 127, 133; A. D. Smith's arrival in, 91–92; A. D. Smith's final year in and departure from, 119–120; description of, 95–97; feud over property rights in, 101–115
Bierce, Lucius Verus, 42, 44–45, 48
Biography, 1–2, 10, 12, 16–17
Birney, James, 115
Bodichon, Barbara Leigh Smith, 131
Bonthius, Andrew, 42
Booth, Sherman, 60, 78–80, 82; arrest of, 83; federal charges and, 72; Justice Crawford argues for release of, 69; as newspaper editor, 65–66, 86; rallies mob and turns on A. D. Smith, 83
Brick Baptist Church, 106–107
Brisbane, Phoebe Adeline, 96
Brisbane, William Henry, 94–99, 101–120, 127
Britain, 26, 36, 41, 46–47, 63
Brookes, Samuel Marsden, 52
Brown, John, 12
Buffalo, N.Y., 29, 37, 40
Bureau for the Relief of Freedmen and Refugees, 123
Burned-Over District (N.Y.), 13, 22–23, 30
Buskirks Bridge, N.Y., 28

Calhoun, John C., 67–69, 86
California, 128, 140
Canada: A. D. Smith as Canadian story, 20; annexation of, 41, 48; border, 21, 36, 38, 41, 45, 49–50; Hunters' desire to overthrow Crown rule in, 15–16; Hunters' Lodge and, 36–44, 47–49, 63–65; Lower Canada, 36, 46, 67; president of, 2–3, 9–10, 19–21, 47, 50, 134; rebellions of, 36–37, 40, 45, 47; Upper Canada, 4, 36, 40, 42, 45–46, 53, 67
Candee, William Sprague, 86–87, 94, 112, 123
Carlyle, Thomas, 49

Index

Caroline, sinking of, 37–38, 40, 46–47
Castleton, Vt., 23, 27–29
Chapin, Lucius Delison (son-in-law), 121
Chase, Salmon P.: A. D. Smith's first official report to, 98; appointment of A. D. Smith to tax commission and, 94; caught up in feud of Direct Tax commissioners in Beaufort, 101–103, 105, 107, 110–118; as Democrat who became Republican, 93; as lawyer in fugitive slave cases, 75–76
Cincinnati, Ohio, 40, 75, 115–166, 128
Clay, Henry, 12, 41, 73
Clemens, Samuel, 128, 132, 135
Cleveland, Ohio, 2–6, 10, 15, 19, 27, 126; A. D. Smith as justice of the peace in, 50; as A. D. Smith's home, 95; concerns about Canada, 36, 38; demographics and description of, 29–30; Hunters' Lodge activities in, 42–44; as Hunters' Lodge western headquarters, 40; Locofocoism in, 32–34
Cleveland Female Seminary, 4, 32
Cohens v. Virginia, 79
Cole, Orsamus, 59, 125
Compromise of 1850, 61, 63–64, 70, 82
Congregationalism, 23, 29, 31
Connecticut, 22, 127–128
Cook, Simeon A., 28
Cooley, Dennis N., 113
Cornell, Rebecca, 10–11
Coryell, Thomas, 102, 114
Courtwright, David T., 95
Craft, Ellen and William, 62–63
Craig, Robert, 45
Crawford, Samuel, 69–70
Cronon, William, 143
Cross, Whitney, 13, 22
Cuyahoga County Archives, 3–4

Dakota Territory, 129
Davis, Jefferson, 90
Degler, Carl, 14, 33–34
Democratic Party: banks and, 42–43; Barnburner faction, 15, 32; as champion of oppressed, 50; civil liberties and, 33; Jacksonian Democrats, 32, 39; Locofoco connection, 14–15, 32–33; nativism and, 57; pro-slavery stance, 82, 116; racism of, 116

Department of the South, 93, 101, 111–112, 115, 118
Direct Tax Act, 87, 92, 97, 101
Direct Tax Commission, 88, 92, 104, 116, 123
Dixon, Luther, 84, 86
Doolittle, James, 85–87, 92–94, 101, 110
Douglas, Stephen, 77–78, 82, 116–117
Douglass, Frederick, 62, 100
Dred Scott v. Sandford (1857), 52, 76, 83
Durham Report, 46

Emancipation Proclamation, 89, 95, 102
Emerson, John, 76
Erie Canal, 13, 29, 54

Faust, Drew Gilpin, 123
Fehrenbacher, Don E., 74–76
Fillmore, Millard, 63
Fischer, David Hackett, 23
Florida, 41, 53, 93–94, 100, 123, 127
Foner, Eric, 93, 99–100
Fraser, Caroline, 129
Freehling, William W., 91
Freeman's Advocate, 41, 49
Freemasons, 38, 48, 97, 122
Free South, 103, 119
French, Mansfield, 101, 102, 104–108, 110–114, 118, 119
Fugitive Slave Act, 9, 14, 16, 61–72, 74–76, 80, 82, 85–86, 108
Fugitive slaves, 62–64, 76

Garland, Benammi, 64
Garrison, William Lloyd, 74, 89–91
Genealogy, 3, 6, 21, 140
Georgia, 62, 85, 93, 100
Gerring, John, 32, 50
Giddings, Joshua, 62, 78
Gideonites, 92, 97
Glover, Joshua, 60, 64–67, 71, 73, 79, 81–82, 116
Grant, Ulysses S., 17, 127–128
Graves, Donald, 41, 43
Greeley, Horace, 20, 72, 85
Guelzo, Allen C., 92
Guillet, Edwin C., 47

Haliburton, Thomas Chandler, 131
Halttunen, Karen, 135–136

Hilton Head, S.C., 119, 123
Huebner, Timothy S., 74
Huggins, Mary Augusta (granddaughter), 73, 94, 121–122, 124, 140
Huggins, William Henry (grandson), 94
Huggins, William Sydney (son-in-law), 73, 86, 94
Hugins, Walter, 34, 39
Hunkers, 55
Hunter, David, 101
Hunter, James, 38
Hunters' Lodge, 2, 19, 133; annexation plans, 41, 48; banking plans, 41–42; demise of, 45–47; election of provisional government, 42; flag, 41; goals, 47; lack of Canadian support for, 45; Les Frères Chasseurs connection, 39; origin of name, 38; rituals of, 38

Illinois, 76, 78, 128, 131, 133
Ingalls, Charles, 129
Internal Revenue Commission, 105, 110, 118
Iowa, 113, 129
Irving, Washington, 132

Jackson, Andrew, 33–36, 39–40, 43, 49, 73
Jefferson, Thomas, 14, 33, 49, 68, 85, 99, 137
Johnson, Andrew, 87, 100
Juneau, Solomon, 58

Kansas, 78, 129
Kansas-Nebraska Act, 61, 77, 78
Kearney, John, 65
Kentucky, 30, 33, 75, 85, 128
Kilbourn, Byron, 81
Kinchen, Oscar, 19, 36, 39–40, 44–45, 47–48

La Crosse & Milwaukee Railroad, 81, 82
Lansingburgh, N.Y., 23, 29
Leach, William, 130
Lender, Mark, 104
Lepore, Jill, 126
Lewis, Joseph, 105, 107, 109, 110–113, 118
Liberty Party, 65, 115
Library and Archives Canada, 4, 19
Lincoln, Abraham, 53, 101–107, 109, 111; A. D. Smith's service to administration of, 10, 20, 87, 93, 101–107, 122, 140; debates with Douglas, 77–78; Emancipation Proclamation of, 89, 102; on racial equality, 117
Locofocoism, 14–15, 32–35, 42, 49, 54, 126
Louisiana, 19, 21, 23–24, 41, 128, 129
Lowville, N.Y., 21, 23, 24, 139
Lowville Academy, 24
Lubet, Steven, 61
Lucas, George, 144
Lynde, William Pitt, 83

Macdonald, John A., 44
Mackenzie, William Lyon, 36–40, 47
Madison, James, 68
Madison, Wis., 6, 20, 51, 55, 72, 82–85, 141, 144
Madison Argus, 58
Maine, 38, 46, 97
Manifest Destiny, 41
Martin, James, 104
Massachusetts, 22, 28, 34, 62, 89–90, 96–97, 127
McDougall, Walter, 135
McFeely, William, 17, 127
McHenry, William "Jerry," 64
McLeod, Alexander, 46–47
McManus, Michael J., 68, 83
McPherson, James M., 11, 63, 91, 137
Melville, Herman, 135–136
Michigan, 29, 41, 54, 73, 86, 94, 121, 133, 142
Microhistory, 126
Miller, Perry, 23
Milwaukee, Wis., x; First Congregational Bethel Church, 23; First Congregational Society, 23; Forest Home Cemetery, 8, 124
Milwaukee Daily Free Democrat, 65, 71, 80, 83, 86, 87
Milwaukee (Journal-)Sentinel, 7, 53, 57, 64, 71, 81, 83, 84, 87, 93, 94, 124
Minkins, Frederick "Shadrach," 63
Minnesota, 129
Missouri, 20, 60, 64, 76, 111, 128
Missouri Compromise, 61, 77, 87
Mitchell, Alexander, 28, 53, 81, 123
Molyneux, Nellie Rice, 21
Morley, Christopher, 16

Navy Island, 37, 40, 41, 47
New England, 10–11, 22–23, 27, 29, 39, 54–55, 57, 61, 95

Index

New Hampshire, 28
New York, 13, 19–27, 29, 32, 41, 43–44, 49, 54–55, 75, 87, 95, 127
New York Anti-Slavery Society, 78
New York Times, 11
New York Tribune, 71, 73, 91, 108
Nova Scotia, 131
Noyes, Thomas, 53

Ochiai, Akiko, 98
Ogdensburg, N.Y., 43
Ohio, 3–5, 29–50, 53–54, 96, 127, 129, 133, 137
Onuf, Peter S., 137
Oregon, 128
Ottawa Citizen, 19

Paine, Byron, 66–67, 83–84, 86
Palmer, Henry L., 59, 81
Panic of 1837, 34, 36, 56
Papineau, Louis-Joseph, 39
Pennsylvania, 63, 73–75, 127
Perry, Mark, 128
Peterson, Merrill D., 33
Phillips, Wendell, 78–79, 139
Phrenology, 4, 27, 30, 134
Pierce, Edward, 104
Pierce, Franklin, 59
Pierson, George W., 127, 135–137
Port Royal, S.C., 91–93, 100, 119
Potter, David M., 78, 86
Powers, Ron, 128
Preemption, 98, 102, 105, 109–111, 118
Prescott, Ont., 43–45
Prigg v. Pennsylvania, 74–76
Puritans, 22

Racine, Wis., 56, 64–65, 71, 73, 94
Racine Journal, 84
Rea, J. E., 39
Reconstruction, 9–10, 91, 99–101, 117, 120, 122
Reed, Curtis, 53
Reed, George, 53, 81
Reed, Harrison, 28, 29, 53, 94, 123, 127
Reed, Herbert, 7, 53, 96
Reed, Juliana, 53
Reed, Martha, 28, 53, 123

Reed, Orison, 53
Reed, Rhoda Fenny (mother-in-law), 28, 53, 86
Reed, Seth (father-in-law), 28, 53
Rensselaer County Historical Society, 28
Republican Bank of Canada, 41
Republicanism, 25–26, 31
Republican Party, 33, 118; A. D. Smith's move to, 83; extreme edges of, 15; nomination of Paine, 83; property rights and, 100; racism of, 117; radicalism and, 93, 100; reaction to *Dred Scott v. Sandford*, 77; states' rights and, 85–86
Rochester, N.Y., 40
Rorabaugh, W. J., 32
Rose, Willie Lee, 9, 91, 96, 104, 109

Sackets Harbor, N.Y., 24–25, 27, 32
Sandage, Scott, 96
Sarmiento, Domingo Faustino, 130
Saxton, Rufus, 89, 97, 100–102, 104–111, 113–115, 118, 119
Saxton, S. Willard, 97, 113, 115
Schlesinger, Arthur M., Jr., 12, 35
Schmitt, Jeffrey, 68–70
Scott, Dred, 52, 76
Scott, Orrin, 41
Scott, Winfield, 37, 38, 41, 46, 59
Sea Islands. *See under* South Carolina
Seward, William H., 75, 78, 117
Sharp, James Roger, 42
Sherman, William Tecumseh, 100, 111, 128–129
Simon, James F., 89
Smith, Abram Daniel: alcoholism, 25, 32, 94, 103–104, 106, 109, 111, 114, 116; appearance, 51; birth, 21; childhood, 21; as confidence man, 135–136; death, 120; Direct Tax Commission removal, 113; election, 42; funeral, 122; justice of the peace, 50; Lincoln meeting, 87; Locofocos involvement, 35; marriage, 23, 29; Milwaukee mayor nomination, 58; name, 22–23; nativism accusations, 57–58; parents, 16, 24; phrenology involvement, 4, 27, 30, 134; portrait of, 51; relationship with Mary Augusta Smith, 141–142; religion, 23, 116; Republican Party adoption, 83; slavery opposition, 30; study

of law, 24; study of medicine, 27; vice presidential possibility, 10, 84; Wisconsin Supreme Court seat win, 59
Smith, Austin, 114
Smith, Daniel Scott, 22
Smith, Maria Cecilia (daughter), 36, 53, 86, 94, 112, 122–123, 124
Smith, Marion Augusta (daughter), 59, 86, 94, 122, 124
Smith, Marius Augustus (son), 8, 54, 124
Smith, Mary Augusta (wife), 8, 23, 29, 50, 53, 59, 86, 94, 96, 121, 123, 124
Smith, Mary Frances (daughter), 29, 53, 59, 61, 73, 86, 94, 121, 122, 142
South Carolina, 89–120, 124, 133; Port Royal, 91–93, 100, 119; Sea Islands, 14, 20, 49, 68, 88, 91–92, 95, 97, 100, 102, 104–105, 113
Spielberg, Steven, 143–144
Stampp, Kenneth, 117
States' rights, 7, 13, 15–16, 66–70, 84–86, 93, 134, 137–138
Steele, Joseph, 23, 29
Stevens, Thaddeus, 100
St. Helena Parish, 98, 105, 118
Stowe, Harriet Beecher, 20, 61
Strong, Marshall, 56
Strouse, Jean, 9
Sumner, Charles, 20, 71, 78, 83

Taney, Roger B., 52, 73–74, 76, 77, 118, 101
Temperance, 9, 13, 30–32, 54, 116, 126, 135
Tennessee, 111
Thoreau, Henry David, 61–62
Tocqueville, Alexis de, 127, 133–134
Toombs, Robert, 85–87
Troy, 28, 59
Troy Female Seminary, 28
Twitter, 7
Tyler, John, 46

U.S. Treasury Department, 98, 108–109

Van Buren, Martin, 12, 15, 34, 37–38, 41, 48
Van Deusen, Glyndon, 2, 35
Vermont, 22, 27–29, 39, 53, 90, 127
Vermont Academy of Medicine, 27–28
Virginia, 63, 111

Washington, D.C., 15, 46, 87, 93, 95, 101–105, 107, 111–112, 114, 140
Washington Globe, 49
Watson, Harry L., 38
Wayne, Michael, 1, 11, 17
Webster, Daniel, 12, 46–47, 73
Webster-Ashburton Treaty, 46
Weisenburger, Francis P., 31
Western Reserve, 29, 137
Western Reserve Historical Society, 3
Whig Party, 33, 46, 55, 59, 126
Whitman, Walt, 131–132
Whiton, Edward V., 59, 69–70, 84
Wilentz, Sean, 14, 34, 62, 67
Williams, Nathan, 42
Wilson, Carol, 62
Windsor, Ont., 44–45
Wisconsin, 49, 70, 85, 92, 131; A. D. Smith's time in, 51–88; constitution of, 55–57; Homestead Exemption, 56; immigration to, 54; *Racine Journal*, 84; railroad land-grant scandal, 81; Supreme Court, 5, 59, 80, 122
Wisconsin Historical Society, 51–52
Wise, S. F., 40, 45
Women's rights, 30, 32, 34, 50, 56, 135
Wording, William D., 93–99, 101–103, 105–115, 119, 120
Wood, Gordon S., 21, 26–27, 31, 99
Woodward, C. Vann, 96
Workingmen, 34

UnCivil Wars

Weirding the War: Tales from the Civil War's Ragged Edges
    edited by Stephen Berry
Ruin Nation: Destruction and the American Civil War
    by Megan Kate Nelson
America's Corporal: James Tanner in War and Peace
    by James Marten
*The Blue, the Gray, and the Green:
Toward an Environmental History of the Civil War*
    edited by Brian Allen Drake
Empty Sleeves: Amputation in the Civil War South
    by Brian Craig Miller
Lens of War: Exploring Iconic Photographs of the Civil War
    edited by J. Matthew Gallman and Gary W. Gallagher
*The Slave-Traders Letter-Book:
Charles Lamar, the Wanderer, and other Tales of the Slave Trade*
    by Jim Jordan
Driven from Home: North Carolina's Civil War Refugee Crisis
    by David Silkenat
*The Ghosts of Guerrilla Memory:
How Bushwhackers Became Gunslingers in the American West*
    by Matthew Christopher Hulbert
Beyond Freedom: Disrupting the History of Emancipation
    edited by David W. Blight and Jim Downs
*The Lost President: A. D. Smith and the Hidden History of
Radical Democracy in Civil War America*
    by Ruth Dunley
Bodies in Blue: Disability in the Civil War North
    by Sarah Handley-Cousins

www.ingramcontent.com/pod-product-compliance
Lightning Source LLC
Chambersburg PA
CBHW030653230426
43665CB00011B/1071